BY THE WAY, DOCTOR

*Don a rubber glove and delve
into General Practice with*

Dr Norman Beale

ELSP

Published in 2024 by
ELSP

Preparation by Ex Libris Press
www.ex-librisbooks.co.uk

Typeset in 10/13 point Minion

Printed by CPI Anthony Rowe
Chippenham, Wiltshire

© 2024 Norman Beale

ISBN 9781912020225

DEDICATION

To Elaine – who always answered the phone with empathy, discretion and without complaint whatever the hour and however inconvenient.

CONTENTS

SAT NAV   7

1 BRIEF ENCOUNTERS
Saturday Night at the Movies   12
The Dangerous Mr Fuddle Wuddle   14
March in November   16
Awash   17
Bathtime to Birthtime   19
David Vernon Thomas   21
Happy Birthday   22
Hobson's Choice   25
After five on a Friday   27
Worthy Farm Blues   30
Break in   31
Whispers   33
Tearful   35
A Summer's Evening   37
Twelve out of Ten   39
White Accident   41

2 PRACTICE PIE
Tacky Tachycardia   44
Earth is Green, Live is Red   46
Percy Geoffrey and Clay but not Monty   48
Plus ça change   50
Eine Neue Familie   52
Bill Gates   54
Cal(culus)   56
Out for the Count   58
Is Doctor Hurst with you?   60
Black Dog   62

A Life in the Country   64
Les Boutiquiers   67
Olga from the …   70
Chitterlings in the sun   72
Best-laid plans   74
The Price of Loyalty   76
A Stranger in the Night   78
Superman   80
Zealous Zoë   82
Taking in Washing   85
Palanquin Progress   87

3 SINGULAR CHARACTERS
Any Old Iron   92
Miasma   94
Smallpox Cottages   98
Fantasy Footfall   101
In Sickness and…   103
When 'Take one at bedtime every night' won't do   106
Cardiac Colin   108
Connie and her Cats   110
June the Sixth   112
Marcel Bloody Proust   114
Matron   118
Councillor Lewis   120
May Bryant   122
One of the Gals   124
The Ingenious Roy Goodmen   126
Trenton Jameson M.D.   128
Dorrie   131

4 MORE BRIEF ENCOUNTERS

Black and blue	134
Grandstand	135
Uncle Bert	137
HWB	139
I think I'll just pop in and see…	141
Hump	143
Gan	144
Daylight Robbery	145
BTM	147
Number Fourteen	149
Lakeside	151
On my way home	153
Morbilli	154
Gardening	155

5 SCRAPES AND TRAGEDIES

Just a check-up	158
Spy in the sky	160
Unwanted tan	163
Lynchet Farm	165
A Motspur	167
Going up	169
Poorly Pauline	171
No smoke without fire	173
Brave little Imran	177
Highs and Lows	179
Although it swims and quacks it may not be a duck	181
Cows that go mad: a Tale in three parts	183
En Passant	186
Not a one-act play	189

6 PERSONAL PERSPECTIVE

Miss Harris and Miss Harries	194
Sidelined	196
Terrorists	197
Moving Day	199
Itadob?	201
We've got one	203
When the weather closes in	205
Party time	208
Maggie on a Monday	210
On being a corkscrew	212
My life on crutches	216
A long afternoon in Reception	219
Travelogue	221
Do you know, I'm so busy?	224
Gee, thanks Fred	226
Attenshun!	229
In the cross hairs	231

Closure	235
Acknowledgements	236
About the Author	236

SAT NAV

When friends ask me if this is a book of my memoirs, the honest answer is no, not in the usual sense. I've dredged up a host of isolated recollections from my professional life as an NHS General Practitioner and arranged them into a set of 100 short stories. After nearly two decades of retirement many memories of my 30 years in practice in Wiltshire are still vivid: vibrant enough to commit them to print. The customary biographical narrative, stretching from 'doe-eyed' enthusiasm to 'seen it all' carapace is very familiar but, I feel, somewhat sterile. I hope that these stand-alone vignettes will better entertain and convey, by their intimate content, what it was like to be a semi-rural GP in the decades leading up to the millennium without being voyeuristic and without veering into off-putting jargon. Each of the stories is an amalgam of actual experiences and the names, of course, have been changed.

The chapter divisions are largely synthetic and not a chronological sequence. But they're an accepted convention if only for the reader who wants to plump up the cushions or put the kettle on. After an introduction, two chapters relate 'brief encounters' – passing but memorable transactions taken from the episodic core of primary medical care. One chapter concentrates on some 'singular characters' that I cared for. Another chapter – 'practice pie' – is a stack of stories, each over a longer time frame, arising from the near-Utopian situation where the patient sees the same doctor consistently. A chapter on 'clinical disasters' and 'close shaves' is, I'm afraid, inevitable. And then a last chapter that is more 'personal' - the only element that might be seen as conventionally autobiographical. It is somewhat introspective without, I hope, being an ego trip.

Nostalgia is a dangerous dude. Does reminiscing self-select only the pleasant, the rewarding and the successes? Does it park, out of sight, the stresses, the frustrations and the failures? Maybe. But, in any case, what is each memory trace that surfaces? Is it trustworthy? Is it true? A far better authority than me discusses this in the foreword to one of his later books:

'To the creative writer fact is raw material . . . . his job is to make it sing. Real truth lies, if anywhere, not in facts, but in nuance.' (John Le Carre, 2016).

I wrap myself up in this quote as a defence against the brickbats. But it is also inspiring. In which case, while each short story is unique and self-sufficient, I dare to suggest that the whole assembly offers, also, a glimpse into the amazing variety and vagaries of humankind.

Having trained in medicine at Cambridge and St. Mary's Hospital, Paddington, I embarked on a series of junior hospital jobs around greater London, my teacher wife having to hop, frequently and frustratingly, from one school to the next. I became progressively disillusioned with hospital medicine and particularly its stifling hierarchy. I still think that the appalling accommodation, the missed meals and the sleep deprivation played only an insignificant part in my disenchantment – these were pretty much as I'd expected. But, navel-gazing aside, I found doing evening surgeries, as a dodgy locum GP in dubious lock-up locations around north London, fascinating and stimulating. I suddenly made a huge life choice and decamped to seaside Somerset, to a training practice, to learn the job of general practitioner properly. My poor wife had to follow me yet again and find yet another teaching post in yet another school. But we both felt comfortably at home in 'different-on-sea'. It was only 40 years later that I discovered one underlying reason - that my great, great grandmother had been born in the workhouse of that very community!

After more locum work – this time clued up – I was short-listed for a partnership in a practice in Wiltshire. I wasn't triumphant. But six weeks later I was unexpectedly invited to a second 'interview' only to stumble over the fact that the job was mine if I wanted it. But what was so wrong with the practice that, on second thoughts, the successful candidate had turned it down? I still don't know, having taken the job and having been a partner for three decades. I started in the practice on a bright April morning having double-checked that all my black bag contents were clean and functioning. I completely forgot to pocket a biro. The senior partner, welcoming me 'on board', gave me his. It was only a drug company 'freebie' but it worked well and seemed to know its way around a prescription pad.

I survived the probationary period, rose through the ranks and, eventually, became senior partner in what was a bustling training practice. As my stories will reveal, we worked all hours, practised obstetrics, triaged major trauma, performed minor surgery and, with the help of our uncomplaining spouses, answered the out-of-hours phone calls personally. We employed all our own staff, interacted with an extensive team of district nurses, midwives and social workers and, in my midstream, we built a gleaming new surgery on a redundant muddy lorry park. I also took up an opportunity to do research, initially in my own time and, having had published a series of papers and taken a higher degree, became an extra-mural journal editor and referee. However, I never wanted to back away from clinical practice, whatever the rigours and frustrations, and saw out my time at the conveyer belt.

General Practice is nothing if not episodic, as these stories relate. I reckon I would have performed not far short of 250,000 consultations during my career, most of them face to face. But irony lies in the other truth of womb to tomb care. Most patients will usually see the same GP time and again (or they did until recently). The episodes therefore fall into a continuum. Then individual quirks, personal history and family dynamics give a patina to the clinical acumen. Burnish this with knowledge of the community, with being part of the community, and you have General Practice at its best.

Here is a powerful spyglass into your GP's practice; front line medicine, warts and all. Many diseases feature in the text but really this is a book about people, people living out their lives in the face of illness, distress and even disaster. We are all the grist of primary medical care sooner or later. Despite a self-generated trend towards cutting their contracted hours, current general practitioners find themselves working their socks off (more than ever). The population has burgeoned and aged without commensurate true expansion of manpower. Clinical medicine is yet more complex, bureaucracy has become more immediate and demanding, and GPs are being inveighed against on all sides. Small wonder that morale is plummeting. Maybe a zenith has been passed but this exercise is not meant to be a political blast. I hope the following pages can be a record of why UK General Practice was – and I hope still can be – a fascinating repository of human interaction and a rewarding career.

Norman Beale
September 2024

1

BRIEF ENCOUNTERS

Saturday Night at the Movies

We all spent a lot of time, too much time, in the canteen at medical school. Compulsory commitments dragged us away and certainly anything social or sporting. But on occasion we were rounded up to go and see something exceptional. Even so, some of us were refuseniks. One dreamy afternoon a flustered registrar burst in to 'invite' us to the paediatric clinic. There was a case of Fallot's Tetralogy, a rare heart abnormality in infants: 'we might never see another one.' There was a scraping of chairs and an almost audible moan but three of us remained seated. If we were never going to see another case, why would we want to see this one? After all we'd had it drummed into us that it's vital, in medicine, to think rationally and be objective. It was, however, a strategic error that I would come to regret.

Saturday evenings were always a popular time at the cinema and now, I suppose, for streaming movies into one's home. I was drowsing in a chair in front of 'the latest' when the family, in unison, shouted 'Da-ad, pho-one.' Without any softening up of any kind, a man was demanding, insisting, that I make an immediate house call. I wondered if he was going to have the grace to provide any details. In fact, he did back off a little when I asked for some basic gen. It was about his new baby son. Apparently, no-one would believe them that their child went blue at times. The midwife had poo-pooed it and the health visitor had spent an afternoon sitting with the family and, when nothing had happened, she, too, was dismissive. He didn't expect me to sit and spend hours with them on a Saturday evening, but would I please come and watch a film?

'You can't mean a Hollywood movie, I assume?'

'No, doctor, just a short video. My brother-in-law has a cine camera and he's brought it over.'

'And the film involves the baby?'

'Yea – please can you come straight away. Only my wife is sure the baby is dying and she's very upset. Our first baby never did this.'

'OK, I should be there in about 15 minutes.'

The small house was overcrowded and overheated. There was a fug of tobacco smoke and there was a surly tension. As is my usual practice, I demanded that they put the dog out of the room. And, as I always find, I had to point out that even 'harmless' dogs will attack someone who appears to be assaulting (examining) one of the household. On this occasion my other usual request – that the TV be turned off – was not befitting. A VHS cassette was already loaded and the image on pause.

Everyone moved around on the scopious sofa to make room for me - in pole position. It crossed my mind to ask if there was any popcorn but immediately dismissed the idea. The 'play' button was pressed. The mother was in the shot, cradling the baby. He was in just a nappy. They were on the sofa just about where I was now seated. Nothing happened for a few minutes and we all began to look at each other. Nothing was said until the father instructed us, rather irritably, to 'keep watching.' We all now saw the baby get agitated and begin to cry. Then it happened. In a very dramatic way, the baby's colour darkened and he went distinctly blue. He stopped crying and went very limp. I had to pinch myself that he wasn't dying – after all he was now on his grandmother's lap next to me on the sofa. We watched on and saw his colour return. The father was still verging on the aggressive – 'so, will the medical profession now believe us?'

Although I had never before seen such a convincing demonstration (my own fault) of a cyanotic attack in a newborn child, I had read about 'tet' spells. I had probably also written about them in some examination or other, pretending an air of infinite knowledge and experience. I explained to the assembled company that we were probably dealing with a heart complaint that suffered from a name that was a tongue-twister. But the essence of the problem was that the chambers and pipework of the heart were slightly skew and when the heart speeds up some blood flows the wrong way. Blue blood that should be going to the lungs to pick up oxygen goes out into the body and hence the colour change. One of the miracles of modern medicine was that this could now be corrected by surgery. I then pleaded that they didn't ask me to go into further detail – it was all above my pay grade. My job was to agree with them, congratulate them on the wit to film an attack, and now go and speak to a children's expert – 'and I mean now, not tomorrow or any other time.' I felt that I had now been accepted, as had my suggestion. There seemed little point examining the child and I shot round to the surgery to ring the paediatric registrar on call.

I saw it as my task to convince the duty registrar how very distressed and anxious were the family and thankfully she agreed to admit the child and the mother immediately.

'Oh, and could they please bring the film. It could be a blockbuster in the medical education world.'

~

The Dangerous Mr Fuddle Wuddle

On the first two occasions that Dawn Reynolds came in I didn't notice or, if I did, it didn't register. Then, during the third consultation, I realised she was always dragging a shopping trolley. And peeping out of the top of it was a monkey. Dawn was a regular, mostly at our asthma clinic, and the nurses knew her well. I happened to mention the toy primate to our senior nurse.

'Oh, that's King Kong' she said. 'Dawn doesn't go anywhere without him. He looks after her.'

'Does she really think that? It's only a stuffed toy.'

'Well, probably. Dawn's an odd girl. Or should I say woman – she's married, you know.'

'Well, I've never come across a Mr. Reynolds.'

'Oh, you won't. He's in Horfield jail – for a long spell this time. He was a local no-gooder who got caught stealing building materials. He was sent down for six months. He treated prison like a university of crime and became a Bristol gangster when he got out. He was soon collared again. Dawn wouldn't have had him back anyway and, as far as I know, she's been on her own ever since.'

'Well, I never knew any of that. But Dawn's asthma – was it from childhood? Her notes are rather sketchy.'

'Yes, but it's odd, you know. She's got worse as she's grown up, rather than better.'

I tended to be rather more sympathetic to Dawn after hearing of her situation but was struck, increasingly, by the frequency of her asthma and related chest problems. Her attacks didn't seem to be seasonal, repeated doses of steroids were not helping her obesity, and I could see her becoming a respiratory cripple.

Then, one morning, a neighbour of Dawn came into the surgery asking for a doctor to call on her. It was her 'chest' again, but Dawn couldn't come in because she had broken her leg.

When I rang the bell to her flat there was long wait before the door half-opened. The first thing I saw was a below-knee plaster cast. Dawn was on elbow crutches and backed off, with some difficulty, to let me in. Even so I couldn't open the door fully and had to sidle into the hall. It was full of soft toys on every available surface and there, behind the door, was King Kong. But then I saw the sitting room. There were literally hundreds of soft toys of all kinds: a stuffed menagerie. I saw dozens of teddy bears of all shapes and sizes including one in lime green, a large plush elephant with red eyes, two pandas, two sloths in a clinch, a Cushingoid frog and dozens of brown bunny rabbits. I spotted Bagpuss leaning against a prototypical dinosaur in knitted wool. The marine world was well represented. There was a large blue and white whale lounging in front of the television. An octopus was in congress with the pouffe – missionary position I thought. There were some turtles and a shoal of fish on the windowsill. In fact, as far as I can recall, there was virtually no free space anywhere in the room. The sofa was occupied by an angry-looking tiger – striped, of course. And when I knelt down on the few square inches of visible carpet to open my diagnostic bag, I was overlooked by a boss-eyed meerkat. And then I saw it – beyond the sofa was a higgledy-piggledy pile of stuffed animalia who were obviously the overflow; a sort of squidgy Eton wall game. Dawn asked if I liked her family. I could only gape.

'Mr. Fuddle Wuddle's been very naughty' she said. 'He tripped me up and broke my leg. So, thank you for coming out, doctor.'

Dawn was obviously a hoarder. My immediate thought was that the very dusty atmosphere must relate to her asthma. Her current attack was more by way of an upper respiratory infection – she blamed the crowded hospital waiting room – but I thought it wise to prescribe an antibiotic now I had some understanding of her ecology. I thought to ask if she slept with any of the toys.

'Well, I only have my very best friends in bed with me. None of these. Tigger, though, stands guard at my bedroom door every night.'

And there, in the small bedroom, was another hundred or more soft toys, all looking rather matt with dust. I began to talk to Dawn about the nature of dust and house dust mite and its potential effect on her asthma. How it would be so much easier to keep the flat dust-free to the benefit of her health if she didn't have so many toys. But she interrupted me:

'Doctor, they're my family. I can't just throw them out.'

'Well, OK, but regular cleaning and hoovering, perhaps?'

'Oh, they hate the sound of the hoover.'

I was going to need more than one bite at this particular cherry, I thought to myself. And I was very careful not to upset King Kong on my way out.

~

March in November

Thursday. Ted marched in to an irregular rhythm and stood to attention, all six feet of black blazer, regimental pocket badge and highly pressed trousers. The military ambience was rather spoiled by the limp, the grimace and the tartan velour slipper opposite the one highly polished shoe. But perhaps marching with a limp is impossible anyway.

He apologised for not going to 'cas' but he thought I might be able to treat his march fracture – diagnosed by the Colonel on Tuesday evening after the rehearsal for the Remembrance Parade due on Sunday. I already knew that Ted had been a long-serving regular in one of the posh Guards regiments and that he was our British Legion's chief standard bearer. Sunday's parade, he reminded me, was a particularly important one: it was fifty years since the end of World War Two and all kinds of dignitaries were due to attend. It was obviously the highlight of Ted's year. He was almost tearful as he outlined his predicament – 'whatever it takes' I really must get him 'on parade' on Sunday. At the moment the pain was so bad that he couldn't even stand the bedding resting on his foot at night and he was sleeping with it out in the cold night air.

He handed me the slipper and I did him the kindness of over-rolling his sock. His big toe was tensely swollen, bright purple-red and you could almost see it throbbing. The signs were concentrated at the base of the toe – which was promptly withdrawn as I reached down to touch it.

'Ted' I explained 'you don't have a march fracture, or any sort of break, but you do have acute gout'. The usual next topic of conversation with new gouty patients is their alcohol 'non-consumption' but he skipped that one.

'If it's gout, doc, does that mean it can be cured by Sunday?'

I explained that there was some hope of it being a little better in a few days but there was no guarantee. 'You need a course of anti-gout tablets and some powerful anti-inflammatory painkillers which you'll have to take for a week or so. In the circumstances we'll leave planning the blood and urine tests that we should be doing until things have started to improve.'

He deflated – 'there is a chance, then?'

We went, as a family, to the parade on Sunday morning. It was very impressive and Ted was magnificent – at the front and rigid with pride. If he was in any discomfort he certainly disguised it very well. There might well have been some march fractures sustained among all the many troops and volunteers that morning, many of them known to me to be very short of regular exercise. But at least the Colonel would be making the right diagnosis.

Awash

In user-friendly terms there has never been a satisfactory definition of schizophrenia. Maybe there never will be. Whatever the trigger, the illness is long-term and can be catastrophic. Sufferers have delusions distorting their rationality, often as a result of hearing voices 'off stage'. Their personality is corrupted: think what a virus does to your computer. Relationships can be destroyed by deep paranoia or bursts of aggression. At worst, imagine your cheery and approachable GP suddenly turning into a salivating werewolf.

Schizophrenia is reckoned to affect one UK adult in every three hundred or so. In our practice we knew of 16 sufferers. By the so-called 'law' of averages we almost certainly had some who hadn't been diagnosed; hopefully none among the partners. Of the dozen or so we all knew there were the representative types – the physically threatening, the paranoid, the relapsing and the 'burnt-out' - now emotionally defunct. Flare-ups in their delusional behaviour were far from rare and could be dangerous. One such patient arrived at our surgery wielding a lump hammer. He smashed every window he could reach before our very brave caretaker tackled him. There was no reason to think that the patient owned a portfolio of Pilkington shares. He had seen his reflection in one of the panes the day before and was convinced that his mirror image was the source of one of his voices. Another patient always clipped a letter to the Queen or the Prime Minister to his repeat prescription requests. Our diligent staff kept a file of them – in chronological order. They were therefore able to predict any impending crisis by a deterioration in the handwriting. But the tribulations at the surgery were as peanuts to the traumas suffered by the close relatives of such psychotic patients.

Cecil, a long-standing schizophrenic on my list lived with his widowed father just two shakes from the surgery. He'd been in and out of psychiatric hospital many times since his first breakdown at the age of 18. I spotted his name on the afternoon appointments list. 'Cess' didn't appear when I rang the beckoning bell. A piece of paper was pushed under my door. It demanded to know if everything in the room had been 'cleansed'. I found Cess waiting outside – for an answer. I eventually coaxed him in. He wouldn't sit – the chair could be 'soiled.'

'I've been told to cleanse myself of all the filth in the world' he announced in a hushed voice. 'Well' I said 'you can relax here. We clean the building very regularly and thoroughly.'

'But I said cleanse not clean. There's a huge difference as you, for one, must know. I only eat cleansed food that no-one else has touched and I drink lots and lots of pure water – from Babylon if I can get it.'

On the face of it there are many more worrying delusions and, in retrospect, I missed the point. I tried to take charge of the consultation, sensing we were in for another crisis. I asked Cess if he was taking his tablets correctly. He was immediately very angry.

'How dare you? How stupid you are. How can I possibly take poisons while I'm cleansing my body? You're a waste of space and you know it.'

Cess stormed out but not without protecting himself from contact with the doorknob by means of a heavily soiled handkerchief.

Two days later, early in morning surgery, Cess's distraught father rang me and asked me to visit Cess. 'He's in a bad way again, doctor. He keeps drinking water all the time and is talking to someone all hours.'

It was after noon before I drew up outside Cess's house. His father was waiting at the open front door and pointed up the stairs. I put a hand on his shoulder and he burst into tears. Cess was in his bedroom, the curtains drawn, the air fetid. He was waist-down naked on the bed masturbating frantically, the more so when he saw me. There were two jugs of water on the bedside table and several empty glasses, one on its side in a puddle.

'Cess, can you stop for a moment so I can talk to you?'

His arm movements suddenly seemed to spread to his other limbs and his eyes rolled up. He went rigid and his back arched. This is no orgasm I thought. It took me a moment to realise that he was fitting – a generalised clonic/tonic convulsion and that he'd stopped breathing. My autopilot threw the pillows onto the floor, dragged him onto his left side and tried to lift his head off his chest. Then he went flaccid – everywhere – and he wet himself, massively. There were some gasping breaths that then became regular. I ran downstairs to the phone – a risk I had to take. Thankfully the ambulance controller answered immediately and I requested an instant response – 'yes, bells and lights please – for a non-epileptic patient who is fitting.' Father was sitting in a fireside chair trying to roll a cigarette but his hands were shaking too much.

I returned and sat with Cess for a few minutes – he was drowsy but breathing regularly, pulse OK. I thought it was safe to leave him again for time enough to ring the hospital. There was a much longer response time and then more delay but eventually the medical SHO on call was on the phone. I rapidly summarised the problem in terms of water toxicity and, of course, explained that my patient was a chronic schizophrenic. The 'duty dog' immediately cut across me and told me that because of the patient's mental illness, I needed to arrange an admission directly to the psychiatrist on call - at which point I became aggressive.

'Look, young man, this patient has already had one prolonged grand mal fit in my presence and could well have more. He could easily go into status and die. It's very clearly your job to admit him under very close supervision until you've sorted out his biochemistry. I'm putting him into an ambulance now – I can hear the siren. Of course, you should ask the 'shrinks' to see him as soon as it's safe. And yes, I will write you a letter detailing his significant history and current medication. Have a good day.'

Sometimes your cuddly GP has to be a werewolf to be the patient's best advocate.

~

Bathtime to Birthtime

Supper when on call for the practice was, to use a cliché, a moveable feast. It could also be suddenly interrupted. A man who sounded quite young, and terrified, was on the phone. It was about his girlfriend. She was expecting their baby and was having a bath. The water was turning red – he thought it must be blood. When I arrived he rushed me upstairs.

Jane, the girlfriend, was sitting on the edge of the bath with a towel dressing gown over her shoulders. She was pale and shivering. The bath water was more than a rosé but perhaps not yet a burgundy. There was fresh blood running down between her thighs. I lay her down. I plied the obvious questions in rapid volleys. She had had no ante-natal care of any kind. It was her third pregnancy and she had thought she didn't need any help. She was planning to have the baby at home. She thought she might be due but couldn't remember the date of her last period. Her massively domed pregnant abdomen was very tense – in fact rock hard. Here, unless we were very lucky, was one of those obstetric catastrophes we all fear. I was trying very hard not to project panic, but this was a serious ante-partum haemorrhage – a potentially torrential bleed. Was it from an early separation of the placenta high in the womb or, even more threatening, a separation of a placenta that was lying across the womb exit – a placenta praevia? Both situations can lead to the mother exsanguinating and our community is 21 miles from the nearest suitable hospital.

Thankfully the ambulance I'd requested before leaving home now arrived. We transferred Jane to the vehicle and the crew prepared an intravenous drip. I explained the dilemma to the boyfriend who was now in the street with two small children. Both little ones were crying – even very young toddlers can detect real anxiety.

'Jane's going to be alright, though, Doctor?' He himself was close to tears. I suggested he get the help of some neighbours or relatives to look after the children and to follow us to the hospital – at a safe speed.

We got the drip running at the second attempt and set off with lights and siren both in action. Jane started screaming and then breathing rapidly. She was obviously now in labour. I didn't dare do an internal exam with the possibility of a placenta praevia. The black humour of medical school – 'when not to put your finger in the dyke ladies and gentlemen' – somehow came up from the distant memory bank. It was therefore impossible to assess the degree of dilatation of the neck of the womb. It was a relief, though, to note that the flow of blood had slowed.

Jane was helped by some nitrous oxide but she was now contracting very regularly and strongly. The ambulance driver was having to vary his speed and was weaving left and right – we were obviously in dense traffic on the outskirts of the city. The hospital was now only a few minutes away. Then, after coming almost to a halt, the driver took us sideways to put two wheels up onto what was presumably a pavement. We all hung on. Jane now began to say she needed to push and I could begin to see the baby's head. Then, suddenly, we bounced back into the road. The ambulance sank down and rocked violently. The ambulanceman with me fell backwards. Jane screamed and arched her back. The baby fell into my lap and I picked it up by the shoulders. It was a boy – fully formed and already breathing. I was soaked in amniotic fluid, blood and vernix. I clamped and cut the cord. A small blanket was produced. I wrapped the baby and gave him to Jane. The ambulanceman and I looked at the cut end of the cord – some dark blood was wicking along it. Now for the placenta. I pushed on Jane's abdomen and thankfully the afterbirth began to appear. Fully delivered it was very bloody and ragged, but this was no time to examine it in detail. It sat, sloppy and redundant, in a bowl while we all took a deep breath. It had caused us all so much trouble. Then the doors of the ambulance were thrown open. Hospital staff were looking in on us. We must have been a gruesome sight – blood splattered everywhere, equipment strewn on the floor, a mother crying, a soaking wet GP and a winded ambulanceman – altogether not a Utopian nativity scene.

The hospital emergency team took the baby off to a warm cot and started to move Jane onto a wheeled stretcher. As she was transferred she asked the name of the ambulance driver. It was John.

'Then, that's what I'll call my new baby' she said. 'He delivered him, really, when he drove us off the kerb.'

David Vernon Thomas

A tanned Mrs. Thomas came in before her husband and indicated to him where he should sit. She was obviously someone in charge of the situation.

'I insisted that David make an urgent appointment to see you, doctor, because one of his legs is very swollen. We've just returned from Ibiza. If it's just from the mosquito bites, why is it only one leg?'

David shrugged his shoulders and, finally, said something – he was sure that the swelling would go down if he put his feet up. His wife's frown clearly relayed a disapproval of that notion!

Trousers and socks off, and up on the bed, it was clear that David's right foot and ankle were significantly boggy, the elastic of his sock leaving a deep, corrugated imprint. There was nothing to find further up the leg, no varicose veins, no inguinal glands. However, the right calf was tender when I gently pressed it and David winced. 'No', he said, 'I've never had this problem before.'

We turned to Ibiza. After a wonderful week's vacation – their first ever package holiday abroad – they had 'run into quicksand' on their return. Banned from their hotel room after breakfast on the last day and with only hand luggage available, they'd been obliged to sit on at the poolside breakfast area until their coach to the airport had arrived. They were in the direct sun for over an hour. Then, at the airport, they had a two and a half hour wait for their flight – more sitting down, chatting to fellow passengers. On board the plane it was announced that there was a 'discrepancy' with the baggage and that there would be a half-hour delay while some of the bags were unloaded and double-checked. It was nearly an hour when the next announcement was made – to groans throughout the passenger cabin. They had now missed their landing slot at Bristol and take-off would be another hour or so. Complimentary drinks would be served.

'So, David', I said, 'three days ago you spent nearly six hours in a sitting position and then a further two to three hours of an aircraft flight – perhaps eight hours in all in a sedentary position. I think you may well have a blood clot in your leg – a deep vein thrombosis – a DVT.'

'But I am a DVT' came the riposte 'David Vernon Thomas.'

We all laughed but I was reaching for the phone. The couple made silent, mouthed conversation while I was making arrangements. Among the mouthing I clearly lip-read 'I told you so'.

David was admitted to hospital and a venogram confirmed an extensive right calf thrombosis. Fortunately, lung scans were clear, eliminating the sinister and potentially fatal complication of a pulmonary embolus – of a chunk of the blood clot breaking free and flying around the circulation to impact in the lungs and cause mayhem, potentially fatal.

David was home again a few days later and our nurses helped he and his wife come to terms with the rigours of daily anticoagulation and with its monitoring blood tests. When I happened to see him in the corridor at the surgery – still trailing behind his wife, I teased them – here they were – 'DVT saved by Mrs. DVT.' That brought on a joint smile but my attempt to push the joke further – 'at least you didn't get a Paul Elliot' – fell completely flat. It probably deserved to, and I had the embarrassment of having to explain – 'Paul Elliot – Pulmonary Embolus.'

'No', David said, in a rather sombre tone – 'we're very grateful for that now that we understand the risk. You'll be pleased to know, though, Doc, that we've booked our next summer holiday already – in Bournemouth.'

~

Happy Birthday

Lunch was on the table and the news was on – still the headlines. Made it! But not for long. The phone interrupted the mid-broadcast reprise. It was the surgery. An old, old lady in a home was, the staff thought, having a stroke. She'd choked on her lunch and was now talking gibberish. And she had wet herself – unusual for her. As duty doctor the responsibility was mine. The home was the biggest on our patch, mixed residential and nursing. It was very familiar territory. I knew my car would be recognised and an escort to the patient would be waiting in the lobby.

In fact, the patient had fully recovered. Her clothes had been changed, she was now in control and fully alert. She knew me by name, knew who and where she was and was somewhat mystified by all the fuss. E & OE she had had a transient ischaemic attack – a temporary stroke. She'd had two before, was already on Aspirin and wasn't fibrillating. I made my recommendations and made to leave. In the corridor I asked about the Union Jack bunting over the entrance.

'Oh, we've a big birthday today, doctor. Dolly Barton is 100.'

'Ah, that's nice – I don't think I know Dolly.'

'No, she has amazing good health for her age though she is very deaf and her eyesight is poor. Would you like to see her and congratulate her?

The Mayor and Mayoress came before lunch and helped her cut her cake.'

'OK, just for a minute or so – it's not every day that someone makes it to the ton after all.'

Dolly was in a standard 'granny farm' chair in a bay window and surrounded by cards including one from Buckingham Palace placed very prominently. There were some crumbs clinging to the fine hairs on her chin and a splodge of thick cream masking one of the corgis on the big card. I was introduced and shook hands with her very greasy paw.

'Doctor who?' she asked the staff.

'Doctor Beale' was shouted into her left ear.

'Never heard of him. What does he want?'

'He's just popped in to wish you a happy birthday.'

'What, like the bloody Minister of Health who sent me a card? I've never even met the man. Who does he think he is?'

Harmless aggression like this can be quite entertaining, I thought, but made to leave. Dolly wasn't ready to let me go.

'Are you Doctor Steel's son, then?'

'No. I'm Doctor Beale' leaning to her left ear.

'Your father, he was a cruel bastard.'

The staff wrote my name on a piece of card and held it for Dolly to see. She just continued her rant.

'Yes, really cruel he was. Said he had to examine me inside once – didn't say why. He hurt me a lot and I couldn't pee straight for a week. It ran down my leg, it did. Bastard.'

I thought I should change the subject: 'I like your card from the Queen, Dolly' and pointed to it.

'Yes', she said, 'very nice' and launched into singing the National Anthem.

> 'God save our gracious Queen,
> Long live our noble Queen,
> God save the Queen.
> Put down that nice young man,
> You dunno know where he's been,
> God save the Queen.'

'Course, I was born under Queen Victoria. A right one her.'

'Really?'

'Oh, yes. Young widow you see. Gagging. Rolling in the heather with that big Scotchman with the beard. And then her Indian toy boy – full of eastern promise he was. Oh, yes, we know all about her. The older women told me all about it when I started work – and I was only 12. Randy bitch.'

Having watched all the chin crumbs cascade as she talked it prompted me to try to distract her again by shouting another question.

'Did you enjoy your cake, Dolly?'

'The cake? Oh, yes, very nice. I let the Mayor have a piece. He's jumped up, you know, like his father was. Bakers, both of them – and swindlers. You'd be dead lucky if you found half a currant in their buns and a lot of their bread is stale. His wife's nice though. Too nice for him.'

I now noticed that several more of the staff had assembled behind me and were obviously enjoying the entertainment. It was definitely time to leave and I pointedly picked up my black bag.

'Well, happy birthday again, Dolly.'

'You see to it, young man, that you tell your father that he shouldn't have been so rough with those big fat hands of his. And, anyway, he shouldn't have put me in here just because my ankles were swelling a bit. I could still get my slippers on.'

The staff were laughing audibly behind me as I made my way out. Back downstairs I saw Frank, the manager, at his desk in the office. He beckoned me in: 'I hear you called on Dolly.'

'Yes, quite a character.'

'Yes, sorry. I should have warned you not to let the staff set you up. Did she get onto Queen Victoria's sex life?'

I nodded.

'And the national anthem with her own words?'

'Aha.'

'And accuse you of being related to poor old doctor Steel? She loathed him and has revelled in 30 years' worth of revenge, slating him to anyone who'll listen. She's long forgotten that he once saved her life. I hope she didn't fart – she often does when she's excited.'

'No, I was spared that at least.'

'Good. But, of course, the day she stops effing and blinding and being so naughty we'll know we're about to lose her.'

~

Hobson's Choice

The parents met me at the front door and stood together on the threshold. It was as if they didn't really want to let me in. My entrance would crystallise their problem; their 19-year-old son. Kevin wasn't in the house. He was in the shed at the top of the garden. He'd been there for 36 hours. The door was barricaded on the inside by his father's heavy cylinder mower and there'd been threats of violence if anyone as much as approached the shed. The parents had tried talking to Kevin through the small side window, but he had now blocked that off with some timber. He had taken in some food and drink on a tray but only if it was left at the door and there was no-one within thirty yards, the length of the lawn. They had no idea what he might be doing about 'toileting'. And for much of the previous day and throughout the night they had heard Kevin talking, sometimes in a very loud voice. And occasionally he had shouted out that 'he didn't deserve to be murdered'.

'Why would he want to think that we are going to kill him?' his mother sobbed as she flopped into a chair. 'And what must the neighbours think?'

No, there'd not been any prior history of any such odd behaviour in Kevin, although his school progress had disappointed them. Several teachers had reported his 'day dreaming' and he had once torn the lid off a desk and marched off with it in the middle of a lesson. The parents had sat through a difficult interview with the head teacher and, perhaps rashly, promised that it wouldn't happen again. But it hadn't and, until the last few hours, this strange incident had been almost forgotten. Kevin was, apparently, making good progress in his apprenticeship and there was no reason to think he was abusing drugs or alcohol. He wasn't a smoker. But he had very little social life (which had been worrying other members of the family, especially his older sister). He had never had a girlfriend and, in fact, seemed to have no friends at all. He would spend virtually all his free time listening to music in his room. He would sometimes rebel against washing and changing his clothes but the parents thought this was probably quite normal in a teenager.

I listened carefully as I crossed the lawn. All was quiet. Throwing my voice, I introduced myself and asked a few questions. The only response was a noise that I took to be an adjustment to the mower against the door. Back in the house I explained to the parents that this must be, in my opinion, a form of psychiatric breakdown. Kevin's fear of being killed was a form of paranoia that, to him, was very real and almost certainly reinforced by hearing voices. Father asked if I was trying not to use the word 'schizophrenia'. I said I was trying to describe it rather than avoid it. He said nothing when I said I would need to obtain, very urgently and for Kevin' safety, the help of a psychiatrist. He nodded and sat down heavily. Mother dashed out of the room.

It was not a good day at the practice. Hardly back at the surgery I was phoned by the police. They were at an address a few hundred yards away. A distraught middle-aged woman had dialled 999 from a telephone box and was still in the street being comforted by neighbours even though it was now raining quite heavily. Her husband, a known sufferer with bipolar disease, had cut his wrists and was bleeding to death inside their house. The police had found the door locked and the windows bolted. They were rather panicky that they might be held responsible for an exsanguination if they didn't break in, but could I accompany them as they'd been told that I knew the patient well.

Once inside the home it was clear that the patient was in no immediate danger. He had cut his wrists – and forearms – but very superficially. There was blood but not a lot. He was sitting, hunched, against the kitchen cupboards, quietly moaning.

'I want to die. Kill me, doctor. Do your job.' He handed me a serrated kitchen knife from the floor behind him.

In the midst of organising some immediate safety measures I was thinking how lucky I'd been not to have had chance, yet, to phone the duty psychiatrist about Kevin. 'Killing two birds with one stone' was an appalling phrase in the context but, effectively, I was going to ask 'the shrink' to admit two patients, rather than one, in a single conversation. Efficiency, and, especially, a time saver.

It was seven o'clock in the evening when I met the duty psychiatrist at the surgery. It was still raining. I'd been home to help to see our children to bed but there'd been no time for supper. Dr. MacDonald ('call me Mac') pointedly locked his large shiny SUV and announced that we'd go visiting the patients in my old Renault. I'd never met him before and tried to give him a cogent summary of the problems. First, we saw the failed suicide. Yes, Mac said, the patient needed to be admitted for a complete reappraisal of his medication. He should be 'sectioned' – for his own safety and in order to enforce treatment.

Then to the detached suburban house and the garden 'sanctuary.' Mac got no further than I had done talking through the shed door. But though his general manner, to this point, had seemed very clipped and business-like, he was extremely empathetic with Kevin's parents when back in the house. He very gently explained the imminent processes, under the law, to take Kevin into safety and treatment.

Back in my car Mac was more his other persona again. I was surprised by the extent of the contrast, enough for me to think that here was yet another 'split personality'. He gave a very professional résumé of the two cases as he saw them. They were on a par, he felt, in terms of priority. Then, as we turned into our surgery car park, he pulled the pin on the hand grenade.

'I've one remaining bed in the whole hospital. I'm leaving it up to you which patient you want me to admit tonight.' He began to get out of the car: 'you'll have to manage the other patient in the parish for what could be several days. I'll get the troops out of course. Well, who's it to be? I'm getting wet here.'

~

After five on a Friday

Oliver Pearson was a patient I'd not met. All I knew was that he suffered from hay fever. Twice he'd asked for steroid nasal sprays, each time in April. He turned out to look his forty years, to be well-dressed, well-spoken and well-versed in on-line medicine.

'Come in, do. Take a seat. We've not met, have we?'

'No, and you'll be delighted to hear at this, the fag-end of the week, that I've not brought you anything too taxing.' He had read, he told me, that there was a pharmacological answer to his poor sleep pattern that I was 'at liberty' to prescribe for him.

Medicine can sometimes be a simple mercenary interaction but no self-respecting GP can afford to be just a grocer. I hoped he 'wouldn't mind' if I asked for more information.

'What, exactly, is wrong with your sleep pattern?'

'Well, if you must know, I sleep through the night OK but don't feel rested when I wake. I understand that there are different depths of sleep and I think I must be having insufficient deep sleep – isn't it called rapid eye movement sleep or something like that?'

'Well, we certainly sleep at different depths at different times of the night and the patterns can be quite complex. You certainly seem well-informed, Oliver. Are you clinically trained in the broadest sense or from a medical family?'

'No, I'm a solicitor.'

This made sense. He was clearly someone more used to conducting interviews than being grilled. 'And how long has your sleep been second-rate?'

'Oh, since my divorce last year.'

'Was the divorce traumatic?'

'No, not at all. I'm a divorce specialist and so is my 'ex'. We met at law school. Negotiating a satisfactory agreement was very straightforward.'

'You sound like the surgeon who removed his own appendix.' Oliver frowned and I felt obliged to apologise. 'Sorry, that sounds rather flippant.'

'Well, your analogy is hardly fitting is it?'

The verbal joust continued for some minutes but told me lots. Oliver and his 'ex' – Donna – had 'got together' during their final year at university. They would revise for their exams together in the evenings and then, fed up with their books, 'comfort each other' before settling down for the night. Weekends at respective parental homes had brought the two families together. A formal engagement and a large wedding with all the trimmings became a foregone conclusion.

'I think we rather fell into a marriage and then Donna announced, completely out of the blue, that she didn't want children. I was horrified and I felt betrayed. Look, I'm not sure why I'm telling you all this but since you seem hell-bent on knowing all about me, I'll admit that Donna and I then just drifted apart – totally in the end. Perhaps we should have tried harder to reconcile but it was all too easy to split up – the legalities cost us nothing of course. We even saved money on selling our house. By then Donna was having an unseemly lunchtime affair with an estate agent and he let us off his fee.'

I attempted to bring the consultation full circle. 'Well, after all I've learned in the last few minutes, I must say that your sleeping poorly is no surprise.'

'OK, Professor Freud, but is there, or is there not, something to help me sleep properly?'

'Frankly, no. Not really. I think you need some counselling rather that pills.'

'I totally disagree. I've come to terms, fully, with my life-story which, I admit, is hardly Utopian. But I suppose I'll battle through my tiredness somehow.' He rose to leave. 'Of course, since you don't seem willing to prescribe any medication I won't be able to take the lot, will I? Well, I must get back to the office, there are several loose ends on my desk.'

'Oliver, on the contrary, I think you had better sit down again! We need to talk further and now!'

Oliver's haughty confidence and chitinous demeanour vaporized and he slumped back into the chair. He had come close to suicide on several occasions he finally admitted. Earlier in the week, in London, attending a refresher course, he had hovered near the edge of the underground platform at Baker Street and had not jumped into oblivion only because a stranger had stepped up to him and asked if the approaching train went to St. Pancras. In the end he had crossed to the other platform, gone to Paddington, and caught the first train to Swindon. He told me this is such a matter-of-fact way that I was seriously worried – and I said so.

'You really are a Freudian, aren't you?'

'No, but I can see that you need professional psychiatric treatment urgently and that can't come from me. I suspect that you've not been entirely honest with me about your sleep pattern. I'll bet you've actually been waking at very early hours every morning and having very black thoughts. I think you're significantly depressed and I don't mean 'fed up'. Would you consider going into hospital?'

'What, a psychiatric hospital?'

'Yes.'

'But can you arrange that?'

'I intend to do my best – to get you admitted this evening if possible. Where will you go from here?'

'Well, Donna is actually in the waiting room. She made the appointment and insisted on bringing me here. She'd heard that I'd abandoned my course and wanted to know why. I think she'll insist that I go with her to her flat. I've got the number here somewhere, so you'll be able to get hold of me.'

'And having broken all this ice, you won't do anything stupid?'

'No. Donna won't let me.'

'OK Oliver. As I say, I'll try my utmost for you. By now there will be only one psychiatrist on emergency duty in our half of the county. And he or she will be on a mission to save any empty beds for cases they consider the most desperate by their criteria - not ours. I'm rather afraid that they will see a caring wife, sorry, ex-wife even, as an ex-cuse. That's the reality in our world, I'm afraid.'

Oliver passed me a card with a telephone number and an address before leaving. I rang reception a minute or two later. The staff confirmed to me that there had been, indeed, a lady who had been waiting for him and that they left together.

And, sure enough, on a return call to me at 8.30 that evening the duty psychiatrist could only offer Oliver an emergency appointment

29

in outpatients on Monday afternoon stressing that it was my job, in the meantime, to impress on Donna that she try to keep him away from sharp knives, railway lines, rivers, high windows and weedkillers. Nothing too taxing, then.

~

Worthy Farm Blues

Bar those relating to accidental injuries, consultations with men in their twenties are not quite unknown but pretty uncommon. The next person on my list was just such a rarity. A fit-looking, tanned young man in very tight jeans and a rude tee shirt (*another day, same shit*) bounced in.

'It's me feet, Doc. As you know' – an invalid assumption – 'it was very wet at Glastonbury this year. In fact, by Sunday afternoon, when it at last stopped raining, everything was under about three inches of liquid mud – well that's the polite word for it. I think I got trench foot although I was in wellies.'

Out of the fetid trainers and socks his feet were a mess. The soles were red and macerated and he had obvious athlete's foot arising between the toes. I reassured him about the maceration – it would improve of itself but put him wise to the fungal overgrowth.

'Oh, I didn't think of ath – e – lete's foot.'

I chose to ignore the mispronunciation that has become a modern fetish, even though it always annoys me.

'Well, it's the athlete's foot that will need specific treatment,' I replied. 'You've picked up what is a fungal infestation that would have been present, perhaps, even before you went to Glastonbury. The fungal threads probably had a better time at Worthy Farm than you did. You'll need to soak your feet in salty water twice a day and then apply some antifungal cream to kill the mould. I'll give you a prescription to get treatment started and you'll be able to get more of the cream over the counter at the Chemist. You may need to persevere with treatment for several weeks.'

The young man dressed and then seemed to hover. I wondered if there was something else on his mind and, sure enough, at the door handle, about to leave, he asked if he could ask, quickly, about a problem a friend of his was having. I pulled a face but said nothing.

His friend had been having a stinging sensation at the tip of his 'todger' when passing water and also had some 'matter' coming from the 'working end' but he didn't want to make a fuss.

I reached down to the third drawer of my desk, a repository for various stacks of paper. I picked out a leaflet that I had in readiness for exactly this situation.

'Give your friend one of these' I said. 'It gives the address and times of the so-called 'Special' Clinic in Swindon – he won't need an appointment but it's vital that he attends, and soon. Until proven otherwise, your chum has picked up a sexually-transmitted disease and needs urgent treatment that only the clinic can provide. Let's call his problem Glastonbury Clap shall we? So, here's the important leaflet and, in fact, here's another one for yourself!'

'Thanks, Doc, for being so understanding. And I shan't forget to treat me feet.'

~

Break in

Generally, at one-thirty in the morning all is quiet and our car park was, of course, completely empty as I drove in. I'd been attending to one of our serious asthmatic patients who had woken in the throes of an attack. The nebuliser had performed its magic but having left the machine and some fluid with the family I thought it best to collect another nebuliser from the surgery. If I took a gamble, and drove straight back to bed it was tempting fate - I was sure to be called to another asthmatic before morning: 'if you don't want it to rain, take an umbrella.' In any case, the pollen count was very high.

It was as I was leaving and setting the alarm on the building that I heard shouting outside. Gladys Pollard, who lived opposite the surgery and whom I knew, was in a state; a coat thrown over her nightie and in slippers. As I crossed to my car she explained breathlessly. Her husband had collapsed in their toilet. She had been woken by a loud bang and finding the bed empty, realised Bert must be in the 'loo'. But she couldn't open the door even though it was unlocked.

'Bert must be behind it, doctor. I think he's died. Thank God it's you – I saw your car and the surgery lights on. I was on my way to knock up my neighbour – she has a phone. Can you see if you can get into Bert – it's a miracle you're here.'

There was no refusing the request – it was certainly not unreasonable even at this hour. Sure enough, Bert was inside the toilet of their downstairs flat, presumably slumped against the door which, in theory, opened inwards. But even the two of us couldn't prise it open enough to get in.

'As you know, doctor, he's a very tall and heavy man.'

Gladys was right but this was no time to debate Bert's dimensions. The flat was at the end of a terrace and the toilet window was on the side of the building. I suggested, for want of a better idea, that I might be able to break in through the window. I dragged the Pollard dustbin under the window. There was a very convenient brick on the lid, as one often used to see. I sent Gladys for a small rug or old blanket and, looking away, hit the window glass with the brick. Surprisingly, the pane held but by hitting it again nearer to one corner it shattered. Large fragments fell into the room and I was able to reach in and open the casement. Fortunately, it opened outwards and, still balanced precariously on the bin, I could now see Bert on the floor – the light was on. I thought he could well be dead. Draping the fireside rug Gladys had procured over the sill and all the glass shrapnel, I was able to pull myself through and into the Pollard toilet.

Bert was breathing and there was a slow pulse. By parting his legs to either side of the pan and dragging him away from the door, I was able to give Gladys enough space for her to open the door fully. We now had room to lie Bert down flat on the floor and he began to revive. Gladys began to cry and disappeared. I rolled Bert onto his left side and pulled his chin off his chest. His false teeth were out. He was cold but beginning to make sensible answers to my questions.

'No, he hadn't had any pain.' He remembered standing at the loo having a wee when his legs began to feel very heavy. He became light-headed and very hot and then he must have passed out and dropped backwards against the door.

He was now able to sit up and stay with it and then, a minute or two later, stand. There were no obvious injuries and I shouted for Gladys. 'Oh, God, another miracle' she said. We helped Bert back to bed and pulled the bedclothes over him, ignoring for the moment, the wet patch down the front of his pyjamas. Gladys disappeared again and I double-checked Bert's circulation and nervous system. He seemed fine and now had enough brain function to thank me. He even laughed when I said that the only serious casualty was their window. Gladys reappeared with some mugs of tea but there was significant spillage – she was shaking so much. No matter, even the over-sweetened dregs were welcome.

I explained the mechanics of 'micturitional syncope' – of the drop in blood pressure in men when they stand to pass water, especially in the middle of a cold night after being horizontal in a warm bed. For safety, all men, and especially those who have had lots of birthdays, should sit if they need to pass water in the middle of the night. Bert seemed surprised and I had to reassure him that safety trumped effeminacy every time. Gladys chimed in: 'Bert, it's either that or I'm having the door taken out.'

The Germans, being a very practical race, and loving to zip words together in their language have a term for a man who pees sitting down – he is a 'sitzpinkler' – a 'gent' who sits. I am certainly one and so, now, is Bert.

~

Whispers

Send reinforcements, we're going to advance.

It had been the home of a succession of 'Knights of the Shire'. There were thirteen bedrooms, four state rooms, a library, a snooker/smoking room and extensive kitchens, all in 35 acres on the edge of the village. The last owner in the family never married. He was a cricket fanatic. He founded the village club, captained the side until well into his sixties and converted a large portion of the grounds to a cricket pitch – close enough to the house to put the windows in jeopardy. And so, when his final innings was over, the family genetic pool dried up and the vacant property came up for sale. New owners – a successful businessman and his wife – a State Registered Nurse – bought it with the intention of making it into a mixed residential/nursing home, the latter housed in a new, purpose-built extension. They were generous enough to offer the cricket pitch to the village club at a fair price and give them time to raise the money.

Pent-up demand for residential and nursing accommodation, a nationwide need, soon filled all the available places. It took very little time for we and our neighbouring practices to become very familiar with the new home and its routines. In confidence, we all enjoyed the ego-boost of playing ersatz consultants in leading an entourage round the wards manning the drugs trolley and issuing prescriptions with a flourish. Regular visiting also allowed us to get to know the personalities of the residents. Two of them were particularly prominent.

Bernadette and Philomena were inseparable. Ancient but reasonably fit, they took to spending their days sitting in what had been the tiled hallway of the old house watching all the comings and goings. It was a great place to pick up gossip and they could often overhear conversations in the old, panelled library – now the office. They weren't interested in cricket and always refused any invitation to watch a match from the terrace at the back of the house. They didn't know, therefore, that the village team had reached the final of the National Village Cricket Competition, traditionally played at Lords.

A few days later the two old ladies were sitting, as usual, in the hallway. They became aware of a conversation in the office in which a coach party to Lourdes was mentioned more than once. As Catholics, they began to whisper to each other that it would be a marvellous thing for them, before they died, to be able to visit the Sanctuary of Our Lady of Lourdes – the young girl who had experienced a vision in medieval times was even called Bernadette. They were still bubbling with enthusiasm when Father Hodges visited that afternoon. As was his custom, he sat with them for a few minutes and he was very intrigued by the proposed pilgrimage. Yes, he would certainly like to be one of the pilgrims. Thankfully he had a passport with some years left before expiry. The mention of a passport gave the old ladies a jolt. Neither of them possessed such a document and they had no idea how to obtain one. The priest said he would speak to Matron and that he was sure something could be organised.

Matron laughed out loud when Father Hodges raised the issue of the pilgrimage.

'Those two old busybodies have it totally wrong.' It had been her husband who'd been thinking aloud about whether there might be any of the home residents who would want to have a seat on one of the coaches going to Lords for the cricket final. Lords – the famous cricket ground, not Lourdes in France. 'Father, are you going to put those two old snoopers straight? Or do you want me to do it?'

Father Hodges gladly volunteered but he said he would wait for half an hour or so – until he was able to keep a straight face. In fact, he was pleased to be able to rehearse the story by telling me, between the giggles, as I walked in to start a ward round that afternoon.

Send three and fourpence, we're going to a dance.

~

Tearful

In the middle of the week, in the middle of the afternoon, in the middle of summer, there would sometimes be an hour's respite between antenatal clinic and evening surgery. Not today. After pummelling the last 'bump' and pronouncing 'it's a boy; or, maybe it's a girl' one of our receptionists appeared with some case notes. One of my patients had just been brought in, by one of his friends, in a very distressed state. The notes were skimpy but when I saw the name I had a flashback.

As a four-year old, Tim Morrissey, during some boisterous play with his older brother, had fallen backwards onto a box of crayons and pencils and sustained a very painful injury. One of the pencils had, like an Agincourt arrow, penetrated his buttock and splintered. His mother hadn't panicked in the face of the screaming but scooped him up and dashed down to the surgery. About an inch of broken-off pencil was protruding from the skin. Our senior nurse and I rolled Tim up in blanket to brace him and then exposed the perforated bum. I was able to grip three fragments of pencil with some Spencer-Wells forceps and withdraw them, each in turn. Mother, I remember, was very sensibly talking the little boy through the 'op'. I can still recall our anxiety as we inspected the retrieved fragments – when we put them together did they make a whole? It appeared that I'd succeeded but the pencil lead had shattered into very small pieces. Many of these were still aboard poor Tim and unreachable. I thought it was probably best just to leave them there and watch for sepsis. I remember ringing our local A & E consultant and that he agreed with our strategy.

Our nurses saw Tim about every 48 hours over the next week and no signs of infection appeared. In fact, he was already sitting comfortably again. But his father brought him in for the final check and was rather aggressive, accusing us of 'not bothering' about lead poisoning. It took some urgent diplomacy for me to calm him down and convince him that pencil 'lead' is actually graphite – in other words carbon and therefore totally inert in the human body. All this flew across my memory in a few seconds. Now, what had our Tim done today, all of 17 years later.

He was sitting in one of our cubicles, his friend standing next to him with a hand on Tim's shoulder. Holding a grubby handkerchief over his eyes, Tim was flexed and rocking in the chair. Even in this submissive posture he was obviously now a very fully-grown and muscular leather-clad male.

'The pain, doc, it's terrible. Can you do something?'

The friend took over. Tim had been welding a new saddle assembly onto one of his motorbikes. The welding kit was borrowed and playing up. After fiddling with the controls Tim had forgotten to lower his mask before resuming the weld. He had arc eye and the damage to his eyes and the headache had become intolerable over the last hour or so. Tim interrupted:

'It's bloody awful, doc, and I'm blind. Without Olli's help I wouldn't have found my way here.'

I persuaded Tim to remove his blindfold and look up at me. His eyes were massively inflamed – reddened, swollen and pouring tear fluid. There was also a patchy scattering of dust across his forehead and I wondered if he might also have foreign bodies in his eyes. Passing the handkerchief to Olli and giving Tim some clean gauze, I went in search of some fluorescein. Instilling the dye caused Tim great distress as I explained why it was essential. Sure enough, there were two dark specks on his left cornea. To distract him as I then dribbled in some local anaesthetic, I asked Tim if he remembered his pencil injury. He didn't but his parents had told him about it. By now the anaesthetic drops were working and Tim was more comfortable. I was able to lie him down and remove the small metal fragments from his eye. Thankfully they hadn't penetrated beyond the conjunctiva. I then began to explain how we would be treating the arc eye – with antibiotic drops and ointment, with painkillers and with strict rest somewhere reliably gloomy. I was mid-spiel when Olli interposed.

'There's a massive problem, though, Doctor. Tim's getting married on Saturday. I'm his best man and tonight's our stag night. Are you going to tell me to cancel it?'

I nodded. 'I think we're going to be lucky if Tim is actually ready for his marriage ceremony, never mind tonight's binge.'

There was a long, long silence ended by Tim, now sitting up but still holding gauze over his eyes.

'But, doc, you've got to get me better for the wedding. We can't cancel that – it's at St. Mary's and it's been months in the planning.'

'No. Obviously we'll do our best. Arc eye usually settles down quite quickly, at least in the initial stages. But the bride's mother will not be the only person in the church with tears in their eyes.'

~

A Summer's Evening

A residential street that is a cul-de-sac can form, on a summer's evening, a natural amphitheatre with an in-built audience. Chapel Close was just such.

I was some miles away, at our local maternity unit. The practice population had just increased by one, one helped into the world by widening the portal. I was repairing the episiotomy – restoring the vulval architrave. One of the midwives brought a message – 'could you ring home about a disturbance.' Free of my gown, apron, wellies, gloves and mask I was able to investigate.

Dennis Watkins, whom we all knew, in the practice, to be a fluctuating schizophrenic had, it seems, gone into a paranoid crisis at home. His psychiatric nurse had been assaulted when visiting him at his flat that afternoon. The duty psychiatrist felt that Dennis should be admitted to hospital forthwith on a 'Section.' In other words, Dennis should be compulsorily detained in a secure ward of the mental health wing. The potential dangers to other persons or property and the risk of self-harm often prove the tipping point in how best to resolve these situations and the necessary paperwork a formality. But staying within the law requires a posse of professionals – the psychiatrist, a GP and a social worker qualified in mental health care all to be on scene, confer, and agree the outcome.

The turning into Chapel Close was virtually blocked by an ambulance, a police car and a 'Chelsea tractor.' A crowd of people were all facing away from me, watching something very intently. They parted to let me through, and I found two policemen, two ambulance men and one of our local psychiatrists in a huddle in the centre of the 'arena.' Greetings done I, too, found myself looking intently at a wide-open window on the first floor of a low-rise block of flats. Dennis Watkins was appearing, on and off, at the window. He was shouting obscenities and gesticulating wildly at no-one and everyone. There would be breaks in the tirade in which we would hear sounds of breaking glass or china, shards of which were being propelled through the window. Self-preservation was keeping all the onlookers at a safe distance and it meant we were able to plan our tactics confidentially. We couldn't do much more than plan until the duty social worker arrived.

With the priority being to move quickly and effectively in order to secure Dennis before, driven by his demons, he harmed himself or someone else, we needed to break into his flat with all speed. The policemen thought they should send for reinforcements and for a 'rammit' enforcer to break down any locked doors. We also thought it might be necessary for two policemen to accompany Dennis in the ambulance. The policemen went to their vehicle to make a radio call and when they returned they had, with them, the duty social worker. Meanwhile the screamed obscenities and the sounds of yet more breakages were continuing unabated. We resumed our deliberations together with the social worker including our best tactics for breaking into the flat. But before we could finish our rehearsal we were interrupted. The social worker said that he thought we were being over-aggressive and lacking in empathy towards 'his client'. We really shouldn't be adopting the tactics of a Fascist state. We were all taken aback. So, we asked, what, exactly, did he propose to do, as Dennis' representative?

'Well, first of all, I do want to talk to my client. I'll go in alone if necessary – in fact that might be best. I'm sure I can calm him down. It could be time well spent.'

We were all agape. And before we could intervene the social worker clutched his clipboard to his chest and strode off up the path towards the communal front door of the flats. He had almost reached the building when a large television set came flying through the window, landing with a splintering crash a foot in front of him. He almost fell forwards into the electronic debris but his feet were of clay. There was a long pause. Then he stood upright, looked at the open window as if expecting another salvo, and then turned and came back down the path, looking over his shoulder.

'OK, let's just sign the documents' he said. His clipboard was shaking violently and we had to steady it in order to pen our signatures on the 'Section' application form.

~

Twelve out of Ten

4.15. a.m. Something is waking me. It's the phone.
'It's my husband, doctor. He's in terrible pain in his side.'
'OK. What's his name and which doctor is he registered with?'
'Bob Stevens, doctor. He's one of Dr. Craven's – I think he's your partner.'
'Yes, and your address?'
'Fairview, High Mesne – on the main road at the top of the hill. Oh, please be quick, doctor. He's doubled up in agony and; oh, now he's being sick.'
'I'm dressing as we speak, Mrs. Stevens. I'll be there in a few minutes. I have to cross town to get to you but I won't be long. Can you put a bath towel over your front gate or hedge where I can see it from the road. There's no need to ring again – I'm on my way.'

Being midsummer, it was half-light and the dawn chorus was warming up. Driving through town was easy enough. I was tempted to jump the central lights but bottled out. Our local magistrates are personal friends, but I could hardly expect privileged treatment if some hidden camera was recording my number plate. The lane up to High Mesne village climbs gently through a couple of miles of farmland and passes a nice pub halfway up where the incline eases. A couple of fields beyond the pub I had to slow down to squeeze past three vehicles which had been reversed into a field gateway; a Luton van and two cars. One of the cars was half into the road as if abandoned in a hurry. After negotiating the pinch point I gave it no more thought. I was beginning to concentrate, looking for a bath towel.

Mrs. Stevens must have been out listening for the car. She came running down the path. I was given the full story as we ducked into the old cottage and climbed the steep stairs. The pain had come on very suddenly and his screaming had woken her. It was down his left side, coming and going, and she had seen him clutch his 'private parts.' He'd now been sick twice. Never seriously ill in his life, Bob didn't take pills – not even vitamin tablets, and had never missed a day's work at the Co-op.

Mr. Stevens was lying on his right side, fetally folded, his knees drawn up tight under his chin. He was pale and clammy. Some of the bedsheet had been doubled over some vomit. When I stretched him out to examine his abdomen the pain came back and I had to wait a minute or two before laying hands on. There was nothing to find. His 'private parts' were also normal. His index finger gave me the diagnosis. It mapped out the course of the pain – a precise line from loin to groin. The poor chap was passing a kidney stone and I put them in the picture. The stone would probably be the size of the proverbial millet seed but while the ureter muscles are trying to propel a stone down into the bladder the spastic activity causes extremely intense pain. If asked to describe it on a scale of one to ten, most patients come up with a figure of at least twelve.

I injected some Pethidine, but long before it could have been working the atmosphere relaxed. Knowing the diagnosis and understanding that it is survivable carries an amazing therapeutic fillip. I asked Mr. Stevens to try to pass some urine into a clean container so that I could test it for traces of blood and he toddled off to the toilet. If proven positive it would secure the diagnosis.

While we were waiting Mrs. Stevens drew the curtains. It was full daylight outside now and their view was spectacular. It took the eye across a crocheted blanket of undulating fields; arable crops including some yellow rape, neatly hedged meadows, and woods up to the dramatic horizon of Salisbury Plain. Seeing my surprise, Mrs. Stevens said that they always felt so lucky to have such a view. They had planned their garden so that nothing interrupted it. But during last summer they had been annoyed by drifts of people edging down past their garden into the field. There had been an invasion of their privacy, their piece of heaven. On one occasion, even a coach party had tramped through, many of them stopping to eye up the garden and make perfectly audible comments, not all of them complimentary. They had all come to see the crop circle that had appeared, one night, in the growing corn.

Crop circle. Of course. Here was the explanation for the clutch of vehicles I'd seen on my way up to the village. Crop circle 'artists' must have been at work in the field beyond. On my way back down the hill I pulled up at the gateway. The vehicles had gone and there were no signs of life. But there, in some tall barley, still green, was a fresh crop circle half hidden by a low mist. Doctors aren't the only people at work in the countryside at night.

~

White Accident

Unless one is very lucky or especially hard-hearted and cynical, medical practice will invade one's private life. After a very pleasant evening at the theatre with my wife we were driving home. In mid-summer it was still not really dark and the roads were dry. There was no reason not to take a short-cut over the Downs even though we knew it was tortuous and narrow in places.

As we negotiated a tight bend through a wooded dip there was suddenly stationary traffic in front of us. We managed to stop in time and to see that some of the cars ahead had doors open and there were people on the road. One of them came to us to tell us, breathlessly, that there was a bad accident up ahead – two cars had collided head-on. Someone was already talking to emergency services. Obviously, I needed to do more than sit in the car and leave it to paramedics. My wife agreed to stay with our car since it might have to be moved to let police and ambulance through.

As I walked down the lane the crashed vehicles came into view – a small minivan half impaled, half underneath, the front of a 'Chelsea tractor.' A tall man was standing next to the 'Discovery', leaning on the offside door and staring at his feet. I took him to be the driver. He nodded when I spoke to him and he said he was unhurt.

There was a strong smell of hot rubber coming from under the concertinaed bonnet of the van. The doors were still closed and for some reason one couldn't see inside; the windows were opaque. Odd. Two men were wrestling with the driver's door and managed to prise it open just as I joined them. I announced that I was a doctor and they stood back – not because of my status or supposed skills but because of what they had just seen inside the vehicle.

The driver, a young man, was white – all over. His right arm had obviously struck the steering wheel and his right hand was hanging at a very funny angle. There was arterial blood pumping into the well around his white feet. I shouted that I needed something to use as a tourniquet and someone behind me passed me a tie. I lashed it around his forearm, tightened it, and thankfully the torrent of blood slowed. The hand and wrist were not a pretty sight – there was a compound fracture of the radius and ulna – spikes of bone were visible. The young man screamed as I pushed past him to release his safety belt and again as I dragged him out of the car. We lay him down and put his arm into a temporary splint by pulling up the front of his shirt. This, too, was white but only at the front. Moaning and shaking with terrible pain, at least he was conscious and orientated – he was very worried about his girlfriend.

The passenger door was still jammed but we could see a young woman inside through the broken glass. This was a serious situation – the van could erupt into a fireball at any moment and we now knew there was someone trapped inside. And those of us now trying desperately to get to her were also in danger of serious burns. From what I could see, after pulling away some shards of glass, the woman inside was unconscious and the impact had half-propelled her down into the legroom below the glove compartment despite her being belted. She, too, was covered in some sort of white liquid – which seemed to be dripping from the van roof. Thankfully we now heard sirens and within what seemed to be longer, but probably only a minute or so, some firemen were with us. They fetched a clever large tool that soon had the door off and the young lady into a neck brace and out onto the road. She was unroused by moving and I put her in the tonsillar position and checked that she was breathing without obstruction. Her teeth were all her own and respiration was regular, pulse strong. It was impossible to judge her colour clinically – it was white – as was her hair and much of her clothing. She was stretchered off with haste and her boyfriend assisted into the same ambulance. My helpers and I, watching the professionals go about their well-drilled tasks, now realised that we, too, were patchily covered with a white wet substance on our clothing. As the ambulance sped away curiosity got the better of me.

The firemen had sprayed fire retardant over the van engine, so I thought it safe enough to open the rear doors. The young couple had obviously been decorating. There were several tins of paint, some boards, some decorating sheets, a small stepladder, dustpan and brush and other paraphernalia all in a higgledy-piggledy heap, thrown forwards on impact. And there, atop it all was a wet nine-inch roller and large paint tray. The tray was virtually empty.

Anxious to get home, perhaps before the pub closed or for a favourite TV programme, the young couple must have popped the tray, still containing a sizeable volume of white paint, into the back of the van with all the other kit. This must have been catapulted upwards and forwards in the instant of the crash, like a rock from a trebuchet. The accident may not have been their fault and I felt anxious for their recoveries – survival even in one case – but the couple had managed to decorate the interior of their van most effectively. It was almost a shame that it was a write-off.

~

2
PRACTICE PIE

Tacky Tachycardia

There are those in life who are lazy. Others are antisocial. And an inexcusable minority are both. Among the latter are those who put a bottle of tomato ketchup in their supermarket trolley and then, three aisles further on, change their minds and plonk it on the nearest shelf – among the blue and white boxes of the washing powders. There it sits, conspicuous and unique. A required skill for a successful general practitioner is the ability to spot the 'Heinz' among the 'Persil'. Easy enough, one might think. But not in real life, where the sauce appears identical to the detergent – in all discernible respects.

Horace Jones was one of the bottles of ketchup I didn't spot. I knew his family well. He was the youngest of six. Father was an agricultural labourer, the family brought up in a tied cottage. Horace was intellectually retarded, perhaps after a difficult birth (suddenly, at home, with no medical input, so no-one knows). He attended a special school, never mastered literacy, and would have found it difficult to hold down a steady job if an older brother hadn't recruited him into his building business. Although his employment could be sheltered, he remained exposed to the shocks and traumas of life outside work. It was especially a shock when his father, aged only 52, dropped dead at the wheel of a tractor. And it was unsettling when Horace and his mother were then evicted from his childhood home and had to move out of the village where he had grown up and felt very much at home.

Falling back on this emotional hinterland led me to think that Horace's repeated consulting about his 'heart thumpings' lay in anxiety. He certainly seemed more worried about his heart than any of his 30-year-old peers. Examining him was unhelpful, at least to me. I could find nothing abnormal bar his mild obesity. On the fourth such occasion I thought it best to take things further and arranged an ECG. Horace was immediately more anxious and the high pulse rate on the tracing seemed acceptable when sister reported how jumpy he'd been from the moment he'd been wired up. I tried going up and down the emotional snakes and ladders again but to no avail. Horace was still reporting a racing heart that just 'came and went'.

Then an off-the cuff remark during yet another consultation took us forward.

'You, know, doctor, my brother says that if I go looking at Penthouse magazine, I could end up having a heart attack. Is that right?'

Here, at last, was a coat hook, something that might allow me to see Horace as washing powder.

'So, Horace, do you look at Penthouse?'

'Well, doctor, only now and again – at my brother's place. He keeps them under the cushions on the sofa. Now I know they're there I usually have a quick look. Then, one day, he caught me. He was really angry. That's when he told me I could have a heart attack.'

'And when you're flicking through Penthouse, Horace, is that when your heart races?'

'You bet, doctor, have you ever seen what's in them magazines. I sometimes think me heart's going to jump out of me.'

Slam dunk, I thought. Tacky tachycardia. Cause and effect established and well within the covers of any textbook on the autonomic nervous system. Treatment simple, cheap, and effective. My job is rarely easier than this – washing powder through and through. Horace seemed to understand when I talked him through the Ladybird book of physiology at the right page and nodded that he did – that his heart was responding to sexual stimulation and only doing what normal hearts do.

'Thank goodness for that, doctor. So, my brother's no right to frighten me?'

'No, Horace, not at all.'

A year later I returned from a longed-for holiday from the practice. Three stress-free weeks; well, at least outside the airports and the car-hire desk. As I was racing through a daunting pile of correspondence early morning one of my partners popped his head in.

'Good holiday?'

'Yes, great – but look at this lot.'

'Yep, I know the feeling. Have you got to the J's yet?'

I shook my head.

'Well, don't jump out of your skin, but your Horace Jones dropped dead from a sudden heart attack just like his father. You'll find the report from the coroner there somewhere.'

I gasped: 'but he was only thirty something.'

'Yes, but it happens now and again - as we all know.'

I nodded slowly. So, poor Horace had been ketchup after all.

~

Earth is Green, Live is Red

The Clarks should have been called Sparks. They ran an electrical shop in the High Street. They didn't sell actual electricity, of course, but they appeared able to obtain or repair anything that ran off electricity be it mains or from a battery. I first encountered their 'Aladdin's Cave' when we needed a replacement aerial for our transistor radio. One of our children had knocked it over and bent the antenna so that it no longer retracted.

'Nice to meet you, doctor, call me Cliff.'

Mr Clark looked lovingly at our 'trannie' and was adamant that repairing it was 'no problem.'

'Although my family have always been patients of your partner, Dr. Heslop, my wife is a patient of yours, doctor. I'll just pop up and get Ivy to meet you. Won't be a minute.'

While Cliff was gone I had some seconds to look around the shop. It was a cramped assortment of museum and department store. There were several large radios that looked pre-war and a timeline of various televisions. There were fans, heaters, torches, toasters, hair dryers, mixers and even electric toothbrushes. Then, behind the counter, was an enormous assembly of deep wooden drawers each bearing a brass-rimmed label. I imagined they contained Cliff's stock of spare parts and components. Then the curtain at the back of the shop was pulled aside, Mrs. Clark came in and I was introduced.

'I don't expect you'll see much of me, doctor' was her parting shot as I backed out of the shop. Fateful words. I'd noticed the ashtrays full of roll-up stubs and that both of them wore the tell-tale brown-yellow staining of their fingers.

The radio was ready to collect within a couple of days and the charge seemed very modest – not that I questioned it. Cliff was keen for me to know that he would always be prepared to fix any household equipment; hoovers, mixers, fan heaters, washing machines, spin dryers, record decks, radiograms. 'Anything that ends in a plug' was how he put it.

'And don't forget, doctor, I'm a fully qualified electrician if you run into any problems with your household circuits.'

The mention of a radiogram seemed from another era although my parents still owned one and I suppose they were from Cliff's generation. But I was certainly pleased to know that we now knew of an electrician that we could call on if ever necessary.

A couple of years later I got to go behind the curtain at the shop and climb the stairs. Ivy had requested a home visit. She was 'chesty' and had a 'bad' cough. She didn't think it wise to go out. Cliff ushered me beyond the curtain at the rear of the shop and signalled for me to go up. Half of each tread up the stairs was occupied by rolls of cable or boxes of fittings and the flat was as congested as the shop itself. Rather disconcerting was the life-sized cardboard cutout of James Robertson Justice as the fierce surgeon, Sir Lancelot Spratt, in 'Doctor in the House.' Suddenly I was back, a perspiring medical student on a ward round trying to remember the average weight of an adult liver. More off-putting were the signs of a couple of litres of fluid at the bottom of Ivy's right lung and a hard lymph node above and behind her right collar bone. She sensed my anxiety and grabbed my hand.

'If it's bad news, doctor, you will tell me won't you. But please don't tell Cliff.'

An urgent chest X-ray strongly suggested that Ivy had lung cancer and I suspected that it had already spread widely. I went to tell her, honestly, of her predicament and she was equally honest. She said she wasn't surprised, having smoked all her adult life. Still coughing and now breathless at rest, she was forced to tell Cliff who had, in any case, been wanting to know the result of the X-ray.

For the first time that anyone in the town could remember, the Clark's shop was closed for a day while the two of them went to see a chest physician. Ivy was assessed, as I'd feared, as already being at a stage in her illness where palliation was the only option. Thankfully we were able to keep her reasonably comfortable over the next two months until she died – in her own bed above the shop. Cliff supported her with great care and sympathy, as did their two sons, one of whom travelled many miles every weekend to be with his mother.

Cliff kept the shop going, telling everyone that he believed in work as therapy. He took on an assistant so that he could leave the shop to do outside jobs without having to turn the rather ancient 'open' sign on the door to 'closed'. This was fortunate for me. We were having an extension built on our house and needed an electrician. Good to his word, Cliff was happy to quote for the work and turned up immediately that the builders were ready for 'first fix' wiring.

I can't remember quite why, but a short time after our build was finished it featured as a coffee time topic at the surgery. My partner, David, asked if Cliff Clark, his patient, had 'done our electrics'.

'Yes, he did. He made a very good job of it and even charged less than the estimate.'

'Mm. Interesting. Now I wouldn't dream of playing with the electrics at home myself, but I can just about change a plug. Is it still red for live and green for earth or have the powers that be played about with the colours yet again?'

'No, red live, green earth is still correct, I'm sure.'

'And you can tell one from the other?'

'Of course.'

'Well, Cliff can't. He has red/green colour blindness. Shall we order a new batch of rubber gloves for you to use at home?'

~

Percy Geoffrey and Clay but not Monty

After his father was killed at El Alamein Jack's mother moved the family back to live with her parents so that she could go out to work. The little boy therefore grew up with his grandparents in the village where 'Gramp' was farm labourer, thatcher, gardener, bell ringer and gravedigger. Jack learnt quickly from his grandfather, but plant husbandry was his obvious passion. Though it was not a formal apprenticeship he tagged along with the team of gardeners at the Manor; formally and full-time as soon as he was 15 and no longer an 'absent from school' statistic.

Though interrupted by National Service, Jack worked on at the Manor through marriage and fatherhood. When the Rosser family bought the property Jack was endowed with the term 'head gardener' though this was rather meaningless since he was now the only full-time employee outside the house itself. But, happy in his own company and not above the many menial tasks, he thrived. The Manor gardens responded to his devotion, as did his own rose garden, vegetable patch and fruit cage. The Rossers were genuinely grateful and allowed the rent of his cottage in the grounds to fall far behind inflation.

Jack's natural talents with plants earned him widespread respect and cup after cup at annual flower shows. He was able to help Mary, his wife, in her activities in the village – spring flowers for Easter services, produce for harvest festival and 'evergreenery' to decorate the church at Christmas. The topiary along the Manor drive, the walled garden, the summer borders, the greenhouses and the sweeping lawns were all admired when the village fete was held at the Manor every summer. Jack was held to be Wiltshire's answer to Percy Thrower, to Geoffrey Smith and then to Clay Jones. He would have become Monty Don but he fell from a wet ladder when he was in his mid-sixties. It took a week to shake off a low back pain but he never stopped work. A friend lent him a corset to help his 'sciatica'. It was some months later that he began to feel an ache in his right groin and thigh and still blamed the fall. Imperceptibly at first, he began to limp as the pain increased. His gardens suffered as he became more immobile, and he began to accept that he would have to retire. The Rossers assured him that he and his wife could stay on at the cottage and arranged a farewell party at the village hall. He modestly dismissed all the 'fuss' and went home laden with gifts and good wishes – and cried.

Jack came to the surgery for the first time in twelve years (and it had been only, on that occasion, for an impaled septic rose thorn). The limp and the grimaces screamed the diagnosis even before he flopped into the chair, his right leg thrown forward. There was barely any movement in that hip and the left was already restricted. The urgent need for a hip replacement was evident. I referred, vaguely, to the likely long wait for surgery but the orthopaedic surgeon was made of sterner stuff – the waiting list was 'between two and three years' even for such severe arthritis. Jack's stoicism had let him down – I would have been justified, I'm sure, in having referred him at least a year earlier if only he'd presented.

By now any gardening, recreational even, was out of the question. Far from it, Jack now needed Mary to help him dress, bathe, and negotiate the tight, twisting stairs at the cottage. Various technical adaptations were installed though they seemed very out of place in the 'chalk and thatch'. But with the apparatus came unwelcome advice – that Jack and Mary would both have a much easier time, indeed a less hazardous one, in a modern ground-floor flat with no garden to maintain – a burden that now fell on Mary alone. Jack was resistant. All his sentient life had been in the village and he knew there was no 'sheltered' accommodation in 'his' community. When it was dry and not too cold he would crab outside on his zimmer frame to sit under the front windows. It was bitter-sweet seeing his garden so unkempt while he was lifted by the fresh air, the view of the downs, the birdsong and by a stream of friends and neighbours pausing to chat. The postie always stopped even if there was no delivery and he was satisfyingly encyclopaedic when any stranger asked directions. But these were the dying remnants of his life in the village, and it became more and more irritating to hear how his part-time replacement at the Manor was so reliant on noisy, brutal machinery.

Within hours of moving, Jack knew it was a mistake. The flat – ground-floor as required – was on the corner of a busy side-street and a main road. The noise, the vibration, and the pollution were merciless. There was constant human traffic too, with pavements next to the building on two sides. Even with the windows closed – as they had to be – he could overhear conversations and he began to think they were about him. For the first time in his life he was unable to get to sleep at night. The dawn chorus was now the trundling of heavy lorries grinding their way to the local landfill. He refused my suggestion of anti-depressant tablets – he told me to put them 'up my ass'. It was a shock to Mary that her wonderful husband could be short-tempered and use foul language. She was glad to have picked up a new social life in the town but began to dread going home. It came as such a relief when the forms notifying Jack of his admission to hospital arrived. But it was very distressing for her to discover Jack in the act of tearing them up.

With the help of the family and some Sellotape, Jack was finally admitted for surgery and things went well. He was virtually pain-free for the first time for years and more like his old self. Getting mobile was the priority back at the flat but his legs remained swollen and heavy. Nevertheless, he was glad to accept a car ride out to the village when one of his sons had an errand to run. Parked opposite the church, Jack remained in the car. He could see the top of the tallest tree at the Manor over the roof of the pub. It was the last thing he ever saw. When his son returned Jack was slumped against the passenger window, his head on his chest, and obviously dead.

The Coroner's post-mortem reported a pulmonary embolus from a leg vein; a clot of blood had broken away and plugged a major vessel. The family wondered whether their tragedy was really a result of the long wait and challenged me to deny it. But they took some solace from the fact that Jack had died very suddenly, without fear, and in his village.

~

Plus ça Change . . .

History never repeats, the saying goes. But I wonder. Little Christopher Cullen was born to first-time parents. He was the product of a third and desperate last chance attempt at IVF and therefore a particularly precious baby. I saw a lot of him because of perfectly understandable parental anxiety. Nonetheless he developed normally. But virtually from the day he was weaned, there was 'high-chair' trauma. Like so many toddlers, his reactions to food were very unpredictable and dispiriting.

Some was consumed avidly, some was simply rejected with a whiplash head turn, and some thrown back at his anxious 'keepers'. Dawn, his mum, harboured a high level of fear bordering on paranoia that she was failing to meet 'little Chrissy's' vital needs. And it didn't help that we were going through a quick-fire succession of new health visitors – the same, and perfectly correct, advice can be given in so many different ways.

Time and again, Dawn brought the little boy in when there was a new spring tide of anxiety that he was failing to develop. Her rather passive husband always backed her but seemed fearful of any confrontation. Time and again we plonked crosses on his 'Tanner' growth chart. Time and again he was growing along the 50th centile. Christopher was consistently 'Mr. Average.'

I sometimes wonder, in idle moments, what happened to Christopher's growth chart but by the time he was seven or eight it was no longer on the front line. Sometimes it takes all that time to convince parents that they're doing a superb job despite the rejected food on the floor, especially anything green. I did see Christopher on a few occasions around puberty – 'no, temporary breast enlargement is quite normal, even in boys, yes even on just one side' – but for nothing serious or threatening. I noticed, though, that he was now already as tall as his mother.

You can well imagine my amazement when, a few years later, a six foot and more, fully grown male of the species called Chris Cullen loped into my surgery. He was in a lot of discomfort with a couple of broken ribs. These, he had sustained, on the rugby field. I could quite understand how he was now second row for the local team. His physique was superb – an inverted triangle of muscle and sinew on powerful limbs and with very large hands; a powerhouse in the scrum and able to clutch the ball high in the air at lineouts. I asked after his mother:

'She hates me playing rugby but Dad's very keen – wants me to have a trial for Bath.'

Chris next came with a young lady, about three years later. He launched straight into rugby gossip knowing I'd be interested. His trial at Bath had not been successful but he was now the pack leader of our local side. 'But we've come in, doctor – this is Angela by the way – because we're not getting anywhere with starting a baby. Angela looked, demurely, at the floor but Christopher was very brassy about the whole business.

'We've been really trying for over two years, in all ways' he said without seeming to recognise the ambiguity. I advised them of the next steps towards success and introduced the eventual possibility of IVF.

. . . *plus c'est la même chose.*

Eine Neue Familie

Registrars of Births and Deaths sometimes found themselves, during the baby-boomer years, having to enter the details of newborn babies with foreign names, a new phenomenon post-war. Some family names were of German origin, some of Italian and we even had one family in our practice with a Hungarian surname. The explanation is obvious enough – some men from the Axis forces who had been captured and become prisoners of war and who had been shipped to Britain had remained here after hostilities had ceased and married local girls.

I was not surprised, therefore, to see the name Kaufmann on my patient list one morning. Judith, a seventeen-year-old, who looked older, came in with her mother. There was a tangible tension between them. It spelt trouble and I waited. Mrs. Kaufmann spoke first and with a familiar local accent. She introduced her daughter, though the striking likeness would never have indicated otherwise.

'Judith's been a naughty girl, doctor. We told her till we were blue in the face not to get into trouble with boys but to no good. We think she's going to have a baby and we want it stopped.'

'Who, exactly, Mrs. Kaufmann, do you mean by "we"?'

'Well, my husband and me, of course.'

'And Judith – what does she want?'

'Oh, she agrees with us, doctor. She knows that carrying the baby will ruin her life.'

'Well, you're seventeen, Judith, isn't that correct?'

Mrs Kaufmann interposed: 'Yes, doctor'. She obviously thought it appropriate to continue an exclusive two-way conversation leaving the actual patient in limbo.

'OK, Mrs Kaufmann but you must see that situations such as these are stressful for the patient but also for the doctor. Judith, at seventeen, is legally an adult and I must speak to her alone and in confidence. How does that sit with you?'

'So, you want me to leave, doctor?'

'Yes, but don't go far. If you could just take a seat in the waiting room for a few minutes.'

Mrs Kaufmann stared long and hard at Judith as if imparting, by means of some strange transference, a very strong message. She then picked up her handbag with some vehemence and left.

I took some routine clinical details from Judith to allow time for the maternal oppression to evaporate. She was, probably, about ten weeks pregnant and being sick. She had a steady boyfriend. They had met in their last year at school and happened to find work together. Her mother didn't like him. They had been using condoms 'every time' and had had 'an accident.' Even in Wiltshire pigs don't fly but I let it pass. Judith continued, telling me very firmly that she didn't want an abortion and that her boyfriend was willing to 'stand by her'. Although it was obviously true that her mother wanted the baby stopped, her father didn't agree.

'He's German, doctor. He was a prisoner of war here. He was wounded and captured in Normandy in 1944. He won't give up any more details, even to mum. Even when I had to talk to him as part of a school history project we did on D-Day. He saw no point in going back to Germany after the war. He has no family there at all now. His parents and his sister were all killed in the bombing of Hamburg in 1943.'

'It's a very sad story, Judith.'

'Yes, doctor but after being very lonely for some years, he met mum. And here I am. I think he sees my baby as the next important part of his new family. For many years he never thought he would have a child let alone a grandchild. Mum, though, is very upset by what people will say. She was born here and grew up here. She's from a very large family and knows half the town. She says that I'm spoiling our reputation as a "nice" family.'

'Judith, from what you've told me I'm afraid I really couldn't refer you for a termination – for an abortion – it's not what you want for yourself. On many other occasions like this I've been prepared to send women to the clinic with my recommendation but not this time. Are you happy with my decision?'

This got a nod, a recurring one.

'Then we'd better get your mother back in – do you want to fetch her?'

Mrs Kaufmann listened in silence when I explained the basis of my decision or, rather, Judith's decision.

'Well, thank you doctor, but I don't know what my husband will say.'

Judith and I glanced at each other in what mother would have thought a conspiratorial way if she had noticed. For my part, I only wish that the traumatic decision-making around abortion requests were always this clear-cut.

There's an inevitability about pregnancy. Some six months later Judith was delivered of a healthy little boy and, later in the year, she married her boyfriend. I've rarely seen more doting grandparents, both of them weeping with joy the day that Judith came back from the maternity wing. Judith's mother even persuaded her, against my best advice, to suppress her breast milk so that 'nana' could feed the baby and relive the joys of parenthood once more. And Hans is already looking forward to more members of his 'neue familie'.

~

Bill Gates

Bill Gates – no, not that Bill Gates – was a dustman. At least that's how his job was traditionally described. It had, however, gone through a succession of wonky descriptive terms. Bill was now a 'waste disposal operative', a term that was far from popular with the workforce. And although the men adopted the numerous changes in the protective clothing provided, everyone in town recognised Bill by the red beret he always wore. I would see him on my rounds.

By late middle age Bill had worked 'on the bins' for over thirty years without missing work for more than the odd few days with 'flu' or the odd 'gippy tummy'. It was a remarkable record considering that his wife, Megan, was severely disabled. In effect he had two jobs – he also ran the home. Before work he would help Megan to get up and get dressed. He would then prepare their breakfast, clear the table and wash up. After making his own sandwiches, he would load the washing machine and then settle his wife with some snacks and a flask of tea, all before going to work. TV zappers had been a godsend – he could leave Megan to decide when to turn on the television and to change channel at a whim. A carer would call for a cursory check around midday and then Bill would take over again on getting home from work.

He may have complained about his twin responsibilities, but I don't think so. I never had any sort of conversations with him except on one or two occasions when he happened to be home on holiday when I called at the house to see Megan. Our district nurses would bath her weekly and sometimes ask me for a prescription for her – usually for emollient or bath oil. They never missed the chance to tell me of their admiration for Bill.

Then the day dawned when Bill came to the surgery on his own behalf. A unique occasion. He walked into my consulting room bent nearly double and found it difficult to sit down. His back had 'gone' when lifting his wife into bed a few days before. After a painful and restless night, he had 'seen to Meg' and then gone to work. His mates on the lorry had thought him a lunatic and sent him home mid-morning. He'd been struggling with back pain and spasms since – even after taking some 'Aspro.'

'Could I have a sustificate, Doctor?' 'There ain't many people would do my job, but I don't want to lose it.'

Examining him was more an exercise in helping him stand and move around the room. On the face of it he had a nasty lumbar sprain, hopefully only muscular. He had no sciatica. I issued a certificate for 10 days and a prescription for some analgesics. I would obviously need to review him. Before Bill left, I tackled him on a few general medical issues – about smoking and drinking but, in his case, not about exercise. I said I would check his BP and weight when he came back, and would he bring a wee specimen? I told him of the widespread admiration of the very selfless way in which he looked after his wife.

'Well' he said 'I look after her 'cos it was me caused her problems. When we was young I had a motorbike and we used to zip down to the coast for a day out, Weymouth usually. Not often, but four or five times a year anyway. You'll remember, Doc, the bad winter of 1963 – you must have been a very young doctor then (I was a sixth-former). Like everybody we were grounded for weeks but we took off one day, as soon as the main roads were clear. But there were black ice in places and I lost control of the bike, just out of Salisbury. We had our leathers on, and helmets. I got away with some bruises. But the bike somersaulted and landed on Meg. She had a damaged spine, a pelvis in bits and a broken leg. I thought she was going to die. She was in Salisbury hospital for weeks and weeks. She's a tough one and pulled through but only with very weak legs and they've got floppier since, as you know.

'Well, it was really just one of those accidents that can happen to any of us, Bill.'

'No, doc, I was going too fast. I owe it to Meg to look after her, poor thing. Anyway, thanks for listening. I must go – you're busy.'

Ten days later Bill was much better. I was able to examine him more thoroughly and I found nothing worrying. It was just 'lumbago', as he was calling it. Bill had also worked out the cause of his back problem.

'It's them wheelie bins, Doc. All my life I've been used to lifting heavy bins and tipping them into the lorry, all day, five days a week. My back was as strong as a weightlifter's and dealing with Meg was no trouble at all. Now I don't do any lifting at work – just run the wheelie onto the bin lift and take it off, empty. I think me back's got weaker and Meg doesn't get any lighter. Me back muscles have gone to pot.'

I think he was right.

Cal(culus)

Fashions in children's names come and go – one syllable monikers were very popular at one time in my career. One little boy brought in to me was called Cal. No, it wasn't a fond nickname – it was what it said on the birth certificate, I was told. Cal had a temperature and, mother thought, a sore throat. He certainly had a fever, a red throat and an ear infection. Bread and butter medicine in a two-year-old but then mother asked me if that was why he would, at times and without warning, suddenly vomit.

'You mean in the last few days?'

'No, doctor. Actually for some time – for months really.'

'Well, I can't see how it relates to his present infection – perhaps what we should do is see Cal again when he's better and have a rethink. Is that OK with you?'

'But if he brings up the medicine, doctor?'

'Well, it's safe to repeat the dose if he's sick within half an hour or so but otherwise not. Keep up the oral fluids, though. Give me a ring if there's a lot of vomiting – we may have to change the prescription.'

Cal wouldn't stand and walk, and his mother lifted him up and carried him out. I handled the door and helped her hitch up her handbag.

A lot of water passes under the bridge in a short time in general practice and two weeks later I'd forgotten about the subtext of Cal's previous consultation. He was certainly fit again. He wouldn't sit on mother's lap and took to practising running from standing starts behind my desk. No matter. Mother reminded me about the chronic, sporadic vomiting. There seemed to be no other history to help us. His appetite was fine (for a two-year-old), he never vomited at night, bowel habit was fine – 'he can fill a nappy for England' I was told. He appeared to be growing well and gaining weight normally – 'his clothes only fit him for a few weeks, doctor.'

The possibility of a rare metabolic disorder – of 'rocking horse dung' – vaguely remembered from medical school ran through my mind but otherwise I was, as my mother used to say, 'flummoxed'. I felt that I had to suggest referral to a paediatrician although I sensed that it would sound alarmist. Mother took it calmy, however.

'Well, it would get my mother-in-law off my back - that's between you and me, doctor. Only she keeps saying there must be something that needs sorting out. None of her four ever did this.'

'OK, I'll do that. But before you go we might just check Cal's height and weight on a growth chart.' In the end we abandoned any mensuration

– Cal had a massive tantrum and the last word – 'No!' He was very clearly a normal child bar his chundering habit. The moon went through a couple of phases before I heard any more about Cal. Then he turned up – a late afternoon 'emergency' appointment with both mum and dad. They were looking very worried. Cal had vomited that afternoon – on the kitchen vinyl and there, in the vomitus, was a small, round pebble. Father spoke up: 'We're very worried, doctor, how many he might have swallowed. The main path down our garden is loose shingle – we made it when we moved in.' Mother intervened – 'we never saw it as anything risky with children doctor, honestly, but we've already arranged to have it decked over.'

It was time to leap on the inappropriate guilt. 'You know, you shouldn't be feeling responsible here. It's known as pica. Lots of children, in infancy and sometimes beyond, will explore the taste of things they pick up off the ground and will sometimes swallow them. It's generally without risk and most things that can be swallowed then pass, harmlessly, through the bowel and are eventually taken care of by our local authority, if you take my meaning. No, take a deep breath, both of you. Pica is very common. By the way, have you heard from the paediatricians yet?'

Mother and father then spoke in unison and then stopped together and laughed. Ice broken. 'Yes, we've an appointment next week. Do we need to go now, doctor?' 'Yes, I think you should. Cal taking on ballast might well explain his vomiting, but I think we should let the experts confirm it – don't you agree.' Cal's mother rang me a week later. Just before going to the clinic Cal had vomited and there had been some blood in the vomitus. The 'nice' doctor in the clinic had therefore thought it sensible to have Cal X-rayed and the film had shown that there were three more pebbles in Cal's stomach. Since they had probably been there for some time and were, perhaps, damaging the stomach lining, the suggestion had been made that Cal have an operation to remove them. 'Do you think we should give permission, doctor? Isn't an operation dangerous at Cal's age? We're due to see a children's' surgeon next week with our decision.'

Since my totally untutored approval was both required and irrelevant, I saw no reason to object to the surgery and said so. Mother seemed to think that my positive response would guarantee safety and success, but I let it ride. What else could I do? Reciting the known risks of anaesthesia and invasive surgery was not going to help.

A letter from the paediatric surgeon confirming a successful operation on Cal – they actually found four pebbles – concluded the episode as far as I was concerned. I didn't see Cal for several months. Then mother brought him in with a new problem. He had grown but wasn't his usual lively self.

There was a nasty discharge coming from his left nostril. 'It smells horrid, doctor. Mum-in-law says it must be his adenoids.'

'Well, mothers-in-law are not always right.' And there it was. Using my auriscope for the wrong orifice I could see the bum of a glistening pebble impacted in Cal's nostril. Home territory, this, for a GP.

~

Out for the Count

Roderick had been a friend and very competitive squash opponent for over a decade. There was a long tradition in his family of being involved in local politics, something we often discussed in the bar after our duels. Cynics had told me that his motive would be shameless and ulterior: inside knowledge of the local economy had long advantaged his family firm. But Rod had broken the mould. He had read engineering at Exeter University and scooped a very good job with James Dyson at Malmesbury. My introducing him, on social occasions, as 'hoover repair man' was wrong on several counts but deliciously naughty. In fact, I always felt that his representing a deprived ward on the Town Council – which he did very diligently – revealed a conscience and generosity of spirit that deserved more credit.

After a particularly gladiatorial game in which we managed to split a ball and break a racquet, we were enjoying our customary beers. Rod launched into a local politics update. He had represented the north-east part of the town for 12 years – for three electoral cycles – as an Independent. Now, for the first time, he was in a contest. An earnest young man, a Liberal Democrat, was standing in the ward in the forthcoming election. Currently unemployed, he was door-knocking every day and making rash promises on the doorsteps. Rod didn't mind the competition – he'd always been embarrassed to be unopposed – but was hurt that 'his people' were being deceived. He knew how difficult it was to tangle with planning laws, to keep the drains clear and reduce the dog shit. 'Well' he said, draining his glass, 'Vick won't be completely upset that we'll have more time for ourselves if I'm not elected. On the other hand – and for God's sake don't let on before it's announced – she was looking forward to being Lady Mayoress next year.'

I was duty doctor on election night and, for me at least, it was a peaceful evening. Until. The phone rang at nine-thirty. It was Vicky, Rod's wife. She was at the count in the Town Hall but phoning from the privacy of her car. She was tearful. Something terrible had happened to Rod. He had suddenly seemed very distant, repeatedly looking around the hall, asking her where he was and what was happening, who were all these people? And although he seemed to recognise the Town Clerk, he had then asked him, twice, what *he* was doing there. Together they'd ushered Rod into the Mayor's parlour and the Town Clerk was trying to hold him there.

'Norman, please, please come quickly. Rod must he having a stroke. Thank goodness it's you on duty.'

It took me only a few minutes to get into town. Although random strangers are not allowed into the count on election night, the Town Crier recognised me standing in the doorway and escorted me in. Rod seemed to know me. He was looking round at the portraits and photographs of all the previous town mayors, protesting that 'of course I know where I am'.

But what are *you* doing here? What's happening?' Although obviously confused, he let me examine him, up to a point, and then asked again, looking at each of us in turn; 'what are we *all* doing here?' I could find no neurological deficit – in the physical sense – and his pulse was regular, blood pressure normal, and there were no gross physical defects. I was getting as distressed as everyone else and then it occurred to me. I had never seen a case of transient global amnesia but maybe this was my first. Rod was middle-aged, under stress (he'd been told the count in his ward was building to a photo finish) and I knew he was a migraine sufferer. I indicated to Vicky and the Town Clerk that we move to a far corner of the room. I whispered my diagnosis, assuring them that, if I was right, it was a self-limiting condition: we should take Rod home on the pretext that he had one of his bad migraines and was feeling sick. The Clerk frowned but couldn't think that there was any by-law that would nullify the count or the declaration if, with due cause, a candidate was unable to be present.

Vicky took Rod home and I followed close behind. He 'came to' sitting in his kitchen about half an hour later. He looked at Vicky and then at his two teenage children. 'What's happened? Why aren't we at the count? If we don't get a move on, we'll miss the declarations. Why the hell are we still here?' Then he looked at me –'and what are *you* doing here?'

I let Vicky explain: 'darling, everything is fine – it's just that you had a kind of temporary blackout affecting your short-term memory and you were getting very upset. We thought it best to bring you home.'

I was more pleased to be in the large audience for the Mayor-Making than any of the rest of the audience. I couldn't reveal why, of course. And, yes, I had refreshed my memory, very promptly, on transient amnesias. In fact, I found I'd forgotten the relevance of multiple simultaneous stresses among the risk factors. Only three of us in the room - the new Mayor, the new Mayoress, and I, knew that I'd recently confirmed a significant hard lump in Vicky's right breast.

~

Is Doctor Hurst with you?

2.45 am. Never a great time for the phone to ring.
'Dr. Beale.'
'Morning, sir. Is Dr. Hurst with you?'
'Well, since she's our unmarried junior partner I hardly think so. I'm at home in bed - though I am on duty.'
'Oh. Well. Can you get a message to her. Only the wife's on the floor. I can't get her up and she's screaming for me to get help. Dr. Hurst has been coming to see her a lot just lately.'
'Well, I'm the duty doctor – that 's why I'm answering the phone.'
'Oh, well, I'd be grateful if you could come and see May as soon as possible. She's over 80 you know.'
Whoever it was then rang off.

Incidents such as this were not exceptional. Callers in the small hours were often at panic stations and before phones became endowed with sophisticated electronics there would be no record of the incoming number. One couldn't ring back and lay fretfully awake having to assume that the caller would eventually ring again along the lines of 'where the hell are you? Have you gone back to sleep, doctor? It's been over half an hour since I rang.' One had to be ready to pounce or the dilemma might easily repeat itself.

On this occasion I had a clue. 'May' had been visited by Ann in recent days. The visiting log at the surgery might solve this one and, thankfully, it did. And, sure enough, the only lights on in the street were at number 25. May was flat on her back in the cramped bedroom. She had slipped on a lurid rayon counterpane that had slithered off the bed. Her husband had given up trying to pull her up by her hands and just covered her over with a blanket and put a pillow under her head. 'Actually', May whispered to me, 'he'd only done that at her command – you, see, doctor, although I've been the patient lately, Harry's mind isn't what it was and hasn't been too grand for a long time.'

May seemed perfectly orientated. She reported no pain and I could find no tenderness. She could move all her limbs and turn her head. After I'd helped her up – to sit, to turn, to kneel and then to stand – she was able to describe, very accurately, how the accident had happened. On the face of it the only thing broken was my beauty sleep

'I really should have put the light on, shouldn't I doctor?' We both looked at Harry. He was asleep in a chair.

I returned to the visiting log next morning and entered the name May Wilding for a follow-up visit. Ann and I tried to be clinical about the case at coffee time. She had already referred Harry to the memory assessment team but in the face of rapidly increasing demand, they had a staff shortage (where had I heard that before?). Ann had treated May for a recent chest infection – she thought successfully – but would happily call in later to check that all was well. 'They're a nice couple', she said, 'but with no family nearby.' In fact, their one son had recently phoned her - from Melbourne, worried about his father. 'He was most upset when I gave him the likely diagnosis. He was astonished that dementia could happen to a maths graduate who used to design jet engine components.'

Six weeks later Ann was on holiday. Harry appeared in reception late one morning. By all reports he seemed perfectly with it. He wanted to know if Dr. Hurst would be 'kind enough' to call on his wife 'in the next day or so'. 'She doesn't seem quite right in herself' was the quote remembered by the staff. They explained that Dr. Hurst was away and that another doctor would call. 'It needn't be today' was the other phrase they remembered him saying.

'Buggins' turn' again. The Wilding household appeared on my visiting list the next morning. 'Yes, I *do* know the way!' Sometimes the staff can't help winding us up but it helps keep us sane. Harry let me in but he didn't seem to know me. His breath was markedly ketotic. I noticed that there was partly consumed food on random plates strewn across the kitchen table but no empty cups or glasses.

'May's in bed. She doesn't want to get up.'

May was very dead. She was stiff and blue but still warm to touch and I noticed an electric blanket was still plugged in through a timer. She had presumably been dead for a couple of days. Harry's dementia was obviously worse than anyone had suspected and now exacerbated by his degree of dehydration. I found a clean glass and gave him a long drink of water. He drank it avidly, spilling some of it, and then burped. I tried to tell him that May was dead in the very simplest of terms and repeated everything I said very slowly. He still didn't seem to understand and just stared into space.

But then a single tear rolled down his cheek.

The Coroner's post-mortem examination found a large sub-dural haematoma inside the back of May's skull. This confined bruise was probably the result of her hitting her head the night she fell even though there were no indications at the time. Slowly and silently it had grown to the point of forcing her hind brain to herniate down into the spinal canal – a fatal outcome; coma followed by death. Beware slippery counterpanes in the dark.

~

Black Dog

Heightened self-consciousness, apartness, an inability to join in, physical shame and self-loathing. These are the components, according to Stephen Fry, of the depressive phase of his bi-polar disorder. He makes the point, if inadvertently, that depression is not just sadness – of which he makes no mention. We all go 'down in the dumps' from time to time but true depression is much more profound. And it's not rare in general practice (nor, incidentally, in general practitioners).

Rosemary Badderley came in, sat down, and sobbed. It was genuine. I waited. She had, she eventually managed to say, 'got through' the menopause and was sure it was not her hormones. It was a very defensive beginning. For a couple of months, she had been 'tearful, weird and ratty.' She had lost her 'get up and go'. She had lost all interest in food, hated cooking for the family, couldn't sleep and, before you ask, doctor, 'yes, I have gone off sex.' The tears reappeared.

'I'm so sorry, doctor, but I'm so embarrassed how aggressive I've become. I know some of my friends are keeping away from me because I've upset them. And my poor family. I can stare at things that need doing for days. I loathe myself for being slack. I was never like this before. I think my kids are avoiding me and I think their schooling has gone off. And our eldest boy didn't come home from Uni at Easter.'

To my knowledge her claim that all this was strangely new was correct. I'd thought that she and her husband had coped extremely well when their younger son had been whipped off to hospital with meningitis a couple of years ago. It had proven to be viral, and he made a full recovery but nonetheless they had borne the trauma very rationally and courageously. I asked her if my understanding was correct, that she was a non-drinker and received a nod. When I asked about sleep pattern she described lying awake for hours not being able to 'go off.' She denied that she and her husband had any financial worries and no, she said without my asking, she didn't think Alex was 'playing away.'

I was assuming that she must have a reactive depression. She had pre-empted my usual routine of going through the common 'tender spots' in life but there seemed to be no obvious provocations. I thought 'reactive' best described her illness – she had no prior history and difficulty getting off to sleep rather than waking up very early was thought to be diagnostic. But was she actually depressed? Could all this be a brain lesion, for instance, or was she wrong about having survived the menopause unscathed?

We were looking away from each other, both deep in thought. I still felt that depression was the most likely diagnosis and decided to lift the lid further. 'Rosemary, forgive me but I really need to ask you. Have you ever thought about harming yourself in some way?'

The sobbing resumed and she gripped her tissues so tightly that her knuckles went white. This was going to need more than kindness and Kleenex. Eventually she looked up. She had been accumulating paracetamol tablets. She had over a hundred but then her husband had found her cache. There'd been a row. He had made this appointment for her – and brought her here. He was in the waiting room.

I grasped at this. Did she have any objection to him joining us? Alex came in and he avoided Rosemary's glance. He declined a chair. He was close to tears. I described what I meant by a diagnosis of true depression and that Rosemary was suffering from many of the symptoms of this real illness. A prescription for an anti-depressant was accepted and I stressed the well-known time lag before we could hope to see an improvement. Alex then handed me a large bag of pills; the paracetamol. They agreed to come back and see me in two weeks and left, holding hands.

Two weeks later Rosemary came alone. She was worse but agreed, reluctantly, to continue with the medication. After another two weeks the couple came together. Still no improvement and they were both very tense. I explained that we now had three broad choices – a change in medication or for me to refer Rosemary to a psychiatrist for more expert advice. Or both. Rosemary said she didn't really want to see a 'shrink' – she was sure they would offer her electrical treatment, something that terrified her. 'After all, isn't that how they kill the pigs at the factory?' So, new pills it was, although I tried to reassure her about ECT.

Four weeks later, a fortnight after another 'no progress' consultation during which I thought that Rosemary was almost pleased to be able to announce that she was no better, she came in, sat down and smiled. She thanked me for all my help and understanding and said she was much better. So much better that she wanted to know how to stop the tablets. Whether this was a false dawn or not, it was far too early to withdraw from treatment. I was very apprehensive. She eventually agreed to continue with the medication for another two weeks. When she returned, with Alex to corroborate, she reported that, without any doubt, she was her old self. 'Sorry, doctor, but I've stopped the pills.' They looked at each other and smiled. Alex put his arm around her. Now the time-bomb.

'Thank you again, doctor, so very much for all your time and patience. By the way, do we notify the desk about a change of address or give you the details. We do hope we can stay on your list. We've just exchanged contracts on our dream home, a house we've always wanted to live in – at the bottom of Black Dog Hill. The vendor has been stringing us along for months.'

All this time I had missed the one tender spot that was relevant, a familiar and protracted stress – the wading through treacle that is the buying and selling of houses.

~

A Life in the Country

Mr. and Mrs. Worsted were new patients. They had made a joint appointment 'just to introduce themselves' they said. They were well-heeled, well-spoken and, on the face of it, well-mannered. I did think it rather ostentatious, however, that a crisply-folded, and clearly unread, copy of the Financial Times was plonked onto the corner of my desk.

'I'm Desmond' he said 'call me Des. And this is Sarah, Sal if you like, my wife. Is it alright if we address you by your Christian name?'

'Well, I can think of many worse forms of address. It's welcome to Wiltshire, is it?'

They nodded. Des had been a trader in 'futures' (whatever they are) in the City of London and Sal had also worked at Canary Wharf. They had just sold their docklands flat that had overlooked the Thames having decided to retire from their careers in finance and move to the country. They had just bought Bidloe Manor: it came with 15 acres of land and they were going to breed goats.

Sal took over in my briefing session. They'd become fed up with their high-pressure jobs, the noise and the pollution, didn't need any more money and, when she'd been mugged, right outside their flat, it was the final straw. Oh, and we don't have children, doctor, in case you're wondering – we did five private sessions of IVF with no success. It seemed appropriate to wish them good luck and to ask if they had any current medical problems.

'Oh, no' they said in unison. Des, again: 'you won't find us bothering you much, doc, and anyway we're BUPA'd up to our eyeballs.' After a few more observations on life in general and advice from me about tetanus jabs they left. I took a very deep breath.

Des and Sal were good to their word and I saw nothing of them, at least at first. Driving through Bidloe from time to time, I noticed cumulative changes at the Manor. The hedges were now manicured, the verges trimmed and a couple of very old and threateningly top-heavy trees had disappeared. The two large fields that abutted the road had obviously been generously fertilised and were now subdivided by some tall fencing. In one corner there was now an impressive wooden building – oak, I thought and with a proper tiled roof. Then, one morning I saw the new inhabitants – goats. I also heard, down the grapevine, that the couple were making significant contributions to life in the village.

It was Des who broke their duck. He was somewhat less bubbly than before and had a curious three-inch circular rash on his right calf. He had been 'Googling' and told me it must be a ringworm. I wasn't so sure. A fungal infection of this diameter would usually be healing centrally – hence the descriptive term, 'ring'. But this bulls-eye dark area was more inflamed in the middle. I wondered whether Des, not a born countryman, had sustained some tick bites. In fact, he may not even have heard about ticks. Perhaps this could be the rash of Lyme Disease? I was willing to prescribe an antibiotic. But Des insisted that, if there was any doubt about the diagnosis, he would rather see a private physician. He rang ten days later to say that the consultant had agreed with me and that he must be treated promptly, and for some weeks, to kill the bacteria. He'd been on the internet again. He sounded rather deflated as he recited to me the horrors of long-term lassitude, weakness, and potential joint troubles. Perhaps he thought I was unaware of them.

'We didn't have bloody ticks in the city' he threw in, as if it was a point that needed making.

There then followed a long spell – many months – in which Des kept complaining of tiredness and hot sweats. I thought it more likely that he had convinced himself that he had Lyme disease 'á la Google' rather than still being infected. Nevertheless, we persevered with the antibiotics and I tried, always, to be encouraging.

It was Sal's turn next. With some irony, she, too, began to complain of lethargy and hot flushes - after a flu-like illness.

'It can't be the menopause yet, surely' she whined.

Impressed by the odd fact that she felt hot on some days and not on others, I suggested she keep some regular thermometer readings. Her temperature was definitely fluctuating. There was nothing else specific. But when I suggested some investigations she, too, insisted on a private referral. It took a few weeks but then she returned with a hand-written note from another of our local physicians. She had Brucellosis, presumably from the goats.

'But they were pedigrees, from a very reputable dealer' she uttered. She then turned away, as if to prevent me hearing: 'though we did pick up a billy and a nanny at a show – they were so endearing.'

Now both of the couple were on medium-term antibiotics. But popping pills was the easy part. Being listless and flat was very difficult in the face of their 24/7 caprine commitment.

It could have been the last time I saw Sarah alive. Just after five o'clock on a very hot summer afternoon that only got hotter and more oppressive, I fielded an urgent phone call. There had been a lightning strike in Bidloe. Someone driving out from the village had seen a body lying out in the open. When I arrived I realised that the incident was in one of the new goat paddocks. It was Sarah. She was alive but unconscious. There was a dead goat next to her and an elongated patch of smouldering charred grass. Even with her breathing and pulse seeming normal I was very pleased to hear the siren of the ambulance that I had arranged to meet me. We transferred a still comatose Sarah into the vehicle, I thanked the passer-by, who had phoned and waited for me in the lane, for her prompt actions and went in search of Des.

Des and Sal came to see me before they removed to London. There was no Financial Times for the desk. They were casually dressed and oblivious to the fresh mud on their boots.

'We thought London was getting stupidly dangerous and life in the country seemed idyllic,' Des said. 'But what with poisonous insects, manky animals and being fried alive, we think we'll be safer in the city after all. We've managed to sell the Manor – to a nice couple born and bred in Wiltshire. We wish them all the best. They're keeping our goats. And we would like to thank you, doctor, for all your care. How on earth do you stay alive, fit and well, living here?'

~

Les Boutiquiers

Napoleon accused the English of being 'une nation de boutiquiers' – 'a nation of shopkeepers'. It's never been quite clear what he meant nor even if he actually said it. We do, though, have retailers of all kinds, what nation doesn't? And many a shopkeeper has a justifiable pride that goes with the calling.

Sam and Doris Green were both children of shop owners. It was in their blood and they were very popular. They ran an 'open all hours' shop that was built in the 1970s as part of a new housing development that included our surgery. The shop was therefore surrounded by dense housing but for a small patch of grass in front with some wooden benches. This was a magnet for people idling away their time having popped into the shop and, sadly, also a focus for trouble and petty vandalism. It was always litter-strewn and a was canine toilet despite Sam's efforts to keep the area clean.

In fact, Sam's efforts to keep his shopfront attractive became something of a fixation. Doris began to worry that he was becoming obsessive. He would spend hours squinting through the shop window display to try to catch 'the buggers'. Although a large man, Doris thought he might be putting himself in physical danger when tackling 'local yobs'. She was quite right to be concerned. Sam chased after one litter lout and a verbal altercation turned into a physical one and he was punched in the face.

Sam was brought over to the surgery holding a heavily blooded handkerchief over his face. From its appearance – already massively swollen – I thought his nose was probably broken. He was adamant that he hadn't been knocked out or fallen and was anxious only to get back to the shop – Doris was with him and they had locked up. He wouldn't be restrained and I had to hope that Doris, at least, would remember my advice that he came back in four or five days so that we could assess the positioning of the likely nasal fracture. However, it was Doris who consulted me - next day and alone. She had a very worrying story.

On several occasions when Sam had rushed out from the shop to buttonhole someone for being antisocial, he'd come back very short of breath and obviously in discomfort in his chest. He put it down to his 'heartburn' from eating stale foods that had passed their sell-by-date. Thankfully, Doris told me that Sam had never smoked or drunk alcohol. But both of his parents – and hers for that matter – had all died in their fifties of heart disease. She had implored Sam, for years, to come and see me and have a 'heart check' but he always refused on the grounds that he couldn't leave the shop. Doris pleaded with me that when Sam came back about his nose I would take the chance to 'run the rule over him' whatever his protests.

I found Sam to be hugely overweight and with a borderline high blood pressure. We agreed on dieting and that our nurses would monitor both his weight and his blood pressure. I would also arrange a blood test for cholesterol. I put a note in my diary suspecting that Sam would default. I was right and he remained persistently uncooperative once his nose had repaired. All we'd managed to do was to add to Doris's anxieties.

Then, late one wet winter's evening, someone heaved a breeze block through the Green's shop window. Sam and Doris, who lived above, hadn't yet gone to bed and dashed down into the street by the side stairs. The offender was casually helping himself to goods from the window display. He wheeled around as Sam approached him and, spilling some of the looted goods, pushed Sam away very violently. Sam lost his balance and fell backwards on top of Doris who had been immediately behind him. It may have been Doris's blood-curdling scream that resolved the threatening confrontation. The looter ran off and neighbours began appearing only to find a horror that would haunt them for a long time. Doris's left leg was broken between knee and ankle and the ends of her fractured tibia and fibula were projecting out into the night air in a swelling puddle of blood. She was moaning quietly. Sam was being sick.

Doris's compound fracture was plated next morning but the fracture didn't heal. Eventually the orthopaedic team had to admit to themselves that their repair must be infected, and the plate was removed. Doris became quite debilitated with the chronic infection and the long-term antibiotics upset her digestion. She lost a lot of weight. Sam became very worried about her and was demoralised when the police failed to apprehend anyone for the crime. Then, when the annual shop rent demand arrived showing a substantial increase, it was the last straw. After 25 years, Sam and Doris decided to give up the shop.

When Doris finally left hospital – in a wheelchair and with the leg bones still not united – she went to live with their son in his bungalow on the other side of town. And when their shop tenancy expired and Sam had managed to find a buyer for the business, he joined her there. There was some good news. At long last Sam sought and began to cooperate with health advice. We started him on a mild anti-hypertensive drug, a baby aspirin and a statin. He began to take regular exercise. He would push Doris around town whenever the weather permitted and they met many old friends made at the shop. And freed from the demands of the business,

Sam seemed altogether more affable and easy-going. Doris was so pleased and her health improved, even in the face of her unresolved injury.

Then, only days after the surgeons had finally thought it safe to book Doris in for a new attempt to fix her leg, disaster struck. Our senior receptionist phoned me in the middle of a consultation.

'I'm so sorry, Doctor, is it alright to talk?'

'Yep, go ahead.'

'Just to let you know that someone's collapsed in Iceland.'

The tone of her voice suggested that this was not the time to crack jokes about the time of the next flight to Reykjavik.

'They think he might be dead. It's your Mr. Green.'

I brought my consultation to a rapid close, apologised, grabbed my coat and dashed. Annoyingly, the traffic in the centre of town was gridlocked. A huge Dutch lorry was unloading flowers. It was probably ten minutes before I reached Iceland. Doris was in her wheelchair near checkout. She was crying and a glass of water was trembling in her hand. The shocked staff pointed me to the vegetables fridge half way up the shop. Sam was folded into it, head down, his feet at odd angles. He was certainly dead and it was far too late to attempt resuscitation. The manager and I managed to lift him out of the fridge and lie him on the floor. Like an idiot, I heard myself say 'mind your back when you lift, he'll be a dead weight.' To the sound of an approaching siren, I went back to talk to Doris. She knew what I was going to say. Her head dropped onto her chest. Then she looked up: 'I expect Sam told you, doctor, as he did everyone, that he was born at a shop and he would die at a shop. He was right, wasn't he?'

~

Olga from the . . . .

Being a public figure in a small community has drawbacks. Some of them are obvious. I always tried to avoid the shops in our high street but its difficult to cop out when we need beer for a barbecue party. Sure enough, I was buttonholed in the booze aisle.

'Oh, I'm so glad I've bumped into you, doctor, I've been meaning to phone.'

'Aha. Well you've got me now.'

'Yes, only it's about our Mum. Her periods have started again. I think she needs more HRT.'

Oh, no, I think, but quickly cover up.

'Well, we can't really talk about it here but if that's the case, you must make sure she comes to see me soon and we can agree on the best treatment. Perhaps you should bring her in yourself. It's easy enough to make an appointment at this time of year.'

I was grateful, at least, with a substantial supply of alcohol in my trolley, that I hadn't been harangued by someone I'd advised to give up the stuff. But I took a deep breath before tackling checkout. Up ahead were, almost certainly, months of anxiety and trauma for my patient. Until proven otherwise she had a cancer of the body of her uterus – womb cancer.

Olga Sheppard appeared a week later. Picking up her case notes reminded me that she had Ukrainian ancestry. The name 'Kravchenko' had been crossed out and I remembered her telling me that her parents had fled Kiev at the time of the 1917 revolution. Her father had been a high-ranking civil servant and therefore a monarchist with no future. I also remembered, with embarrassment, the puerile joke that once did the rounds at medical school – what does a gynaecologist find inside a Mamushka – another Mamushka. Olga's post-menopausal bleed was even less amusing. On coming in she immediately apologised for her daughter's impudence.

'I've told her to wait in the waiting room' she said, 'the interfering hussy.'

After grinding through the obvious questions and answers around Olga's bleeding I explained that I really needed to do an internal examination. She happily agreed and I sent for the nurse and the 'smear' kit – Olga was almost due for her five-year check anyway. Before proceeding I asked one of our routine questions when choosing an appropriate speculum.

'Olga, are you still sexually active?'

'No' she said 'but my husband is.'

Nurse and I roared with laughter and Olga joined in, realising what she had said. In fact, the mirth was very helpful in taking the tension out of the two-fingered probing. Although Olga was somewhat overweight and the bimanual examination difficult, the uterus was, I thought, enlarged for someone knocking on the door of sixty. It also seemed to be tethered across to the right side. Olga was also quite tender there – more than I expected, certainly. She obviously needed urgent referral to a gynaecologist. I suggested that her daughter join us and we all sat down while I explained, as gently as I could, that the possible diagnosis was a growth in the womb and what we should do about it.

Sadly, the assumed diagnosis of uterine cancer proved to be correct, and Olga was given high priority for surgery. Her womb, Fallopian tubes and ovaries were all removed. However, there were some 'dodgy' lymph glands found inside her pelvis and she was referred for follow-up chemotherapy.

Although Olga tolerated the surgery very well and recovered quickly, she was reduced to a shell, physically and emotionally, by the chemotherapy. Her family rallied supremely but she was able to do very little except lie on a day bed and try not to vomit. When she stood up she needed to be propped in order not to fall. Perhaps inevitably, trusting to luck one evening and fed up with being a burden – her husband was snoozing in a chair – she tried to cross the room and fell against a door jamb. She fractured her right neck of humerus – broke the main arm bone between shoulder and elbow very near the top. This very painful injury cannot be immobilised using plaster of Paris and her arm was put in a sling. Being right-handed she was now even more significantly disabled: unable to dress or wash properly or even do her knitting. She also found that the painkillers offered made her even more nauseous. It took the combined efforts of her husband, her two daughters, our nurses and myself to convince her to finish her course of chemotherapy but somehow she did it. She remains well and cancer-free as of today and is very grateful that we 'insisted on the torture'. Perhaps her caustic wit is a Ukrianian trait?

It may very well be that her 'hussy' daughter saved Olga's life – or was it my shopping? But when we next had a family barbecue, I took the soft option of phoning and ordering the beer from the local wine merchant. It's rarely easy to reach the right diagnosis based on a flippant remark by a patient or relative across a supermarket trolley. And there's certainly no guarantee of forgiveness if you get it wrong. One may be off duty but the patient isn't.

~

Chitterlings in the sun ...

Richard Minnis was someone I hadn't seen since he was a teenager. The name took me back a decade or so, to a painful memory. His father had been my first death when I arrived in the practice. It had been gruesome. Arthur Minnis, an agricultural labourer, died from a malignant melanoma. When I first met him he had only days to live. The cancer was everywhere and, to my horror, black tumour had replaced his left eyeball. He was amazingly stoic, refused to leave his own bed and died there. Richard was the only child and, I remember thinking, much taller and sturdier that either of his parents, something of a cuckoo in the nest.

Richard came in. He was now huge, dwarfing the chair when he sat down. Wasn't he Mongo from Blazing Saddles? I snapped out of my reverie when he spoke. The voice was jarringly high-pitched and slurred, not the rich baritone I would have expected. His breath odour would have blistered paint at a hundred yards and the right side of his face was very swollen. He had a large dental abscess arising from an upper molar. He desperately needed the ministrations of a dentist.

'But I ain't got no dentist, doctor.'

I explained that all I could do was prescribe an antibiotic, which I would do. But he must find himself a dental practice and let them take over the care of his abscess.

'I will, doctor, promise. T'll be nice to be able to quilt and get rid of the rotten smell.'

I nodded, not quite knowing what he meant.

A week later Richard was back. He had registered with a dentist but, as a new patient, he had been told by the receptionist that he would need a full thirty-minute appointment for the dentist to 'get to know his mouth'. There wasn't one available for almost a month. But at least his abscess had receded.

'They antibiotics, doctor, gave I diarrhoeal but can I have some more?'

I hoped my irritation was suppressed enough for it not to register. But I could see no alternative but to prescribe.

'Thanks, doctor, yous a gem. Shame about the smell at home though. You know, I think it's coming from our mother and 'er don't seem right. Tis like chitterlins left out in the sun.'

Something told me to push this button.

'Are you saying, Richard, that you think she's ill?'

'Well, 'er don't complain but that don't mean much.'

'Would you bring her in to see me?'

'Er wouldn't come, doctor. P'raps you'll call in and see 'er. Anywhen'll do. I shan't tell 'er you're coming mind, or I'll be in the doo-doo.'

It appeared that I was committed. I made a note lest I forget and called in a couple of days later. The old cottage, once rural but never bucolic, was now a miserable oasis in a desert of smart new bungalows and semis that had been put up in the past decade. The chalkstone walls were screaming for some fresh whitewash, were green on the northern side and the rotting thatch was slipping. The half-acre of garden was still exclusively for unkempt vegetables but for a stack of wooden pallets in one corner. I knocked at the back door but to no effect. It was ajar and I went into the scullery, calling out. Everything was exactly as I remembered it, the flagstone flooring, the cracked earthenware sink, the ancient piping and even the perforated zinc meat safe hanging from a rafter. Richard was right, there was a smell in the place – the smell of rotting flesh. Eventually I heard Mrs. Minnis answer. She was in the bed where her husband had died. The smell was much stronger. Mary was pale and her face thinner, even, that I had remembered. She was obviously very unwell.

'Thank you for calling in, Doctor. Richard told me you were coming. Him can't keep a secret for toffee.'

Mary seemed resigned to my wanting to examine her. It was difficult not to turn away as I removed the bedclothes. Her nightdress was bloodstained and crusted with pus. Underneath it, after I'd pulled the clothing away from her chest like a piece of Velcro, and with Mary wincing in pain, was a fungating breast tumour. There was a gaping cavity extending up into her right armpit. She must have been in agony for weeks.

'It's a bit teart' she said. 'I'm sorry I've let it go, doctor. You won't be angry with me will you? Dr. Wilkins used to growl. Mind you he always come out if Richard was poorly.'

I was shaken but not angry. I explained to Mary that she would have to go into hospital for urgent treatment of what she presumably realised, was a breast cancer.

'Yes, I know, doctor. My mother had the same.'

I spoke to the breast surgeon at Swindon – the hospital now had a dedicated team - and Mary was admitted that day. There was some possibility that they could buy her some time but in fact Mary died within hours. Richard seemed remote when I went to see him but he'd had the wit to fall back on an uncle to help organise the funeral. He followed me down the path to the gate. To lighten the conversation, I remarked on the impressive size of the potatoes he'd been lifting when I arrived.

'Mine are peanuts compared to yours, Richard.'

'Oh, you'll be needing some cowclap, Doctor. Nothin like it for dead dirt. Thanks again for coming to see us and for looking to our mother.'

Ten days later I drove home from surgery on a warm evening. Turning into our drive I had to brake sharply. There was a six-foot high pile of fresh farmyard manure, steaming gently. My wife appeared on the far side of it.

'Sorry, I haven't had chance to ring and warn you. Two men on a tractor reversed a trailer in here about half an hour ago and tipped this lot out. They said you were expecting it. One of the men was, well, a giant almost.'

The pile of manure had to wait until the weekend for me to have time to shift it. It was upwind of us for those few days and there was a nasty smell in the house.

~

Best-laid plans

Bending over backwards in the face of a patient's foibles doesn't always pay off. But pure human sympathy will sometimes push one into what sees, later, to have been rash behaviour. Audrey Lightfoot, a middle-aged patient of mine had a horror of death. Nothing so very unusual there, you might say, but over and above the fear we all have, more or less, her recurring nightmare was that her 'death' would be mis-diagnosed and that she would be disposed of whilst still alive. Nothing would convince her that this was as likely as the moon not rising after dark. Whatever the current cause of her latest consultation with me, her dreaded non-demise and subsequent live burial always bubbled up.

Over many years I had called on every conceivable type of reassurance for Audrey but to no avail. And although I had never summoned up enough courage to tease her, I had often wondered whether I should tell her of the old Royal Naval tradition of sewing a dead sailor into his hammock before burial at sea and proving total absence of life by passing the very last stitch through the nose. Perhaps we could promise a deceased Audrey some sort of equivalent needlework security? But, in reality, the only time that a living interment appeared to take second string among her myriad of anxieties was when there was a real possibility of imminent death – when I thought her life might actually be in jeopardy.

Vague abdominal pains were one of Audrey's frequent complaints. Her self-diagnoses varied from irritable bowel syndrome to a host of specific food 'allergies', some more difficult to dismiss than others – at least with any confidence. And, on occasion, my attempts to reassure her depended on examining her abdomen. One memorable Wednesday afternoon I did a quickfire second pummelling to convince myself. Yes, there *was* a significant central mass, and *yes*, it was pulsating regularly. An aortic aneurysm? Exactly the finding, with its potentially serious consequences, that one would not want to have to reveal and explain to an endlessly anxious neurotic. Audrey knew immediately, of course, that something was up: we were entering a tricky bend, and against the camber, on our journey together. I did my best to make light of my findings and heard myself pussyfooting.

'I think one of your tummy blood vessels is slightly swollen, Audrey, and we'll need to do a scan. Nothing urgent, I'm sure. But just to be on the safe side, I'll ring the expert I have in mind personally, someone you will like, a very sympathetic, understanding man.'

Eventually she stopped asking the same question – 'so am I dying, doctor' in a dozen different ways and took off.

I found time to ring James Kirklees, the vascular surgeon at Bath, next morning, Thursday. He happily said that he would see Audrey in his outpatient clinic in the next week or so and I thought he had absorbed my massive rider that Audrey came from the outermost orbits of anxiety neurosis.

'Just send a quick letter giving me your patient's details, Norman' and he gave me his fax number. Duty done, I relaxed.

Monday morning came the deluge. Audrey appeared as an extra extra at the end of a painfully long surgery. After waiting for two hours, she was apoplectic. Why hadn't I been honest and told her the truth? Apparently, her aneurysm was about to burst and the chances of surviving the operation were far less than 50:50. And would the surgeon – 'a very nice man, by the way, as you said' – be bothered to double-check that she was really dead?

I was mystified. Had Audrey been to a catch-up weekend outpatient clinic or attended accident and emergency at Bath? Somewhere, somehow, she had obviously met Jim Kirklees. I explored the possibilities.

'Oh no, doctor, your surgeon friend was so really, really worried about me that he came to see me at home on Saturday afternoon. It was very kind of him, don't you think? He's obviously more worried about me than you are.'

Audrey did prove to have a dodgy aortic aneurysm threatening to burst. Jim did a superb operation before it dissected. If it had split it would have killed her. Audrey was extremely grateful and soon well enough to return to her enduring catalogue of fears and anxieties.

A few months later I happened to see Jim Kirklees in the corridor at the hospital. I stopped him and thanked him for saving Audrey's life.

'Well, Norman, you saved her really – well spotted. I think she realised that the credit is mostly yours. I hope she expressed her gratitude to you?'

'Mm, actually, Jim, she taught me an important lesson – always to tell the full truth however anxious the patient. But, Jim, I was surprised that you came out to see Audrey at home, kind though it was, especially to someone likely to have her neuroses crystallised by your sudden appearance on the doorstep.'

'Oh, it was no problem, Norman. I didn't actually go out of my way. I was collecting my daughter from school at the end of her term, anyway. And, as you well know, St. Hilda's is just round the corner from your patient's house.'

~

The Price of Loyalty

All of Ralph's extensive family were patients of the practice. Many of them, if not most, had worked or still did work, in the factory; turning pigs into pork products. Ralph's great-grandfather, his grandfather and his father and mother had all been employed there and all had been presented with the long-service medals that the company awarded after 25 years of continuous service. Ralph was only a year short of his, having re-started as an apprentice butcher in the slaughterhouse after National Service.

Ralph was now the charge-hand in the boning department and a shop-steward. He was much respected, a reputation built on his skills with the knife and his guile in wage negotiations with management. But not all such meetings were about pay and conditions. The Union had recently requested a special meeting with the top brass to discuss the growing rumour of possible large-scale job losses among the workforce. This had been strongly denied by regional executives brought in to reinforce the local management team. The stories were completely unfounded, the shop stewards were told. And as evidence of a secure future, they were told of on-going negotiations to secure a European Union grant sufficient to build a new abattoir. This apparent good news was welcomed and taken in good faith by the workforce who had, after all, a strong tradition of loyalty. Half of believing something is wanting to believe it.

There was total shock, therefore when, only a few months later, the workforce, on the stroke of midday, crossed the road to the canteen to the sound of the hooter. Or, rather, tried to cross. They found themselves surrounded by a large contingent of reporters and photographers, microphones and cameras poised. 'What did they think of the news that the factory was going to close?'

Most of the workers were too numbed to make sensible replies and staggered into lunch, many wondering if they were in a nightmare. Once they were all seated, a manager from head office stood forward and apologised for the brutal way in which the news had been broken. He protested that he and his team had no idea how the announcement they were scheduled to make had leaked into the public arena. However, very sadly, it was true. The controlling company had decided to close the whole enterprise in six weeks' time. Everyone would be made redundant, including local management and the site would be put up for sale.

The shop stewards all looked at one another and one stood up and demanded an urgent meeting – that very afternoon. The spokesman from head office responded curtly with a refusal, picked up his papers and left. His team followed him. There was a profound silence as people avoided each other's eyes and looked at their food. Much of it remained untouched. Not knowing how to pay the mortgage, the balance on the next holiday, the car loan repayments, school uniforms, even food on the table; minds were racing, painful notions tripping over each other. The future looked as bleak as the cold food on the plates.

Ten days later, at home during the evening, Ralph suddenly complained of a very severe headache and flopped back in a chair. His wife was talking to him as he went unconscious. She dialled 999. The ambulance crew found him in deep coma. He was cold and clammy, and his blood pressure was 190/120 - which they didn't believe. One pupil was widely dilated and as they lifted him onto a wheeled stretcher his breathing became irregular and noisy. He never regained consciousness and died in the small hours of the next day. The death certificate stated 'cerebral haemorrhage.'

I went to see Ralph's wife at home. She put the television on for the children and we talked in the kitchen. She was, of course, devastated. She was also angry. This was somewhat earlier than usual for the normal grieving process. Following the terrible news at the factory Ralph had been a different man – 'not my husband.' She had watched him stare into space for hours, totally distracted. He would break down in tears, pace the house at night, refuse food and drink, and for the first time ever, in her experience, he had dreaded going to work. His mood had frightened the children.

Finally, he had begun to talk – a lot. He told her, in the middle of what was to be their sleepless last night together, that the atmosphere at work had become poisonous. Life-long friends were avoiding him and some of his workmates all but blamed him for being 'a sucker' in trusting 'the bosses.' He couldn't concentrate and his butchery skills had 'gone to pot.' There would be no bonus at the end of the week, but so what. His wife was sure that it was the loss of camaraderie and respect in the slaughterhouse that had killed him. The casual, 'couldn't care less' attitude of the disingenuous senior management had made her a widow. And she now had to finish bringing up their two teenagers alone.

'He was a redundancy death, doctor.'

~

A Stranger in the Night

Alice Dew was an ongoing concern. She had become a recluse since her husband had died. She rarely left the second-floor flat that had been their home after they had given up the Verger's cottage when Jack had retired. It was her daughter who had first noticed her mother's growing absentmindedness and irregular hours. It might have been bereavement but the problems had continued well after the anniversary of Jack's death.

The family wanted me to call, as if 'on the off chance' but I told them that, as a ploy, this never worked. It was better to be honest and tell 'Mum' that they had spoken to me and asked me to call in. A five-minute chat revealed nothing amiss – to me at least. But I was well aware that a brief home visit can be deceptively misleading, the 'patient' being on their mettle and best behaviour. I was less reassured when I returned and asked Alice some closed questions. She knew her address, the month but not the day. She hated the Prime Minister but couldn't remember her name. She thought her daughter had 'popped in' yesterday but didn't seem sure. She denied sleeping poorly or that she felt 'down' or 'weepy'. Overall, she seemed too casual and relaxed about things, almost once removed from reality. But did all this add up to onset of dementia? I wasn't at all sure and wasn't surprised when, after doing nothing further for a few weeks, her daughter again got in touch.

Now Alice began to tell me that her neighbours were watching her and tapping on her wall. She had also been woken by flashing lights at night. And, at one point, she suddenly froze, looked at me, and asked 'had

I seen it?' She was now also a different personality – pushing me aside at one moment and then staring into space beyond me. And I wasn't totally convinced that she knew who I was any more.

Failing memory, paranoia, mild aggression, visual and auditory hallucinations put me at a loss. It was high time to ask Don Brooks, our local geriatrician to see Alice, ideally at home. He was much more community-orientated than other local physicians and we always valued his common-sense approach and advice. He also lived locally and we were all on first-name terms. It was a relief to me to be able to phone him and speak to him and he was as cooperative as usual.

A few days later, winter suddenly arrived. Heavy snow fell for three days and was whipped into deep drifts by strong east winds. It was bitterly cold and difficult to get around the practice. After a quiet weekend muffled by the snow and the phone not ringing much (for once) I walked to surgery on the Monday morning. There was an urgent phone call about Alice early during surgery. It was from her daughter. She sounded very distressed; frantic almost. Her mother had been adamant, that morning, that a very nice man had called to see her at midnight. He had partly undressed her and touched her body. She had been adamant about the time and the details and, like the daughter, I found this new development very worrying. I said I would need to ring the geriatrician again and stress the need for him to see Alice very soon lest it not be safe to leave her at home.

When I got through to Don he was pleased that I'd phoned. He listened patiently to my description of Alice's latest hallucinations and my consequent worries.

'I don't really know how to tell you this, Norman', he said with a barely suppressed giggle. 'You know, Alice's story about a strange man calling late last night and getting rather personal is absolutely true. It was me! I've been unable to get out of the village for three days until yesterday and although it was Sunday I tried to catch up on things. I even went back out after supper and, though it was not midnight, it was easily after nine that I called on your patient. I agree entirely that there are things we need to investigate although her delusions are not, perhaps, as frequent or intense as it appeared this morning. I'll arrange a formal memory test and a brain scan – the hallucinations and the change in her personality that you've noticed are worrying. There may be a growth – I'll write to you of course and won't mention the "strange man".'

It was some months later that Alice died of her brain tumour – two days after the second anniversary of her husband's death.

~

Superman

Lorry drivers are a largely unsung link in society, their vital importance only being noticed when they go missing. They do not lead healthy lives, even if they try. Their job is sedentary and stressful. In the UK, at least, when they break their journeys, facilities are second rate. They are forced to park in disregarded areas of service stations that are often hundreds of yards from restaurants and toilets. Otherwise, and often overnight, they are obliged to park in litter-strewn, noisy laybys that also reek of stale urine. And the 'full English' food and drink made available to them would make a hardened dietician blanch. On the other hand, they are a very upbeat section of life's highway and, being isolated for much of each working day, somewhat garrulous in company. In my experience, they always had a fund of stories to tell.

HGV drivers were therefore always popular when they came to the surgery – which they did in significant numbers. This was not because they were ill, or even because they thought they were ill. We were less than a mile from a large international haulage company who sent their drivers to us for their regular and mandatory HGV medical examinations. These could be tedious in the extreme, but one had to stay alert and not be distracted by the friendly banter.

The drivers were, almost without exception, overweight or even obese, but always had a bluff explanation. How are large bones defined, I wonder? Many of them smoked but played down their tobacco consumption in self-delusion land. We also generally suspected them of bingeing on alcohol although perhaps not when working. In other words, they were a high-risk group for diabetes, heart attack, stroke or cancer. I still swallow consciously when passing a lorry on the motorway.

Bill Crump was as loquacious as any of his peers and in a very good mood. After all, he had been given the afternoon off and the company were paying for the medical. The initial questioning and examination proceeded as per usual – in other words with many an interruption by Bill – until, asking forgiveness as I always did, I felt inside his underpants. It was like receiving an electric shock. His right testicle was twice normal size. I finished the examination and then said that I would just like to check his scrotum again. Bill put on a quizzical expression but said 'Go ahead, Doc. Be my guest.' On lowering his pants properly it was clear that my first impression had been correct. The right testicle was clearly abnormally large and rather hard.

'Bill' I said 'your right testicle, your right ball, is quite large.'

'Isn't that a good thing, doc? Doesn't that make me Superman?' he asked cheerily.

I took a very deep breath. This was not going to be easy. Bill was 54 and hadn't the faintest clue of the significance of testicular enlargement.

'Bill, I'm very sorry to say that it means the opposite. It probably means that you have cancer of the testis on your right side. I'm so sorry to be blunt but I have to be frank. I'm afraid it will need to be biopsied – a little snip cut out for examination – and then almost certainly removed – completely and very soon.'

'Bloody hell, doc. Are you sure?'

I nodded. 'I can't be one hundred percent sure just by groping with my fingers but I wouldn't be having this painful conversation with you if I wasn't on fairly safe ground, medically. Let's look at the good news. If you hadn't come in for a routine medical today this probable growth in your private parts could have gone on swelling and increasing the risk of its seeding itself and spreading round the body.

'But, doc, what about . . . . .? Will I still be a proper man?'

'Bill, there are hundreds, no, thousands of men out there who have had only one testicle all their lives and they function perfectly normally – including sexually. I think that's what you mean isn't it?'

'Well, that's some relief. But what now? Can I work? Does the rest of me pass the medical?'

'Yes, Bill, you do, and you can work. But you need an urgent appointment with a urological surgeon. I'll be phoning one in the next half an hour. I don't want you going off on a road trip to Bulgaria or even anywhere beyond Bournemouth. We may need to get hold of you very quickly. Do we have your home telephone number here?'

'Well, you don't mess about do you doctor. Thanks, anyway, for being so honest – and thorough. Wow, me with cancer. I never . . . . . .'

His voice broke and tears appeared.

'Bill, we'll sort it – and quickly.'

Bill had a right orchidectomy two weeks later and also a course of radiotherapy for some suspicious glands up in his abdomen. He recovered quickly and was soon back at work full time. He also told me, with a grin, that he still 'worked.'

Bill reappeared in normal surgery many months later – in the middle of a spell of very hot weather. We had reason to return to the contents of his underpants. He had developed a tinea cruris – a fungal infection in his groin. He was sure it was because he couldn't shower for days on end on some of his long trips and I was equally sure he was correct.

'You know what, doc? With all the long hours at the wheel you get to think about things. I now check my left ball every day and if I ever find it's getting bigger, I've decided not to have anything done. I'd rather die than be castrated. Is that alright with you? Would you look after me anyway?'

~

Zealous Zoë

Occasionally one comes across people who have remarkable and instinctive talent for understanding human behaviour and know exactly how best to respond when there are conflicts. Their native instincts are easily more perceptive than the acquired skills of the average GP – even one who attended every undergraduate lecture on human psychology and even stayed awake.

Like his father before him, Kevin Dibben was an agricultural labourer. He'd been very keen on tractors from a toddler and would often accompany his father in ploughing, muck-spreading or spraying. He could never see the point of schoolwork but was complicit enough to become literate and numerate - enough, anyway, to cope with everyday life. On the other hand, his knowledge of farm routines, of agricultural machinery, of crops and animal husbandry was both passionate and profound. He loved the land, could read the weather, he knew all the trees and the birds that sang from them, and was even able to tell one variety of wheat from another – all familiarity acquired on the 'edgerows of hexperience' as a famous post-war politician once told the King. It was pre-destined, then, that Kevin would look for work in agriculture when he left school. In fact, he was able to replace his father who suffered a disabling heart attack in his mid-fifties. And when a bungalow became available to rent at the farm (the younger son of the farmer had decided to emigrate to New Zealand) Kevin was able to move in with his young wife, Zoë, just in time for the birth of their first child. I knew none of all this when I first met Kevin. It would have been so helpful.

When I did meet Kevin – in surgery one evening - he was tense and restless and making no spontaneous conversation. I had to ferret my way into his problem. It was soon pretty apparent that he was depressed, indeed fighting off tears. I had no idea where to start. With time pressing, the priority was to engineer, somehow, that this consultation would be only the first of a sequence and then, perhaps, we could eventually come to understand this emotional cataclysm. Kevin accepted a prescription for an antidepressant which I justified in terms of a replacement chemical for one he was lacking in his brain, thinking the mechanistic explanation would be acceptable. I reassured him that it wouldn't make him sleepy and that he would need to see me in a week 'for a possible adjustment in the dosage.' He didn't ask to be put off work and I let it pass.

Kevin returned, as bidden, but brought his wife who was carrying their little child – fortunately asleep. Within a sentence or two Zoë took over. She had seen Kevin's whole personality change when Andrew, the son and heir of the retiring owner had taken over the running of the farm. Kevin had always got on well with Andrew – the two of them had known each other since infancy after all. Although technically boss and employee they had always been on very friendly terms, Kevin never giving the slightest concern about his work ethic and proficiency. But the relationship had soured. Andrew also had recently married. Deirdre came from a commercial background – her parents ran a manufacturing enterprise and she had been to business school. 'Hard-nosed' was the description Zoe offered me. She and Kevin had been subjected to a host of pettifogging intrusions since Deirdre had grasped the reins at the farm. Kevin now had to report for work at the farmhouse every morning and seek permission to go home at the end of each afternoon. He was required to regularly clean all machinery he was using, but now in his own time. He had to log all fuel and lubricants used. He must wear the monogrammed overalls provided and Zoë had to wash them regularly. Kevin's steel toe-capped boots had to be inspected and approved and so on and so on. And, as a couple, they'd been told that they must allow regular inspection of their bungalow, decorate rooms in rotation - at their own cost - and repair any minor damage detected, again out of their own pocket. Kevin had found it increasingly difficult to be friendly with Andrew who was being used as a lightning rod. Zoë was obviously very astute. She had seen that the new regime at the farm was not only an annoyance to them both but that it had played on Kevin's mind, alone in his tractor hour after hour, day after day, until he had come home early one afternoon and completely broke down.

Through all this sad story Kevin sat staring out of the window, stony-faced. My advice - rather pathetic I thought - was to continue antidepressants and that I should put Kevin off work. He suddenly erupted:

'oh, no, don't do that, doctor, I'll lose my bloody job and we'll lose our home in the bargain.'

This seemed rather melodramatic, but I couldn't really deny the possibility.

After a couple more evening consultations, Kevin did seem better but it was more thanks to Zoë rather than any clinical skills or biochemistry. Besides being canny, Zoë proved to be very enterprising. When, on two occasions, she had come home to the bungalow and could smell Deirdre's perfume she was outraged. It was time to go. Through a family connection, she arranged for she and Kevin to take over the tenancy of a terraced house in the town. She also persuaded Kevin to leave the job at the farm and find work at a local factory. She felt that Kevin would no longer be so isolated and able to mix with more people. My chemical intervention was clearly now irrelevant, and I stopped Kevin's treatment. Multiple problems solved at once. Or, or so it seemed, for some eighteen months.

Kevin seemed to thrive in the new circumstances – his hours were more regular and fewer, the pay was slightly better and, as Zoë hoped, he did make new friends. But it didn't last. Gradually Kevin began to be withdrawn and distracted again and a crisis blew up when he couldn't face the job any more. Zoë's antennae again detected the real cause. It was the attitude of Kevin's new workmates. They were, in general, work-shy and cynical. They would foul up the machinery by various ruses, spend ages on toilet breaks, knock off early by clocking each other out and mock anyone with any pride in their work. Kevin began to find it annoying, and then very distressing, even though he managed to hide his real feelings lest he be ostracised. He also missed the variety of the work and weather at the farm. Kevin was back with me in surgery and although I now knew far more of the background and could diagnose reactive depression with confidence, I wasn't at all sure that medication was going to help much. I think Kevin sensed my lack of confidence but didn't argue, this time, when I put him off work.

Once again Zoë came up with the answers. She had heard, on the grapevine, that Andrew and Deirdre had separated. Their nemesis at the farm had left. She had also been told that there had been three replacements for Kevin and that none of them had lasted more than a few months. She scooped Kevin up from his doldrums. They drove up to the farm and waited for Andrew to come in from the fields. They were greeted warmly and all was settled within a few minutes. Kevin could return to his job and there was every prospect that the bungalow would again be empty in a few weeks. It was theirs if they wanted it. Once again, I was able to withdraw the antidepressants and though I haven't seen Kevin since, Zoe is again attending my antenatal clinic.

~

Taking in Washing

Somewhere around the middle of the 1990s there was a full-page article in our local newspaper on the subject of asbestos and its newly recognised dangers. I remember reading it. Swindon, the largest town in our county was, it appeared, a hot-spot for asbestosis and for the cancer it causes – mesothelioma. This stemmed from the steam engine boilers and their maintenance, and then their scrapping, at the British Rail works there. Asbestos had been a very popular and effective fire-proof material for insulation in railway engines. But there were many cases of the tumour reported outside Swindon – in plumbers and in many other trades in the building industry. One of my patients also read the article and it prompted him to come to see me.

Trevor Ford was a self-employed plasterer. He was always in demand and made a good living. Unmarried, he had ample spare cash for his hobby – restoring vintage motorbikes. For many years, he told me, he'd been using Artex, a very popular wall and ceiling coating. It came as fine, dry powder and was mixed, on site, with cold water. Easy to apply, it could be given a textured finish. All of us will have looked up, at some time or other, and noticed a swirly pattern on ceilings. 'It was' Trevor said 'the giveaway that the finish was in Artex. But did I know it contained asbestos?' He'd heard from friends in the trade that the government was about to ban the presence of asbestos in the product – some years after other countries, apparently. He apologised for being a pain but mates of his had been to their doctor and had a 'once-over' because asbestos could get into the chest and cause cancer; as I probably knew.

'And however hard you try, the mixing process for Artex always throws up a cloud of fine dust. I know I should always wear a mask but they're such a b..... nuisance.'

Trevor had no symptoms but knew this was a trap. One chum he used to know well had recently died from the asbestos disease never having had a single warning sign.

On examination Trevor had no signs of chest disease, no abnormal lymph glands, and his peak flow was normal. But I knew that none of this was unfailing. He needed a chest X-ray and perhaps further investigations. He rang me three weeks later and I was able to report that his X-ray was entirely normal. Thankfully he didn't ask me about having regular check-ups since there's no easy answer. I had already told him to have a low bar for reporting chest symptoms like cough or breathlessness and reminded him in ringing off.

It was eighteen months later that Trevor reappeared. He'd been on holiday with his brother and family – to Croatia. Compared with his older sibling, he'd been more breathless in the swimming pool and on walks. And, as if he needed any more reminders of mortality, an old friend who'd been a plumber, had just died of the 'mesowhatsit'. Once again, I could find nothing amiss and his peak flow was well above expectations. It seemed politic, however, if not obligatory, to take another X-ray. Thankfully, this one was also normal. Reassured and euphoric, he agreed not to do any more Balkan bathing.

I didn't see Trevor again until I bumped into him at his mother's house. I'd been treating her for a stubborn chest infection. That morning she had phoned the surgery and asked for a house call – she was more breathless and the cough was worse. She hadn't felt well enough to walk in. As I arrived, Trevor was just leaving. He apologised. He could have brought her to the surgery if he had known but 'she will keep things to herself, you know'. I examined Ethel very carefully. I was concerned that she wasn't getting better. From listening to, and from tapping her chest I thought I could now detect an effusion – a collection of redundant free fluid – low down in her left chest. As she was getting dressed a regular beeping noise started up. I was more surprised than Ethel.

'It's only my washing machine' she said 'I'll just go and see to it. Sorry, Doctor.'

When she came back she told me about the machine, with some pride. 'Trevor bought it for me and had it installed a few years since. It was top of the range and probably very expensive. But it's never given any trouble and copes well, even with Trevor's heavy overalls.'

My pulse rate took a leap.

'So, do you wash all Trevor's clothes, Eth?'

'Yes, of course. It's why he was only too happy to buy me the machine. I've always done it, doctor. As you know, he's not married.'

Without making further reference to the laundry routines of the family, I explained to Ethel that I was worried about her chest and that I would like a specialist to see her. She didn't quibble and I referred her very urgently. Investigations supported my worst fears. Ethel had an extensive methothelioma of her left lung which was half submerged in sinister fluid. She died in less than three months – wasted, blue and very breathless. She had gone into a hospice once we could find her a place. Her admirable dedication to her son was her downfall. Trevor's guilt was difficult to manage but at least his chest remains clear.

Palanquin Progress

The first London Marathon was in the spring of 1981 and raised the profile and the popularity of long-distance running in the UK. GPs came to learn how to best advise on some of the unwanted consequences – plantar fasciitis, shin splints, stress fractures and even jogger's nipple. But everyone assumed that being fit enough to run 26 miles (or even only 13 miles) conferred a long, healthy lifespan. Not so; at least not always. Len Rivers, one of my patients, was well-known locally as a distance runner who often entered competitive races with success, even into his seventh decade. He was rightly proud of the cups on his mantelpiece and the medals in the glass cabinet.

Now his wife, Lillian ('Lil') and his youngest son, John, were in front of me in surgery; a deputation. It was an SMBD situation as we knew it in our practice lexicon – 'something must be done.' Not that there wasn't ample justification. They were worried about 'Dad.' He had stopped running and wouldn't even be persuaded. On the contrary he was now spending his retirement plonked all day staring at the television without really watching it. John, on leave from the navy, had noticed a dramatic change since last at home – 'Dad didn't even seem to know me at first.' And then, earlier in the week, Lil had returned from home to find Len not in the house or garden. After an increasingly anxious hour a neighbour had brought him back from town. He had been going into every shop in turn 'looking for me Missus.'

It sounded very much as though Len was dementing. I said I would put all the necessary gambits into play and gave some obvious short-term advice. John then asked me if it would help to 'line up Dad' for more household chores – cleaning the windows for instance. This seemed a good idea to me and I said so, adding that he would probably need to be supervised and encouraged. Perhaps I was naïve but I don't think I could have foreseen what happened next.

On a bright but cool morning a few days later Lil had set up Len to clean their outside windows and, for a novice, he had 'made a good job of it.' Lil was very encouraging and, without really thinking, had allowed her husband to get the ladder out of the shed and make a start on the upstairs panes. A friend, passing along the street, had shouted the age-old banter – 'Hey, Len, you can come and do mine next.' Len, forgetting where he was, had turned to reply and fallen from the ladder. Although he had landed on the lawn he was unable to get up, even with help. In fact, to Lil's horror, he let out a terrifying scream as she pulled him to a sitting position. His right leg was in an odd position and shortened. Their friend, equally as shocked as Lil, used their phone to ring 999 and an ambulance took Len to hospital where his right hip fracture was confirmed. He was operated on the next day.

The shock, the anaesthetic and the alien surroundings all compounded to cause a quantum leap in Len's intellectual decline. Lil was very upset and felt guilty when Len, for some days, didn't seem to know her and broke down completely when he finally did. It took the physiotherapists much longer than is usual to get Len on his feet again. They did eventually manage it and with her husband more orientated, Lil was glad to get him home. But his domestic rehabilitation was far from successful. We put in all the professional help we could and arranged a twice weekly place for Len at the day hospital. However, the bulk of his care fell, inevitably, on Lil. It was very frustrating for her when he refused food and drink, wouldn't change his clothes or wash, even after being incontinent and could be aggressive and threatening. She hid her tears from us and didn't report how often she was up at night trying to stop him breaking out of the house.

In only a few weeks there was another deputation. Another appropriate deputation. John came to see me again by himself. While valuing all the help we'd been able to organise, he'd been horrified to find, coming home on leave again, how much trauma his mother had been hiding from us 'because she doesn't want Dad taken away.' But he could see no alternative.

An impromptu family discussion was a very useful outcome of the home visit I made the next day – we were joined by John's older brother and sister and their spouses. Everyone agreed that 'Dad' would have to be admitted into appropriate care – for their mother's sake.

Arrangements were made for Len to be transferred to a nursing home a few miles away – by ambulance if I would sanction it. I did but there was a crisis on the day. I was phoned by Lil who was extremely distressed. Two 'lovely' ambulance men had been trying to persuade Len to go with them for over twenty minutes but with no success and he had become very hostile.

'Could you call by, doctor, and give him a sedative injection?'

I didn't see a chemical straitjacket as a good strategy but went along to the house as soon as I could. The two ambulance men were big strong lads but clearly and rightly reluctant to exert any force to resolve the situation. Len was sitting in a fireside chair staring straight ahead. There was foam around his mouth and something told me he had soiled himself. Nonetheless, I knelt close to talk to him but having pushed me away with surprising force he resumed his iron-like grip on the arms of the chair. Making encouraging platitudes I tried to help him up, but he spat at me. We were back to SMBD.

Signalling them to join me, I spoke to the ambulance men in the hall. Did they think, I asked, that they would be able to manage to lift Len – still in his chair – into their vehicle. They nodded and the ruse worked. Len was carried out like a Roman emperor on his way to the Colosseum.

Lil looked up from her tears. 'I never did like that chair' she said, and we both laughed - inappropriately.

~

3
SINGULAR CHARACTERS

Any Old Iron

Local knowledge can be priceless. We knew we had a problem at home when one of our children came downstairs carrying the handle to the toilet flush in the main bathroom. A steel spindle attached to it had obviously rusted through. It was the link to the actual lever in the boxed-in cistern. A replacement was urgently needed. I raised our dilemma at coffee time at the surgery and was told I needed to go and see 'little Freddy Wilkinson'. The senior partner knew him best.

'He's a wizard with steel and wrought iron. His father was a blacksmith but Freddy can't do the heavy work with his disability. Don't bother going to the front of his house. If he's in, he'll be in his workshop down the garden. Go along the path to the back. And be sure to have a good look at the numbers, the handle and the latch on the gate – they're good examples of his skill. Incidentally, I think you'll find he's a patient of yours, but I bet you've never seen him.'

Freddy was small and very affable. His left arm was shortened, a peculiar shape and he seemed to let it hang redundant most of the time. I explained my problem showing him the two parts of the rusted spindle.

'It's got a sort of kink in it – will that make it difficult to make?'

'That's called a crank, doctor. It's no problem – I'll cut some soft steel and bend it to shape this evening. Call tomorrow sometime – I'll be here all day.'

I looked forward to telling the family that we'd soon no longer be hauling on a length of wet string in the bathroom. Freddy saw me looking at his arm.

'The arm? It was a German shell did that to me. Our regiment was in the Battle of Loos in 1915. There's still a big piece of shrapnel near the elbow. It plays up from time to time and there's a hole that some muck comes out of. No-one's ever been keen to go in there and chase after it and I'm used to it now. The shell knocked me out and, when I came to properly, I realised I was a prisoner behind German lines. After sort of patching me up, they sent me to a POW camp in Germany and I was forced to work down a coal mine. With my bad arm I couldn't hew coal at the face – the worst job – but it was hard for all of us. We damn-near starved. I know I'm a tiddler, but I was only five stone when I got home in 1919. Dad gave up any ideas of me taking over the smithy. I worked in the ticket office at the station till it closed but Dad did teach me how to work small scale with metals. Sorry to go on, Doctor, you're probably much busier than me.'

I collected the new spindle on my way home for lunch the next day and it was exhibit no. 1 at the table. I was telling everyone about Mr. Wilkinson's war when my wife suddenly interrupted. A historian, she had suddenly seen the possible import of the name Wilkinson. In the eighteenth century, in the Midlands, hadn't there been a famous iron manufacturer of the same name; John Wilkinson, she thought. She'd check on it. Perhaps Freddy and his late father were descendants?

Some years passed and my partners were quite correct. I never saw Freddy professionally. Until, that is, I was asked to call and see him at home. Glancing at his skimpy notes as I waited at the door I saw that he was now 88. I was surprised – I'd assumed him to be seventy something but had forgotten that he was a World War One veteran. A middle-aged woman answered the door – it was Ann, his niece. Freddy had felt very dizzy on a couple of recent occasions and had nearly fallen. He was finding his iron work much more tiring. He looked a lot older than at our 'spindle' meeting. He was pale and thinner than I remembered him. Even so, he had a unique and impressive way of undressing without using his crippled arm. I could find nothing else untoward on examining him but he obviously needed investigating. He agreed to see our Geriatrician as an outpatient. I took the liberty of a side-step and asked him if he was descended from John Wilkinson, the famous iron master. Neither Freddy nor his niece had heard of the man and were both adamant that they were 'moonrakers' since the year dot.

'Well, your namesake was quite a character. He was the driving force behind the building of the famous iron bridge over the Severn and my wife told me that he even wanted to be buried in an iron coffin – and was.'

'Well' said Freddy 'that won't be my wish.'

I suddenly realised how insensitive I'd been with Freddy possibly harbouring a sinister disease. I made a hasty tactical retreat.

By the time Freddy saw the geriatrician he had also begun to find it difficult to swallow food. An urgent endoscopy was organised and he was found to have a stomach cancer encroaching on his oesophagus. He also needed urgent treatment for iron-deficiency anaemia. I couldn't help seeing a paradox in the fact that his bone marrow was screaming for more iron when, at home, he was surrounded by the metal and that there were several ounces of Krupp best steel embedded in his left arm.

As soon as the endoscopy result arrived, I went to see Freddy again. His niece had moved in to look after him and Freddy had been planning his preferred approach to his illness.

'Whatever you do, Doctor, please don't send me off for another of those inside telescope exams – it was bloody awful.' No surprise there but then he shook me.

'I've been thinking a lot, doctor. Your specialist friend was very honest. He told me I have a cancer and that they can't operate safely at my age – well, in any case I'd refuse. So, knowing my furnace is nearly out I've decided just to have little drinks so as not to be thirsty, but no food. I don't want to linger. Ann's happy to look after me and she knows what I want and don't want. Is that alright with you?'

I resorted to a cliché and explained that my job was to cure sometimes but to care always. However, it was sometimes a legally difficult area. I would want to organise some back-up that I was acting properly. In fact, the geriatrician agreed with me that although we were walking a fine line, just supporting Freddy passively would not be an 'assisted dying' scenario.

'And if Freddy's steely determination is genuine there's little that we can do anyway.'

I don't think he intended a pun. Freddy died only two weeks later. When I went to confirm the death his niece handed me a steel spindle with a crank.

'Uncle Fred wanted me to give you this. He made two of them knowing that soft steel always rusts and you'd be back one day.'

I choked up.

~

Miasma

As in life generally, some problems presenting in general practice remain unresolved. Or they fester for a considerable time and only then unravel.

Marian Hickman came in to surgery to introduce herself and ask for a prescription for her psoriasis. Her skin had been a lot better, she said, whilst living in Australia – she was sure it was the sun. She and George, her husband, had recently come back to live in Wiltshire where they'd both grown up. They'd been teenage sweethearts and married at 18. But George, unable to find work during the late 1930s, and determined not to go into the local pork factory, had joined the Wiltshire Regiment. His timing was not good. Within 18 months his Battalion – the 2nd - was in northern France trying to hold back a rampant German onslaught. He'd been wounded in the buttock by shrapnel near the town of Arras and then captured on the way to Dunkirk. He and Marian were separated for the next five years.

I'd finished writing the prescription by now and Marian sensed that I had no time to listen to any more of her life story. She stopped midstream, apologised, and we agreed on a suitable schedule for repeat prescriptions and the criteria for reviews.

Some months later, Marian was back. Her psoriasis was worse. She was also complaining of stiffness in her joints and that she was ever dropping things. George was getting fed up with having to replace so much china. He'd be quite happy, apparently, with tin plates and cups from the 'Army and Navy'. I wondered if Marian was developing psoriatic arthropathy – arthritis related to her skin complaint. The joint stiffness and loss of dexterity was suggestive but maybe I'd been watching too much Dennis Potter. I noticed, also, that Marian was emotionally more brittle than when we'd first met and there was no part two of the biography. She returned to get the verdict on some obvious blood tests. They were all normal, but Marian wasn't. It was handkerchief from the handbag time and she blurted out that she felt so guilty.

'Guilty of what crime, Marian?'

'Of keeping on at George for us to come home from Australia. Even after more than twenty years I was still homesick – not that life out there wasn't very pleasant. But when no kids appeared for us and George was working all hours, I used to watch the planes taking off over Botany Bay – we lived near Sydney airport, doctor - and ache to see my sisters again. And there were now lots of nieces and nephews I'd never met. In the end, George agreed for us to come home – we'd saved enough money for the fares and even for a deposit on a house of our own.'

'But coming back to the UK has caused problems?'

'Yes, doctor. One problem specially. George is having nightmares again and has gone back into his shell. He's short-tempered again and I know he's having thoughts about jacking in his job. We're back to what it was like when he first got back from the war. We'd both imagined that being back together would be wonderful, but it was awful. George was not the man I'd married. He was restless, couldn't hold down a job, often got angry for no good reason, and we'd both be up at night with him in a cold sweat and screaming. Sometimes he'd lash out at something that wasn't there. And then he'd settle down to sleep again, but on the floor. In the end we decided that we needed to make a completely new start and because he'd been in the army we were given a free passage to Australia. It took a year or so, but George got better, much better. And the nightmares stopped completely.

We both got good jobs and enjoyed them. We even bought a bungalow with a large yard – that's Australian for garden.'

'Were the nightmares because of his war traumas then, Marian?'

'Well, I thought they must be. He wouldn't talk about the war – even to me. Said he just wanted to forget about the bloody army. He would just play comedian if other people asked him: "just got shot up the arras and was stupid enough to get captured" is all he would say.'

'I think he must have been more traumatised than either of us know, Marian.'

'Oh, yes, I'm sure, doctor, but what can I do? We've come full circle and I'm so unhappy. It's all my fault for bringing us back to the UK.'

'Well, do you think George would come and see me? I've never met him and I think I need to persuade him to have some counselling. There's something now called 'post-traumatic stress disorder'. It can last for years. No-one had organised the thinking around it in the 1940s and, in any case, any attempt to deal with it professionally then would have been swamped by the huge numbers of men returning from the Services. Do you think he would come in?'

'Frankly, doctor, I doubt it. But I'll try. Thanks for being so understanding. Look, I must leave you get on.'

George didn't come in. The problem rather blew over as far as I was concerned – for over two years. Marian then came in with bronchitis: 'the English winter's got me' she said. Chest infection aside, she seemed less tense, less anxious.

'All well at home now?' I threw into the mix.

'Oh, yes, doctor. Thank you for asking. George is so much better. His nightmares suddenly stopped and his mood improved. And we've been so very happy since – very close - if you'll pardon the expression.' And do you know – the reason was the smell.'

'The smell?'

'Yes, that awful stink from the by-products department at the factory. You know they've closed it now – thank goodness. All the pig skins, gristle and bones are now being sent somewhere in the Midlands according to my sister – she works in the sausage department. We always have a laugh that the only part of the pig not used for something or other is the oink. But George. Yes, since getting better he's begun to tell me bits about being in prison camp. He was in Stalag VIIIB in Poland. I knew that, of course, from writing to him and sending parcels and things. But like all the ordinary soldiers he was sent out to work by the Germans. 'Hitler's slaves' they called themselves. He was in Stalag for about two years while his wound dried up and then he was sent as one of a party of men, under armed guard, about a hundred miles further east, to a place called 'Ouswitts' – I think that's how you say it.'

Marian had to stop for a prolonged spasm of coughing. She was grateful for a glass of water - I needed her to continue.

'Thank you, doctor. Yes, George and his mates were put into a huge factory and forced to work alongside prisoners from the concentration camp there. These men – 'poor buggers' George calls them – were lousy and starved and if they collapsed the SS guards just shot them there and then in front of everyone. And if one of our blokes tried to give them something from a Red Cross parcel or the odd cigarette stub you'd get the butt of a rifle in the back. It must have been awful and George was there until the Germans took all our POWs back to Germany – another horror story. George couldn't talk for some time after telling me all this, said he'd sworn to himself that he'd never tell anyone. But the worst thing about the factory at Ouswitts, he said, was the smell. Unless the wind was very strong and from the west there was always a sickly smell. It reminded him, he said, of the by-products boilers here in town. When he came home it was as if the smell came with him. The by-products stench took him back, every day, to being in Poland and all the horrors he'd seen. And it was common knowledge that the awful smell had been the Germans burning bodies. I felt so sorry that I hadn't had a clue of what he'd been through. And we thought the war was tough here at home with rationing and the bombing.'

'So the fresh air of Australia was good for you both, then?'

'Yes – looking back it was. It was as if George was reborn – as the young man I'd known at school. And, fool that I was, I dragged us back home and back to the stench again. And back came the nightmares – until By-Products closed last year. And since then George has been sleeping very well again. Funny isn't it, doctor, that smells can bring back so many memories – even horrible ones.'

~

Smallpox Cottages

Some of the most amazing people one can come across are those who have overcome disability, mastered disfigurement and, in spite of the depressing odds, developed impressive skills. Sally Winspear was among them. She had shown the first symptoms of rheumatoid arthritis after her second pregnancy, when she was just shy of her thirtieth birthday. Now, at double that age, she relied on her wheelchair and her retired husband for any locomotion beyond shuffling, on a frame, across the small rooms at their cottage. And she had to haul her whole body round to face you to talk to you if you weren't dead ahead. Most striking was the 'pick-up-sticks' configuration of her fingers and thumbs. They were massively distorted from the knuckles outwards, some even crossed, and it was a daily miracle when she took up her needlework. One gasped to watch her skill with needle and thread or steering material through her sewing machine with the flat of her wrist. So adept a seamstress was she that she spent much of each year making the costumes for the village pantomime. The excruciating acting and the insulting asides aimed at the audience were leavened by her superb costumes, a new set every year. Sally herself never went to the shows though - her admirable, but unnecessary, modesty kept her at home.

Over three decades Sally had been tried on every known therapy for her arthritis. In truth none of them had really helped but her rheumatologists had never dared to admit defeat. She had also had several joints fixed including two dangerously unstable ones in her neck. Through all this her morale remained surprisingly high. That is until she had been given gold. No, not gold in the sense of top dog at the Olympics but real gold salts in suspension. The published side-effects indicate that patients are at risk of developing rashes. This might have been alarming in Sally's case. The family lived at number 5, Smallpox Cottages, a terrace built on land that was once remote from any habitation and where burial pits were dug for smallpox victims.

A few weeks later, Garth, Sally's husband, made an appointment to see me in surgery. He was worried that he was developing a rupture. He had a recurring pain in his left groin when lifting Sally. I could find nothing convincing but the moment he'd finished belting his trousers, he started weeping and flopped back in the chair.

'I don't know how much longer I can put up with it, doctor.'

'I take it you don't mean the pain in the groin, Garth?'

'No, it's not that. It's Sally. She's suddenly become a very different person. She's a spitting cobra, doctor. I'm always in trouble now. Her tea is too hot or too sweet, the sheets on the bed aren't straight, the washing has been left out too long, my socks smell – oh, I could go on and on. And she keeps going on about her 'bamboo spine' and that no-one's doing anything about it. I think I'm right in saying that her spine isn't made of bamboo, is it doctor?'

I nodded. 'No, it's just a phrase. She probably overheard it in outpatients. It's a descriptive term sometimes used when looking at X-rays of the back.'

'Well, anyway, Sal was never like this before those gold injections were started. Never.'

He dried his eyes self-consciously.

'Well, Garth, the rule of thumb with drug side-effects is that anything can happen, there are no absolute rules. But to the best of my knowledge, I don't think gold therapy can cause personality change as profound as this.'

'But can't you find a reason to stop the injections, doctor?'

'Well, perhaps. I think I'd best speak to Sally's rheumatologist at Bath. He will know more than I shall ever know about the side-effects of gold and he may have a better answer than just stopping Sally's treatment. If you can hang in there, Garth, for a few more days, shall I then call at the cottage? I can weave my suggested tactic into the conversation.'

'Yes, thank you doctor. But for God's sake – sorry – for my sake don't let on to Sally that we've had this chat, will you.'

'No, Garth, I'll call in on the pretext of needing to review Sally's treatment after, what's it been now, a month?'

'Yes, a month of hell.'

On visiting Sally, a few days later, I 'spontaneously' noticed her change in mood and raised the issue with her. She was very cross with me while Garth pulled a face behind her back. I said I would speak to Malcolm Hunt, the rheumatologist, and he rang me back at the end of his morning clinic two days later. He'd never come across such a change in personality on starting gold therapy. He even took a quick peep at his favourite oracle while we were talking, but nothing was recorded. He was intrigued, and anxious to know more (was he thinking of writing a paper, I wondered). He suggested seeing Sally in one of his next clinics.

'Can the husband hold out or will there be blood on the carpet?'

Sally came back from the clinic in Bath with a sealed envelope for me. It was from Malcolm and in his own handwriting. His suggestion was that we reduce the weekly gold injections to fortnightly to see if it made a difference to the 'tongue-lashing index'. It was, he added, a rather simplistic and empirical manoeuvre but he could think of nothing better. He didn't record that Sally had been very short with him and surprisingly aggressive - Garth told me so outside as I left. He also told me that Sally was no longer doing her needlework. She just sat staring out of the window most of each day, finding fault with the neighbours. Perhaps I should be treating her for depression, I wondered.

About six weeks later I called at number 5. To my great surprise I could hear laughter inside. I knocked and a smiling, giggling, Garth answered.

'Come in, doctor. Nice to see you but mind where you tread.'

There was a flood of soapy water in the corridor to the kitchen. Sally was wrapped in a huge bath towel and was also giggling.

'We've had one of those sit-in baths put in for Sally, doctor, you know – with the door on one side, and we used it for the first time this morning. You'd think that grown adults like us would know to let the water out before opening the door.'

So, what on earth was it that had turned these overgrown water babies from spitting to giggling, I wondered? Malcolm Hunt would be fascinated but, in fact, the gold proved to be absolutely irrelevant. Sally told me the story while Garth continued to mop the floor.

Not seen for its profound significance, Sally had received a visit, now three months back, from the chair of the village pantomime committee. There would be no need for costumes this winter – there was to be no pantomime. A retired actor from Bristol, having just moved to the area, had rounded up all the local pantomime buffs and suggested that they all pool their resources and put on a week of 'proper' drama at the main Town Hall each Spring. With modern plays there would be no need for 'flashy' costumes; the actors could wear normal clothes. His persuasive personality had won over any sceptics and many of the annual pantomime plans had been dropped. Sally's services would not be needed. It hit her hard after a week or two – she was unwell, now unwanted, and suddenly very unhappy. Long-suppressed anger got the better of her and poor Garth was collateral damage. But there had been a recent twist in the tail. The Bristol 'luvvie' had been arrested on a child abuse charge two weeks ago. I'd read something about it in the local paper. The Town Hall drama season was in free-fall and someone had called at the cottage, yesterday, to see Sally and ask if she would be kind enough to make the costumes for the forthcoming village pantomime as usual. The new chairman was Scottish and was currently writing the script – 'Jock and the Beanstalk'. Garth had already taken Sally to buy some tartan fabric.

~

Fantasy Footfall

In any health service where consultations are at cost it would save some patients a lot of money if they could buy a season ticket. And there are some who would make even more savings if they had a family pass. At the beginning of his trainee year with us I introduced Euan, our new trainee, to the concept of dis-ease as opposed to disease. It's a very flexible interface. There are some patients – a minority, thankfully – who seem to need regular and repeated reassurance that their lives are not being endangered by everyday discomforts. Euan and I agreed to construct a joint timeline of all the interactions with some of these regular 'customers' and discuss it from time to time. We could use it to review strategies for dealing with such patients, sympathetically and safely, but without feeding their introversion and without inflating our workload.

Trevor and Andrea Coulter were, to me at least, obvious candidates for our learning exercise. I had known them for over a decade. Childless, they were in their late forties. They both worked for a local removals firm, travelling to and from work together. In fact, they seemed to do everything together, sharing their lives and, very often, their symptoms. These were manifold.

Each working day in general practice is a myriad of staccato interactions in which only the alarming or the bizarre are likely to impinge on the memory. In fact, it is only by referring back to our training substrate – the sequences of consultations that Euan and I kept (coded) - that I can remember many of them at all.

The first 'saved' consultation involving the Coulters was with Andrea. She had a nasty taste in her mouth. There was nothing to see and she seemed happy with simple reassurance. Trevor came next. He had been passing 'sloppy poo' for a few days and 'my bum stings.' His anus was unremarkable. I suggested he bring a fresh specimen of stool to the surgery if things continued. He didn't seem keen. I made an entry in his already bulky notes and updated our timeline.

Christmas Eve was usually a quiet interlude at the surgery, patients' preparations for the big day taking huge precedence over their health. But Andrea and Trevor were in – together this time. They both had skin lesions. They had heard that there was an outbreak of scabies at a local school. This was news to me and neither of them had any skin blemishes suggesting that they had been within a hundred miles of a Sarcoptes (Scabies) mite. I was left wondering what the real reason for their attendance had been.

It was St. Valentine's Day when Trevor next appeared. He thought he had 'flu. I thought he had a cold and confirmed that the menthol vapour rub his mother had given him was perfectly good treatment. And, yes, he *could* go to work. Andrea next appeared in our Easter Saturday surgery – supposedly for emergencies only. Her 'emergency' was backache that had been bothering her all week. She seemed perfectly content with my diagnosis of a slight muscle strain. I hoped I was right. She then asked me whether she might be menopausal. She had missed a period. I had to point out that we were in an 'emergencies only' session, it being Easter weekend. I asked her to come in and discuss her hormones during a normal working day. She agreed and apologised. She didn't come back.

Euan and I met over lunch after the holiday and had a wide-ranging discussion on patients who attend for what appear to be flimsy reasons and perhaps come close to wasting NHS resources. We even debated the possible significance of patients who only show up on Bank Holidays. Perhaps this was idle chat, perhaps not. And in any case, the Coulters didn't wait until Whitsun. Trevor was back in a fortnight. He'd been sent by Andrea. We'd had a few hot days and she was complaining that his feet smelt. To her this was a sure sign of athlete's foot and that he needed urgent treatment. Trevor's trainers were rather offensive – more so than his feet, I thought and there were no signs of a fungal infestation. I remember him barely waiting for my verdict. As far as he was concerned, he'd fulfilled his contract with Andrea and could go home for supper.

The next time I saw the Coulters – both of them – was not because they were being neurotic. The problem was, though, self-inflicted. They'd been on a holiday to a Spanish costa and over-grilled themselves on the beach. Their sunburn was easily self-treatable and I resisted issuing any sort of prescription lest it create a precedent.

Trevor's next problem was a wasp sting. I couldn't really whine that he was abusing my time. It had gone septic and there was some ascending lymphangitis. He needed an antibiotic. He was up to date with his tetanus protection. Of course he was. Andrea was next. She saw Euan while I was on holiday. She was 'tired all the time' and 'not sleeping properly', phrases that will give any GP heartsink. Euan detected nothing abnormal and was surprised that she happily left while he was still wondering how best to reassure her. I was glad that he had recognised this snippet of patient behaviour. It's not uncommon. It's as if they've prepared a meal but can't wait for it to finish cooking.

Euan and I wrapped up our timeline for the Coulters towards the end of his year with us. By then Andrea had consulted six times and Trevor eight times. From our clinical standpoint, it was only on one occasion out of the fourteen that either of us diagnosed a problem where medical intervention was essential. We had to recognise, though, that this would not have been the patients' perspective. Nevertheless, we did consider it legitimate to wonder if some of their symptoms had been imaginary – that Trevor and Andrea had been fantasising. Perhaps not, but their very low tolerance of everyday niggles that we all suffer has to be seen as a potential threat to practice capacity, practice efficiency and practice morale. Somewhere out there is a compromise and Euan was very glad of the insight before launching into his own practice.

Then, out of left field, came striking news. In yet another consultation concerning something 'that few peoples dies of' as they say in Wiltshire, Andrea announced that she and Trevor had bought a house in Cornwall and were moving away. I waited until she had gone before punching the air. It was wasted effort. Within the year the Coulters were back. They didn't like the doctors in Falmouth.

~

In Sickness and ...

Old Dick Barr had something of the Buddha. Not only was he considerably overweight and always seated, he had a sunny disposition. He was always in the large old chair by the hearth, as much a fixture as any of the other brown furniture. He was 91 when I first met him, a long-retired farmer living opposite his farm – which he now rented out. On my first ever visit to see him I was admitted by a middle-aged woman I took to be his daughter. She soon put me right. Betty was his wife.

'Although I'm only half his age' she told me, pointedly.

I forget what, exactly, was wrong with Dick on our first meeting but it couldn't have had much pathological significance. Next time the complaint was of being thirsty all the time, of a sore mouth and of having to totter, on his two walking sticks, to the 'lav' too often. Sure enough, he had become diabetic and had oral thrush. Seemingly free of serious complications, his high sugar levels responded to tablets. He rebelled against the dietary advice. His mouth improved with antifungal drops and his thirst abated. There was also less wear and tear on his toilet Oyster card. Betty seemed very keen to know, exactly, what complications to look out for as we chatted on my way out of the cottage. I dropped a few hints but was intrigued by what I thought was a Yorkshire accent.

'Yes', she said, 'I grew up in York – in one of the not very nice parts. I sometimes had no shoes to wear and was always hungry. Joining the WAAF in the middle of the war got me away. I was posted down here.'

My next non-routine visit to Dick was requested urgently. Whilst helping him into his pyjamas the previous evening, Betty had noticed a 'large' lump on his abdomen. It proved to be an umbilical hernia. No surprise with his 'embonpoint' as the French call, with exquisite politesse, a pot belly. It reduced easily and had probably been there for some time. I was able to be reassuring. Dick beamed a smile but Betty seemed almost disappointed that the diagnosis was so mundane. Again she followed me out to the car.

'So, did you not go back north to your family after the war?'

'No, I'd met Sheila – also a WAAF; Dick's daughter.'

'And that's how you met Dick?'

'Well, in a roundabout way. Sheila's mother died of her bad heart just before VE Day and, being an only child, Sheila came back to the farm when demobbed. She saw it her job to help her father and I came with her.'

There was obviously more to this story, but I had to dash. Betty understood and I looked forward to the next instalment.

Calling to see Dick from time to time I was impressed how well Betty looked after him. His diabetes didn't deteriorate although he developed mild heart failure. At 95 he was still fully alert but less mobile. Bathing and dressing him were now very difficult for Betty alone and a private carer was recruited for three times weekly. At the end of her first visit the carer took Betty aside. Keeping her voice low in a curiously conspiratorial way she asked if Betty realised that Dick had a nasty rash on his body, that there was a likely skin cancer on his left temple and that his breasts were too big – she was sure there must be a hormone problem. Betty summoned reinforcements – me.

Dick did have a small discrete lesion on his temple – I thought it was an incipient rodent ulcer. I explained to Betty that though a form of skin cancer it would never spread and, at his time of life, unless it grew rapidly, we could probably leave it be. His rash consisted of Campbell de Morgan spots – 'age spots' – totally harmless and only telling us what we already knew. And Dick's 'man boobs' were just part of his obesity. Betty seemed disappointed, almost, that I'd found only one potentially harmful issue.

'At least he's got cancer' she said rather surprisingly.

By now I knew that Betty and Sheila had been very close and had very happy times at the farm in the post-war years. They had been a 'unit' to use the modern jargon. I couldn't resist asking Betty what had happened to Sheila.

'She died on me. It was the year of the coronation – how can I forget? One morning Dick was at market and we were enjoying our 'privacy' when she suddenly complained of a terrible headache and she collapsed unconscious in my arms. I can feel the telephone shaking in my hand right now and have you ever tried to dress someone who's unconscious? You'll know the diagnosis doctor. It was a bleed on the brain. She was only 36. She was in and out of coma for 24 hours until they decided to operate. I saw her off to the operating theatre, but she never came back. Her last words to me were a plea – would I look after 'Dad'. I promised. And here I am.'

'I'm very sorry to hear that, Betty. But you married Dick?'

'Sheila was the love of my life and, looking back, I was in a terrible state for years. I was so emotionally off-cock that when Dick asked me to marry him, I agreed. We were both fed up with the gossip and sniggering in the village anyway. I told him that there would be no 'hanky-panky' and in any case he was past 60.'

I beat a hasty retreat.

Not many moons later, Dick complained of chest pain. Betty immediately rang the surgery and I let myself into the cottage within the hour. Dick did seem distressed – there was no smile to greet me. We began to take off some of his clothing. He put his hand on his right lateral chest and then withdrew it very quickly. It didn't seem likely that he had had the heart attack that Betty had diagnosed. There were no abnormal signs in his circulation nor in his chest but he did seem hot and not himself. I suggested a 'watching brief'. Betty said nothing but I could tell that she was wanting him hospitalised. Two days later I returned. Dick was in more pain and very restless. We hauled up his cardigan, shirt and vest at the back for me to listen to his chest and there was the problem – an angry blistering rash, the 'belt from hell' – Dick had shingles. I explained and sat down to write a prescription. As usual, Betty followed me down the path.

'I know you're doing your job, Doctor, and doing it well but can you not come over one day and tell me that Dick has something fatal, that he is dying? He's 97 soon. I look after him because of my promise to dear Sheila. But I only married him for his money, and I think I've waited long enough.'

~

When 'Take one at bedtime every night' won't do

To me, at least, Cyril Reekes was a shadowy figure. His wife was dying, at home, and I was visiting just about every other day. He would let me in, show me upstairs to Maureen and then duck out and disappear. I would never see him on my way out and I raised his 'hide and seek' behaviour with Maureen. Even in her breathless predicament and knowing she was dying, she had 6:6 emotional insight.

'Cyril hasn't ... come to terms ... with my going ... Every time ... you come ... doctor, it ... punches a hole ... in his thinking ... that all will be ... well as long as ... he looks after me ... and he certainly ... does that ... I couldn't want ... for better care.'

'OK. I do understand but ...'

'I don't mind you ... saying it ... doctor, it ... won't be long ... now ... will it? ... If you need to ... speak to Cyril ... I know ... full well where ... he'll be hiding.'

'Well, Mo, maybe soon. I'll look in again before the weekend and nurse will tank up your pump and dress your sore tomorrow if that's OK?'

Maureen had presented with bloody urine about a year before. She had an aggressive renal cancer and the kidney was removed – but not soon enough. Having recovered from her operation, she had her future hopes dashed by the reappearance of tumour and fluid in her left lung, making her very breathless. The surgeons abandoned their attempt to remove the lung when they saw, at operation, the wide reach of the tumour; it was throughout the chest cavity. They sewed Maureen up and were rightly honest when she came round. She showed amazing courage and had come home to die. We were now at a late stage. Thankfully she was reasonably comfortable on Diamorphine but Cyril's 'head in the sand' stratagem was certainly a worry.

When I did sit down with Cyril at the beginning of the week in which we thought Maureen was going to succumb, I found it difficult to read his reactions. He said very little, his body language was wholly flaccid and his facial expressions impossible to assess because of his very long-standing and severe Bell's palsy. Only one side of his face had any movement. It always took an effort not to react visibly when confronted by his endless winking in 2:4 time.

Maureen died the next weekend. I'd been off duty and called at the cottage on the Monday afternoon. I was worried how Cyril would have reacted to the inevitable, his bizarre bubble of optimism having been pricked. At the very least he was at risk of becoming isolated. Maureen had repeatedly miscarried in her youth, the couple had remained childless, and Cyril had retired early to look after Maureen. My anxieties were brushed aside when the door was opened. A stranger appeared. She was big, blowsy and noisy – all the opposites of Cyril. She introduced herself as his older sister, Corrie, and that she had come down from Gloucester to 'help him over the next difficult days.' It was soon obvious that Cyril had 'passed over the reins' or, perhaps, had had them wrenched away. It was difficult, embarrassing in fact, to talk to him without Corrie repeatedly interrupting with skin-deep platitudes and I was glad to get away.

I remembered our boys being on Whitsun holiday from school when Maureen had died and they had just gone back to a new academic year when I next saw Cyril. He came in to see me, guess what, on the orders of his sister. He'd been getting headaches (even after she'd gone back to Gloucester) and then, a week ago, a profuse nosebleed. Corrie had told him to 'see me or else' and he apologised. Corrie had told him that he had 'blood pressure' but 'what did she know?' But Corrie was right. Cyril's blood pressure was high enough to make any re-readings or subtle adaptions to his lifestyle irrelevant. He needed urgent treatment.

A week later he returned and thankfully his medication had already brought down the readings without him suffering any side-effects. A couple of blood tests in the meantime had shown him to have, also, a high 'bad' cholesterol level and I suggested another tablet – 'one to be taken every night before bed.'

'Sorry, Doctor, but I can't do that.'

'Sorry, Cyril, I don't follow.'

'Well, doctor, you see, I don't go to bed every night – only every other night.'

'Really?'

'Yea. After Maureen died and Corrie had buggered off I couldn't sleep – much if at all. I'd never been on my own in bed for 40 years. So I thought I'd stay up every other night to do the housework and the washing and things and get meself so tired that I'd sleep the next night – and it works'

'That's amazing Cyril. And you feel well on it?'

'Yes, doctor and I even shop now in the middle of the night. As you know, Tesco in Trowbridge is open 24 hours. They know me there now and I get personal service.'

'OK. Well, good for you for being so inventive. I'd suggest then, that you take these statins for your cholesterol with your blood pressure pills, every morning, never mind the small print in the instructions. Can you let me check your blood pressure again in about six weeks' time?'

'Thank you doctor. I'll bet you sleep well – given the chance.'

There was no answer to that and there was many a leaf on the ground when Cyril next came in. All was well. He was still only going to bed every other night and showed no evidence of any problems. With his Bell's he could only half yawn but I didn't see any such. There was one issue, though.

'Hope it's alright to ask you a question, doctor? Only Corrie keeps on at me on the phone.'

'Go ahead, Cyril.'

'She says I must get married again because having no love life is so bad for men that they can drop dead. That's not true, is it?'

'Certainly not, Cyril. I don't know what your sister's motives might be but she seems very much out of order to me. If you do meet someone you like very much and build a relationship it need not be about sex.'

'Thanks doctor. That's a relief. I haven't told Corrie or that would be wrong but as you'll understand, I couldn't be a very good husband any more anyway. One night I'd be too tired and the next night I wouldn't be in the bed at all.'

~

Cardiac Colin

'Cardiac Colin,' as I shouldn't have thought of him, was a very familiar figure to everyone at the practice. Throughout his middle years he battled with a recurring fear of having a heart attack. There was no rhyme nor reason why he should worry about his heart, certainly no more than the rest of us. In fact, the reverse. He was not overweight, he didn't smoke or drink. He had no relevant family history and his cholesterol – measured more times than was sane – was entirely normal. He probably didn't take as much exercise as was ideal although his large garden was always well maintained and we were often the beneficiaries of fresh produce at the surgery. But if his phobia was irrational, as many are, it was certainly real and long-standing.

Colin's medical record envelope groaned with documents. On any number of occasions over some fifteen years he had presented with chest pains – at the surgery, at numerous local accident and emergency departments and, once, even in Devon on holiday. There were enough

ECG tracings to make paper chains for Christmas. There were cardiac enzymes results galore – all normal. Colin had even, once, had cardiac angiography (again normal). A desperate cardiology registrar had thought, mistakenly, it would convince him that he carried no current risk of coronary thrombosis.

Then, during a house call by one of my partners on a very busy Monday in winter, Colin once again complained of left-sided chest pain and difficulty in breathing. This time there *was* something wrong. Colin's heart was racing, and he was hot and clammy. On questioning he agreed that the pain was worse when he took a deep breath. He also admitted that he and his wife had had 'bad colds' the week before. Surely, my partner thought, this must be a lung infection even though the chest sounded clear and there was no cough. Colin didn't really react on hearing of the diagnosis of pleurisy and that he should be admitted to hospital. Silently convinced that the problem was really with his heart, he readily accepted the need for further tests and an ambulance was requested.

Ten days later I found Colin's name on my daily home visits list. On the simple grounds of geography and for no better reason, I made it my first call. I was admitted to the home by his daughter who was grateful that I had 'come so quickly'. The patient was lying back in a recliner chair and, I thought, looking pleased with himself.

'It *was* my heart, Doc' he said, almost gloating 'I knew it was but will you thank your partner for sending me in. He was definitely on the ball.'

He handed me a brown envelope. Inside was a discharge form with some hastily scrawled jargon written, no doubt, by an overstretched and sleep-deprived houseman (none of us ever forget). The word 'pericarditis' jumped off the page.

'Well' I said 'it *was* your ticker, Colin, but you still haven't had your heart attack. You had a virus infection of the membrane and fluid around the heart – a knock-on effect of the bad cold you'd had the week before. Didn't they explain on the ward?'

'Yes, I suppose they tried but I didn't really understand. They don't use everyday words like you do, Doc. They kept on about having a fusion but I didn't have one done in the end – I suppose they thought I wasn't worth the expense.'

'I think you mean an ef-fusion, Colin. We're talking about a large collection of fluid around the heart that can stop it working properly. It's good news that you didn't get one.'

I suddenly realised that Colin's wife was not with us. It was very unlike her. Despite her husband's chronic neurosis and the endless false alarms, she was always caring and attentive, an unacknowledged heroine.

'Where's your mother?' I asked the daughter.

'Oh, I expect you haven't heard, Doctor. She's had a heart attack.'

'Really?'

'Yes, she's in the coronary care ward. She was visiting Dad at the weekend and popped down to the hospital shop. She passed out coming back up the stairs. They told us she would have died if she hadn't actually been in the hospital. I've come over to look after Dad until she comes home. They said, last night, that she's improving but may well need an operation.'

The irony was running down the walls of the kitchen like condensation on wash day. All the many occasions when Colin had persuaded himself that he was having a heart attack had so drained our energy and common sense that we had never given his wife's health a fleeting thought. It was a sobering reminder of how not to doctor the middle-aged. Women, too, can develop coronary artery disease once their protective hormones go missing.

Colin had had his heart attack – by proxy.

~

Connie and her Cats

In any clinical interaction in medicine both parties are human. Whilst stating the obvious is tedious it is, nonetheless, a point worth making. But why hover on the phenomenon at all? Because, of course, it can go wrong. Professional boundaries can be crossed and it's not always the 'News of the World' scenario of a doctor sleeping with his patient.

Connie Archer was someone we all knew in the practice. She was a type-2 diabetic, considerably overweight and a cat-lover. She also had a human lover – her partner Joy. Joy was twenty years junior to Connie but, on the face of it, their lesbian relationship seemed very stable. They lived comfortably enough in an orderly rented house, one of the terrace opposite the surgery. Joy worked shifts at the large factory in the centre of town and did most of the shopping and housekeeping. As an ex-bookkeeper, Connie was happier managing the couple's finances, settling bills and organising their social diary – mainly bingo twice a week. Their friends always saw Connie as 'wearing the trousers' though it was almost certainly more complicated than that.

Connie had a tortuous past in terms of relationships. She had even been married – conventionally – at one time. And from repeated and frequent consultations, not always centred on her diabetes, it was very clear that she felt insecure in the current relationship.

Whether Connie tripped over one of her four cats in the house – all mollies – which she denied, or simply slipped on a wet kitchen floor, which she claimed, is immaterial. The result was a deep graze down her left shin and it rapidly turned septic. I had already noted the near absence of arterial pulses at ankle level and poor peripheral circulation was, I assumed, the reason that her filleted leg refused to heal. In fact, the ischaemic infected tissue died off and Connie was left with a significant deep ulcer with exposed bone surface at its base. It was unsightly, putrid and the smell was sinister. It was also very painful and Connie found it excruciating to bear weight on the leg. We arranged for her to have a wheelchair with an elevated leg rest. After a month our district nurses could detect no signs of a healing process and, after a joint visit with them, we deliberated outside on the pavement. It was time to refer Connie to the hospital clinic run by the vascular surgeons.

Connie was very upset and cantankerous. There was no way, she insisted, that she would be able to get up the hill to the out-patient department from the car park – she was encyclopaedic on the hospital geography after attending diabetic clinic for many years. As a compromise, she finally agreed to go by ambulance, in her wheelchair and with Joy providing the motive power. Joy, in her turn, agreed to swap shifts with a series of workmates so that she was always on the (hugely unpopular) late afternoon/evening shift. Negotiations were, then, finally concluded successfully but Connie wasn't to know that the arrangements were to be a big mistake.

A letter from the vascular surgeon was, in essence, a pat on the back for our team. He thought we had been treating Connie's ulcer optimally. He simply carried on with our approach, seeing Connie twice a week and leaving us to change dressings once during each weekend. The surgeon did have the advantage, though, of regular input from his microbiological colleagues and he did try Connie on vasodilator drugs. He was also more aggressive in his approach to Connie's blood sugar control which Connie didn't appreciate. Nor was she compliant.

Then, one Sunday running into Monday came a crisis. Our leading district nurse was waiting for me as I arrived at surgery on the Monday morning. She had found Connie in floods of tears the previous afternoon and it had taken time and patience to get to the hub of the story. Joy had left. Behind Connie's back, she had struck up a relationship with one of the two regular ambulance drivers that had been taking them to outpatients – both female. After a huge bust-up on the Saturday morning when Connie had discovered a text on Joy's phone that was by way of an electronic love letter, Joy had packed two bags and stormed out. Now, and very understandably, Connie was refusing to go for her hospital appointments. You could hardly expect her to be happily transported there by her betrayer and, in any case, she was saying that she didn't want any more treatment:

'If I lose my leg, if I lose my life, so what. If it wasn't for my cats, I would already have taken all my diabetic pills.'

But there was more trauma. By Wednesday Connie had realised that two of her cats were missing. Of course she blamed Joy and was even more inconsolable. Her diabetic control was completely lost when she started bingeing on food for comfort and she ended up in hospital in pre-coma. Almost inevitably, her leg went gangrenous and it was amputated just below the knee.

Three months later I was told that Connie had been discharged into one of our local residential homes. I went to see her. She was pleased to see me, smiling and joking. I asked about the leg and, using her left hand, she pulled up her skirt to show me her stump. Her other hand, I noted, was holding that of another lady resident sitting alongside her.

~

June the Sixth

I first met Jock MacKinley after he had been discharged from hospital into a local nursing home. The staff were immediately anxious. He was having difficulty swallowing his medication and, also, some foods. It appeared that he had been lucky to survive his stroke. At first the physicians had considered his care to be palliative but he had rallied and rather surprised them.

It was just about possible to juggle his drug regimen to give him liquid alternatives but his problems with eating rumbled on. His carers were always on tenterhooks at mealtimes – was he or was he not going to choke. For some weeks, until they got used to it, his dis-ordered speech also gave concern. His guttural Glasgow accent didn't help matters and it became clear that his aggressive outbursts usually related to his frustration at not getting what he wanted. His most common request was easily understood. However, he was not given the whisky he craved. We arranged for him to attend the Day Hospital each week where he saw the speech therapist.

Despite what was an obvious challenge for her she was able to help Jock begin to articulate more words clearly. However, slowly but surely, he lapsed into articulating just one phrase, time and time again. It was bizarre and always out of context – it was 'up the beach on D-Day.' A daily sequence of Kafkaesque conversations kept everyone on their toes and having to guess the answers to routine questions:

'How are you today, Jock?'

'Up the beach on D-Day.'

'Are you warm enough?'

'Up the beach on D-day.'

'Do you need the toilet, Jock?'

'Up the beach on D-Day.'

Among Jock's few possessions in his bedside cabinet there were some tarnished medals with their ribbons. He was also fond of wearing a Tam O'Shanter, even in his pyjamas. A visitor recognised the cap badge of a famous Scottish regiment. Everyone therefore assumed that Jock had served as a soldier during the war and that he had been among the first troops landed in France on D-Day.

As June 1994 approached – the 50th anniversary of the Normandy invasion – some of the staff thought they should help Jock celebrate his bravery – he having gone 'up the beach on D-Day.' Various events were planned for the big day including a visit from the Mayor and there was a rumour that the Lord Lieutenant might look in and that the local press would be very interested.

The plans were never secret, of course, and Jock's daughter, on one of her occasional visits, heard about them. She immediately asked to speak to Matron who reported the conversation to me.

'I'm sorry about this, Sister, but it would not be right to celebrate Dad's war.'

'But any of our lads charging up those beaches on D-Day must be heroes. Surely it's only right that we should mark the occasion with any survivors.'

'But, Sister, Dad didn't take part in D-Day. I know it for a fact.'

'Oh.'

'No, you see, during Spring and Summer 1944 Dad was serving a four month's prison sentence for desertion. He went AWOL in February that year, a few weeks after he had met my mother while on leave. They led the military police a merry dance, flitting from one of my mother's relatives to another, all over the Midlands. I think they both considered it an exciting and tacky adventure. In fact, I've always assumed that it was when I was conceived. No, making Dad out to be a hero could be very embarrassing for everyone if the truth came out. Of course, he would be more than happy to play the part and to be fawned over.'

The plans to put Jock in the limelight on D-Day+50 were quietly shelved. The staff at the home were told, in confidence, that it had been an understandable mistake that Jock's echolalia should be taken literally. His criminal record was kept confidential. Just the same, it was difficult for the staff, on the day itself, to disguise their amusement when, inevitably, Jock spoke, as usual:

'Up the beach on D-Day.'

For once it was appropriate as the familiar brief spools of black and white film came on the television.

~

Marcel Bloody Proust

The next patient was Clifford Stiles. I remembered his last consultation. It had been interrupted by my having to help with an emergency in Sister's room and 'Cliff' couldn't wait for my return. He had been very talkative. I hoped it was just from fleeting anxiety.

'Good morning, doctor. You look in the pink and, I must say, you're doing well this morning. Do you know you're only running nine and half minutes late today? Better than last time, certainly, and wasn't it a pity that we were so abruptly interrupted? But I suppose some people can't resist having dramatic outbursts can they?'

The 'attention-seeking' patient that morning had actually died in the ambulance taking her to hospital but I let it pass for the moment. The quoted half minute was a bad sign, as was the plastic bottle of water he was cuddling.

'Anyway I expect you'll be wondering why I'm here on such a lovely day?'

I nodded but was given no time to formulate a reply.

'It's about my weight, my w-e-i-g-h-t not my, um, w-a-i-t although, as I say, it hasn't been too long this morning. Well, about my weight then, or, more accurately, my body mass index which is, of course, a measure that you will understand more than me. It's 22, well just over actually, and I want it to be no more than 20 now that I'm rapidly approaching my 30th birthday. I feel that I'm on a slippery slope. Naturally, you'll tell me all about calorific intake but that's the rub. I'm very confident that my diet couldn't be bettered. For breakfast this morning, for example, I started with some freshly squeezed orange juice. Incidentally, isn't it good news that we can now recycle peel and skins. And incidentally also, you should know that I never keep fruit - of any sort - in the fridge so that the vitamin C is at its best. Then I had a thin piece of wholemeal toast with some smashed avocado and a light dusting of red pepper. Thin toast mind, I hate doorsteps of bread. Don't you?

My chance to intervene was in picoseconds and I lost it.

'And then a handful of blueberries with black coffee – freshly ground of course and seeped through a filter. I always use two filter papers to be sure to hold back any impurities. Don't you think, like me, that coffee filter papers are getting thinner – I'll swear some brands are almost transparent in strong sunlight.'

My repeated attempts to interrupt Cliff all failed but as he embarked on the intimate details of yesterday's lunch I jumped in forcefully.

'Well, all this is interesting in a way but if we are to focus on your weight gain and what best to do, we'll need to . . . .'

'Oh, I wouldn't want it said that I have put on any significant amount of weight, doctor. Going up by two points on the BMI scale is not really a major weight problem, you must agree. No, no, no, on the contrary, I just want to offset my potential for obesity, shall we say. Actually, my normal lunchtime preferences might be more relevant than you seem to think. And I will be concise, believe me. I usually go for something that's half animal and half vegetable. Yesterday's midday meal is a good example – two ounces of prime steak, medium rare, and a rocket salad dressed with virgin olive oil. I really don't see the point of the vinegar they always throw in do you? Although I suppose you would call it acetic acid? I try to go all day without going anywhere near any carbs – well, after breakfast I mean – and I always try to stay well hydrated using a top quality mineral water. I think it's true, if I'm not mistaken, that the water from Malvern has royal approval?'

A question of a sort but it gave me another chance to stem the tide. In my growing annoyance I fluffed it.

'I have to say that my downfall stems, perhaps, from my evening meals. Normally I eat between six and seven. After that I don't sleep too well but sitting down to a meal before then somehow doesn't seem altogether satisfying. Evenings when I'm expected to work late or on the really rare occasions – I can't for the life of me remember when it last happened – when I might go for a drink after work – 125 millilitres of a good red wine at most – can be hell with my digestive tract. I expect you notice the same if your duties upset your routine? Anyway, when it comes to what I actually eat for supper I have to say that I focus on introducing some variety. I understand that's important when it comes to minerals and vitamins that are so essential for all of us. Do you do the same, doctor?

'Well, my own diet is not really relevant here, Cliff – nor are the minutiae of yours. No! Let me continue for the moment. We must get back to focussing on your BMI and whether you really have a problem.'

'Oh, please, doctor. I really don't want us to embark on any controversy. It's just that you're the one person with known expertise in these matters – at least that's the general understanding. Even top people appear to respect their doctor and believe what they're told. Are you saying that I can ignore what my body is telling me – surely not? Isn't obesity becoming a major public health crisis in this country? That and neglecting to take adequate daily exercise. There are alarmists everywhere one looks and many of them are, I notice, much stockier than me – and maybe than you, too, doctor.

My toes were curling up inside my shoes and the tip of my biro was making its way through the skin of my palm. This was 'heartsink' squared.

'Yes, I have to say that when it comes to physical activity I do try to treat my body with the respect it deserves. We're only endowed with one body in life, after all but you'll be more aware of that than the rest of us doctor, I'll bet. I walk to and from work every day and unless the weather makes it totally impossible I always take a daily stroll at the weekend, taking in some light shopping and the paper shop on Sundays. I hope you're one of those people, like me, who thinks that the shops should be kept to restricted opening hours on Sundays. Anyway, if I have to avoid a soaking at weekends I walk around the flat for an hour. I reckon 40 times in and out of the three rooms is a good mile although it is a very tedious mile. No, I much prefer to get out for a walk even when winter is pinching. I don't suppose you get much opportunity to take exercise, doctor, but then I'll bet running round this desk all day keeps you pretty fit. As desks go it's pretty big isn't it. Nice though – looks like good quality oak and your leather top is very attractive.

It was high time to put a stop to this time-wasting. There were probably thirty odd people in the waiting room, a third of them to see me, some probably harbouring serious disease.

'Cliff – I must stop you there and if you crosstalk me again I'm afraid it'll have to be the end of the consultation.'

There was a very silent silence. Then . . .

'Oh perhaps you want me to go now, doctor. Of course, I'd have to consider whether I would have grounds for a complaint. You're not giving me chance to fully delineate my problems – my weight was only one of the things I wanted to discuss with you and even there we seem to have got nowhere. Of course, I do understand the pressure you doctors are under and there must be dozens of timewasters who pester you about nothing every day. I have to say I like to think I can be empathetic with people. Perhaps you'd like me to leave problems two and three for another occasion? I guess they will wait for a few days but I really do need to get to grips with this weight issue before I slide any further down the slippery slope to which I have, if you recall, already referred.'

By now I wasn't really listening. It was time to out a stop to this stream of consciousness. I was plotting an escape strategy. It was Tuesday. The practice weighing scales would be in my side-room for the afternoon antenatal clinic. I reached for the bottom drawer of my desk – for a diet sheet.

'Cliff – Cliff – just stop for a moment. I'm suffering information overload. Here is a thousand calorie per day diet sheet. With it you can match your daily intake to the numbers – 'guestimating' the weights and therefore the caloric values of food items is surprisingly accurate and you can then keep track of your intake. Then the answer to your anxiety is in your own hands – the only place where it will work. If you can stick to a thousand calories per day you'll be fine'

There was no way I was going to open the cupboard harbouring his second and third problems today. His introverted logorrhoea was almost certainly masking one or more serious problems, relationship issues maybe, but they would need to be explored using very structured conversations with me asking carefully closed questions.

'Now, if we could just pop next door and put you on the scales, we'll have an objective reference point on record won't we.'

He began to remove his jacket – 'that's right. No, bring it with you.' After weighing him – twice at his insistence – I ushered him out into the corridor and indicated the way back to the waiting room. He was still talking – something about his jacket feeling tighter that it used to be. Hopefully he still thinks the pressure on his back when I propelled him down the corridor was the 'tight' Harris Tweed.

~

Matron

Sister McFee had been matron of our cottage hospital for nearly twenty years before she retired. She had trained at St Thomas' in London, a 'Nightingale Nurse'. She rose through the ranks to become sister on one of the surgical wards there. Having then married a distant cousin, a bank manager in our town, she had moved from London when nearly forty. She and her husband never had children and her removal had coincided sweetly with a vacancy for matron in our local hospital.

Everyone agreed that she had been a breath of fresh air – a whirlwind was how some people expressed it. She gave off an aura of no-nonsense discipline and demanded very high standards of herself and everyone else. Our own Betty Boothroyd, someone suggested, but she had never been a Tiller Girl. We all saw the hospital staff respond, after early trepidation, to her firm management. Even those who had wilted under a verbal lashing had to agree that she was always fair and just. It was fascinating to watch how patients and their relatives in the waiting room at the hospital, stretched out with a magazine, would sit to attention if she appeared at the desk. It was an urban myth, though, that the bedsheets would straighten themselves if she joined a ward round. Staff loyalty and stability increased, bed turnover improved, and we began to think that clinical outcomes were better. We certainly saw a drop in infections. It was also clear that after she had joined the Area Health Authority as our representative, local needs and priorities were never brushed aside. But for those of us who got to know her socially, we knew that she was only nine-tenths starch.

Beyond medicine, 'a discipline that takes no prisoners' as she would often remind us, she and her husband were a fiendish bridge partnership and they won many a trophy on the badminton court. We were all very sad when she was suddenly widowed and more upset, in a shame-faced, selfish way, when she decided to retire a few years later.

'Matron' as she was ever known was a patient of our practice. It was Doreen, our main telephone receptionist (whom no-one envied on Monday mornings) who first noticed an oddity. She realised that Matron was requesting house calls that always seemed to be on Mondays. She was rather imperious on the phone but 'more up tight than ill', Doreen thought. Mondays are always very busy in the practice but none of us would have refused to have gone to see her. However, with holidays, courses, and other hiccoughs, it had not always been her own doctor – me – who had visited. One day Doreen asked if she could see me in private. She sheepishly told me what she had spotted but 'I'm sure it's nothing'. Looking through Matron's case notes did, though, reveal a strikingly regular demand for house calls - every fourth Monday for some months. Doreen was quite right. The series of symptomatic problems recorded didn't seem related and had required no investigations or follow-up. What to do? After congratulating Doreen on her 'antennae' and asking her to be very discrete, I spoke to one or two of my partners. We all felt that a 'wait and watch' tactic was best. 28 days from Matron's last visit would fall on a bank holiday so we prompted each other to be on alert the day after.

Our secret hypothesis fell apart when Matron rang in asking 'for the doctor to call' on the Friday before bank holiday weekend. I went to see her. The problem was a vague abdominal pain and reported diarrhoea. There was nothing to find and I was at a loss whether to challenge her that the symptoms were fictitious. I bottled out but did talk to my partners during an in-camera meeting the following week. None of us could rationalise the situation. Why was it that Matron, the acme of common sense and practicality and who had never shown a scintilla of neurotic behaviour, had needed our support every twenty eighth day (at most) for the last eight months. We did spot that it matched the length of her retirement but couldn't see any significance. We certainly could not go on like this, maybe for years.

The following week I called on Matron at home. She was surprised to see me and let me in with a frown. After some small talk I asked if we could sit down and talk. She seemed very apprehensive and even more uncomfortable when I said that I wanted to discuss the number of home visits that she'd requested and that I felt that we were somehow missing something. Was there an on-going problem she perhaps wanted to air? Thus confronted, she came straight out with it. She had developed a phobia of post-mortem examinations – about 'being cut up after death'. As a massively experienced nurse she knew it was completely irrational, but it stemmed from the Coroner having insisted on a post mortem on her husband when he had dropped dead.

She had thought that by being examined, even just superficially, by one of our partnership every twenty-eight days at most, I would be able to sign a death certificate for her if she died suddenly. That I would then not have to report the death to the Coroner (as the 'patient not having been seen for 28 days or more' rule dictated). I let the silence expand until she broke it – by sobbing. She obviously needed some professional input, someone qualified to explore her anxieties and resolve her fears; some counselling. Composing herself, she asked me to send her to someone privately and at some distance. Money was not a problem but would I write any letters myself by hand and protect her privacy. She didn't want to be seen as a 'bloody crackpot'.

I referred Matron, privately, to the Professor of Psychiatry at Bristol – we'd been housemen together and he was a 'Tommy's' man. The visit requests stopped and I heard that she had joined the weekly walking club and was already its schedule secretary.

~

Councillor Lewis

To the best of my knowledge, George Lewis had always been known as GL, perhaps from school, even. He and his older brother had run a small pig farm started by their late parents after the war. When it had been swallowed up by an arable consortium the brothers had been able to bank, each, a considerable sum of money. GL bought a bungalow in town and kept himself busy with various odd jobs, some of them for some very odd people. He never married. Goaded by what he saw as local injustices he stood for the town council at an unopposed by-election and would probably have become mayor if his political career had not imploded. I had learned all this very much out of sequence as I got to know him as a patient: he was prone to chest infections. What everyone knew was how he came to leave the council. He was stopped by the police late one evening, driving erratically. He was way over, way way over, the legal limit for alcohol when at the wheel. He was banned from driving for three years and in a hail of damaging publicity he resigned his seat on the council.

In recent months GL had been coming to surgery complaining of 'indigestion.' His story would vary somewhat but he usually admitted to poor appetite, bloating and 'heartburn.' He seemed to mean acid reflux, especially at night. Never a smoker, he was adamant that he had stopped drinking completely after his brush with the local magistrates. There was nothing to find on examination except that he was rather thin and was a little tender in the upper abdomen. I noted that his personal hygiene was rather neglected but not everyone showers and dons clean clothes when going to the doctor these days. I asked him to see the nurse for some basic blood tests and report back in about a fortnight. Two or three weeks elapsed and I'm afraid I didn't spot his failure to return. I might have been prompted by blood test results but there were none.

A month later there was a request to see him at home. Apparently, he was 'loose' and didn't dare cross town in case he was 'caught short.' There was quite a wait before he let me in and he seemed flustered. He reached down hurriedly to close a cupboard door as he walked ahead of me through the kitchen. Whatever he was anxious to hide there was no disguising the offensive smell of stale cooking fat and the dirty crockery piled high.

His 'looseness' turned out to be frequent sloppy stools rather than uncontrollable diarrhoea. He denied nausea or vomiting. His appetite was still patchy but he seemed very unsure how to answer some of my other obvious questions. His tongue was coated and there was an offensive breath odour wafting over neglected teeth. Once again he was a little tender in the upper abdomen and he had now definitely lost some weight. I challenged him on the blood tests I'd ordered. He seemed bemused – was I sure I had wanted some blood taken? He couldn't remember me saying so. I was beginning to wonder if, despite his strong denial, that he was, in fact drinking alcohol again, and to excess. The bowel problems, the self-neglect, the memory lapses, and the tremor I'd noticed as he fiddled with his fly buttons getting dressed were beginning to form a familiar pattern. Again he denied that he was drinking – this time with some aggression. 'I learned my lesson' he said 'when I lost my licence.' He did agree, however, to allow a district nurse to call and take some blood and apologised for all the 'trouble.'

As I collected my things together and began to leave I suggested, gently, that he take more watery drinks and that he was inviting dental problems by not cleaning his teeth. I had one last try on the alcohol front, 'Was he absolutely sure that he wasn't boozing again?' He shook his head and again said 'absolutely not.' We were in biblical, thrice denial, territory. As I crossed the kitchen again and reached the hall the front doorbell rang. Instinctively, I opened the door. I recognised the caller – the counter assistant from the local wine shop. (Yes, we did know each other). He was holding what looked like rather a heavy box. I stood aside and he put it on the hall table. Inside were two bottles of brandy, some mixers, a carton of beer cans and a half bottle of a single malt. 'Just GL's weekly order' the delivery man said cheerily.

I let him out and closed the front door. I headed back across the kitchen carrying the box. It was time to start the consultation all over again.

~

May Bryant

Like many thousands of her generation, May Bryant was evacuated, from South London, in September 1939. She was four at the time, a tiny, lost sidekick to her two older brothers of six and nine. Thankfully the authorities at their Dorset destination kept the three of them together. They were taken in by a childless couple who found themselves on the fast track to learning how to look after young children.

After a bitter winter, a glorious summer and another winter, May found herself, confusingly, on a train back to London. Her lonely mother had come to collect her, wanting her 'baby' back. The blitz had eased and the war, for May's family, as for so many others, had settled into a numbing stalemate of fear, separated families, austere restrictions and the daily dread of very unwelcome telegrams.

May was nine when the war rebounded on her in a terrible incident. During 1944 Londoners had become accustomed to the 'Buzz Bombs' – the German V1 rockets launched from northern France. When their motors stopped – when the 'buzzing' ceased – you sought cover; they were about to fall from the sky. But the more advanced V2 rockets – from launch pads further afield and more a feature of early 1945 – gave no warning of approach. There would be an instantaneous and enormous explosion and firestorm covering several acres. Whole buildings could vaporize, and hundreds of civilians be killed or badly burned.

May suffered such a bomb. She had been walking back from the shops with her mother when a huge explosion and violent hot wind threw them across the road and into a garden hedge. Both were concussed and were still lying where they had landed when strangers, and then the police, and then ambulances arrived. They were checked over and propped up as minor casualties as the services looked for anyone who might be saved from death. In their state of shock, May and her mother watched, unavoidably, as police and firemen pulled charred bodies and body parts out of a wrecked building just a few yards down the road. May's mother suddenly realised that her daughter was transfixed by what she was watching. She pulled May into her chest and tried to obscure her view. It was too late. It was only after some time that blankets and tarpaulins were brought to hide the gruesome human remains now lined up along the road. For the rest of her life May would have flashbacks and a deep-seated phobia of fire, of things charred, of naked flames, of gas appliances, of lighted matches and even of cigarette smoking. In fact, she had the classic features of post-traumatic stress disorder before it was ever defined.

At the end of the war the Bryant family were reunited but had to move to Wiltshire if Dad was to go back to his old job – his employers had been bombed out of London during the blitz. May never married and although her brothers established their own lives and families she was left, rather, to look after her ageing parents. And, after they had died, she became something of an emotional cripple, developing an increasing anxiety state and recurring agoraphobia. She became a familiar figure to everyone at the surgery. Despite desperate efforts to prevent it, she became dependent on sedative drugs, first Barbiturates and then the Valium-like compounds. Several counsellors and psychiatric nurses did their best to support her but with little success.

May was unable to hold down a steady job because of her recurring panic attacks. These could be so easily provoked by associations with fire. Guy Fawkes celebrations were a nightmare every year. A neighbour's garden blaze would provoke terror and she once had to flee a nephew's birthday party as the candles were lit. She lived a life repeatedly interrupted by periods of significant tremor, racing heart and sleeplessness. One outstanding attack of panic was brought on when she went, with a good friend, to see the film, Rebecca; the burning of Mandalay saw her rush from the cinema and almost cause a motor accident when she stumbled into the road.

Eventually we managed to find her a flat that was wholly electric and all of us continued to support her as best we could. A crisis came along when the Government tightened up on the regulations covering the certification of those 'unfit for work'. It fell to one of our junior partners to have to tell May that we couldn't renew her long-term sickness certificate after she'd been called in for an independent medical exam by the Job Centre. May took umbrage and left the practice. Without being selfish, we were somewhat relieved, particularly when we heard, down the grapevine, that May had suffered a florid setback on 9/11.

You can imagine my surprise, therefore, when, some years later, one of the town's undertakers rang to ask if I would be able to countersign a cremation application form.

'The deceased', he said, 'is a Miss Bryant.'

'You mean May Bryant?'

'Yes, do you know her?'

'And she wished to be cremated?'

Yes, her two brothers came into the office yesterday afternoon and were quite certain it had been her wish.'

I was speechless for several long seconds.

One of the Gals

The Cabinet War Rooms under Whitehall are now a tourist attraction. But during the Second World War the subterranean offices – converted cellars – were a place of very serious activity. A pool of young typists, mostly female and all cleared by security, worked very long shifts not knowing whether they would have a home to return to if there was an air-raid. One of them was Molly Simpkins. Privately educated and from a well-connected family, she was recruited without any real background scrutiny. That her typing was 60 words per minute and her shorthand excellent was almost subsidiary. A hasty marriage late in the war failed after only a couple of years, after which she remained single. She worked on in the Civil Service in London and on retirement she moved to a bungalow in a Wiltshire village – in our practice area.

Molly became a good friend of our senior receptionist, Mary and it was she who first expressed concern. An obvious choice for clerk to the parish council, Molly had always impressed by her prompt and accurate production of immaculately typed minutes. She always tried to summarise accurately what people had actually said, dropping, with some difficulty, the Whitehall practice of recording a formulaic, sanitised version of what they should have said. Recently, however, there had been a difficult conversation between Molly and the committee chairman. He had noticed that there had been more and more flaws and gaps in the minutes and the typing was no longer accurate. Mary, too, had noticed a change in Molly who had resigned from her post but didn't seem to care. Then, when her muscles had locked in trying to pour tea from her favourite teapot, Mary asked me if she could bring her in to see me.

The first thing I noticed was that Molly was moving slowly and that she had fine hand tremor. The failing muscle memory, the episodes of 'freezing' and the characteristic tremor made the presumptive diagnosis easy - Parkinson's disease. Our local neurologist agreed and started Molly on some treatment. She responded and for some time she was free of stiffness and muscle-locking. She had no balance problems and regained some of her sparky wit. The on-going war between symptoms and medication continued for several years but we all knew, and Molly accepted, that there could only be one outcome. The 'Parkinsons' would win unless nature called time with some other pathology.

Eventually, Molly decided that she should sell her bungalow – and her beloved garden – and move into a 'sheltered' flat where there was a warden on call and some meals could be provided. She probably left her removal too late and it seemed to provoke a rapid deterioration. She began falling and we arranged for her to have a Zimmer frame and a pendant alarm. After a particularly heavy fall in her kitchen, I was asked to go and see her. She had dramatic bruising on her bottom and, from the midline tenderness, I thought she had bruised or even fractured her vestigial tail bones. I was able to reassure her but thought I should review her medication before giving her strong analgesics. Molly pointed to a kitchen cupboard and inside were boxes of pills and a bottle of laxative. They were all pristine – unopened.

'But where, Molly, are the pills you're using at the moment?'

'I don't use the proper tray' she said 'I can't get it in my pocket.'

'So, what do you use?'

Molly reached into her skirt and brought out a little silver make-up compact. It was a familiar object used by many older women but not usually for this purpose. Inside, normally, is a small pad, some compressed face powder and, up in the lid, a small mirror. In this instance, there was no face pad and the mirror was cracked. But the outstanding discovery was that the tablets inside were all coated in the same nondescript beige colour – that of the sandpit of loose powder residue.

'I can see why you keep them here, Molly, but how can you tell one from the other when they're all coated with powder?'

Molly just frowned. Silence. It was pure luck that I had stumbled on her medication randomiser. Small wonder she was falling.

Sadly, even when taking medication correctly, Molly continued downhill. It was miserable to see her struggling with the simplest daily routines and we could all see that she was heading for a nursing home placement. But nature took a hand. She fell again – this time in the middle of the night. She lay on the floor in agony until her 'breakfast' carer went in. I was called before starting surgery. She had obviously broken her left hip and I was reassured to know that an ambulance was on its way. Molly wasn't wearing her pendant alarm and I wondered why she had taken it off and, more importantly, why she hadn't used it in the small hours.

'Oh, she said, I never wear it in bed in case I roll over and damage it.'

~

The Ingenious Roy Goodmen

All GPs are well aware that 20% of their patients create 80% of their workload. On the other hand, there will be a sizeable number registered with them who are never seen and cause no work at all. Roy Goodmen was one of them. On taking a phone call about him, I challenged the caller that he was not actually on my list and asked her to wait on the line. I sent for the medical record envelope. It was old, cloth-backed, wafer-thin and empty. But Roy Goodmen *was* actually registered with me. I let the conversation resume. The caller introduced herself – the daughter of John and Vicky Brown who farmed in one of our outlying hamlets. I knew them and I also knew that Mrs. Brown had recently had a stroke – as her daughter was now reminding me. She explained that her mother had, for many years, looked after Roy following the deaths of his parents. He had lived on in one of the cottages at the farm – indeed, the one where he had been born. He had always been a bit 'slow' but well enough, physically, to work on the farm all his life. 'Mother' had shopped for him, pressed him to keep himself and the cottage clean, and looked after his paperwork; he was unable to read and write. Now that 'mother' was in no state to carry such responsibilities there were worries about Roy's welfare.

Frankly, I was a little irritated. I protested that the problem was not, on the face of it, a medical one: that the appropriate agency was social services. The conversation became a little hostile and when a story of weight loss and a 'nasty' cough emerged I even wondered if they were symptoms invented to force me to accept some responsibility. In the end I agreed to visit Roy during the next few days and accepted a rather curt 'thank you, doctor.'

The terrace of Victorian cottages formed one side of the farmyard. Roy's stood out from the others for all the wrong reasons. Someone had recently scythed down the nettles and brambles in the small front garden. The beheaded stems had been left to rot and were now a tangled brown mesh. There was no response when I knocked at the front door. As I waited, a neighbour drew up in a car and shouted: 'try the back doctor, it won't be locked.' The path along the rear of the terrace was bounded, on one side, by a low breeze block wall. On the far side of it was a higgledy-piggledy morass of rusting machinery, old milk churns, compressed stacks of black polythene and tangles of baling twine in lurid colours. It was all semi-submerged in a rank slurry. Many farmers are too fond of fly-tipping in the remote corners of their own yards.

I pushed on Roy's back door and it opened. There was an immediate rip tide of stale cigarette smoke, the only response to calling Roy's name. The man in question was sitting over a pathetic wood fire in a cold and very dusty front room. I didn't hear him cough but it would not have been a surprise in the thick atmosphere. There were ashtrays filled beyond capacity everywhere and dozens of empty cigarette packets thrown onto a soiled old sofa. After a one-sided conversation, Roy let me examine him superficially. He was very 'unwashed', his hair was long, matted and greasy and he hadn't shaved, I assessed, for over a week. He did have some signs of recent weight loss but nothing to suggest an urgent medical problem. He refused to lower his trousers and it prompted me to ask about his toilet – was it upstairs or down? He pointed to a door off the kitchen. Behind it was a standard lavatory (for 1950 or so). The pan was bone dry and empty. I didn't dare pull the chain. Emboldened by the need to make a fuller assessment of Roy's circumstances, I took to the staircase and went upstairs.

Two bedrooms. In the front was an ancient brass bed with a mound of bedclothes roughly layered. The pillows were a variegated grey as was a trail of soiled underclothes thrown onto an ottoman at the foot of the bed. There was a huge cobweb across the window.

I stood in the doorway of the rear bedroom and gaped. No furniture. On the bare floor stood at least fifty Pringles tubes in a rough circle of varying density. They were unlidded but not empty. The crisps had been replaced by a yellow fluid. It was urine, some of it stale enough to have a green film over it. The smell was characteristic but not particularly strong. Here, obviously, was Roy's 'toilet' when he rose to pee in the night. For a man who was illiterate and 'slow' and who was a public health menace, he certainly didn't lack ingenuity. Back downstairs I challenged Roy.

'You don't seem to have a proper toilet, Roy. What do you do with your poo?'

'I go over to the farm or throw it over the wall.'

Enough. It was my turn to pass the parcel. When I spoke to someone at Social Services – a stranger to me – there was a rather unseemly professional boundary 'ding-dong.' 'They' were of the opinion that Roy needed to be admitted to hospital, that his problems were medical. I persisted and, in the end, it was agreed that someone from their department should, at least, go out and make a full assessment of need. I was later informed, via a peremptory call to our receptionists, that Roy had been admitted to a residential home in the neighbouring town.

I later heard, from our attached social worker, whom we all knew and trusted, that Roy had died; a victim of the nasty 'flu we had that winter. There was irony, I thought, in the fact that he had not survived being clean, warm, and well-fed for very long. This often seems to happen. And there was, surely, further irony that he had succumbed to influenza, an Italian term introduced into British medicine in the eighteenth century by the Queen's physician and President of the Royal Society, Sir John Pringle.

~

Trenton Jameson M.D.

When a retired doctor joins your list of patients it provokes mixed feelings. It could be a boost to the ego that you've been chosen to look after a comrade. On the other hand, there's the old adage that doctors make the worst patients. And when a husband and wife are both doctors there could be double trouble. But after signing up the Doctors Jameson neither of them came into surgery and didn't appear when invited to have 'elderly MOTs'.

Then, one fine day in mid-summer, I was bidden. The wife – Marjorie – had asked to speak to me on the phone. She said she was very worried about Trenton, her husband, and thought it very unlikely that she could persuade him to drive to the surgery since he denied any health problems. She seemed very tense during our brief conversation, and I wondered if she was anxious not to be overheard. In fact, she rang off abruptly and before giving any more information.

When, next morning, I drew up outside the Jamesons' bungalow, I replied to a call on the mobile that had come in while I was driving. Mid-conversation I realised that an elderly woman was peering through the car window. She suddenly realised that I could only get out if she backed off. She seemed very twitchy, constantly looking over her shoulder. She was thankful that I had arrived when I did – her husband was in the garden - and it gave her chance to speak to me alone. It was not going to be easy, she said. Her husband had always had a 'thing' about GPs – that they were the 'odd-job men' of medicine, that they were 'second-rate', and that what they 'got up to' had no intellectual basis. She was sorry that he was so prejudiced – they had both been hospital consultants and had always been able to call on colleagues at the hospital when they or their children ever had health issues and neither of them had, really, any knowledge of general practice.

'So, what was your husband's speciality?'

'He was a consultant anaesthetist.'

'And what would you say is his main problem at the moment?'

'He keeps falling asleep.'

Trenton Jameson was in a lounger at the top of the garden. He was fast asleep, the Times newspaper across his chest. Marjorie woke him and introduced me. Trenton looked around and then fixed a stare at me.

'And what do *you* want?' were his first, and far from pleasant, words.

There followed a difficult conversation. Obvious questions from me and monosyllabic answers from him. I learned nothing that was useful except for the daily drowsiness (denied), and a recent poor appetite (another prompt from Marjorie). I noted scratch marks on his arms, the skin seeming very dry. His colour was also pallid. Clearly the consultation was not going to be valuable and in what was now very bright sunlight both of us were squinting and beginning to sweat. I backed away, saying that I would call and see him again. I ignored the sarcasm of 'well, do if you want to.'

Marjorie came with me to the car. I told her that I thought Trenton looked pale, possibly anaemic and that, at the very least, we could get one of the district nurses to take some blood, assuming patient cooperation. We could use the results as an excuse to revisit. And having some laboratory data - something that her husband might accept as more like 'proper' medicine - might induce him to be more cooperative. She seemed pleased with the tactic and then had to jump backwards once more – this time to let me into my car.

Sometime the gently ambling pace of chronic medicine is overtaken by a hell-ride of something sudden and acute. Four days later, at nine o'clock on a Saturday evening I was on call. Marjorie Jameson was on the phone. Her husband was extremely distressed – I could hear moaning – he hadn't passed water for over 24 hours and was finally demanding help. I explained that it was no longer considered best practice for GPs to 'just pop in a catheter' in these circumstances but she said she was certain that Trenton wouldn't get in an ambulance. I thought he was probably ready to do exactly that from the noises off but I said I would call round – I did have a suitable catheter, as it happened, and I might be able to offer him immediate relief.

Trenton was grey with pain, restless and desperate. I felt very sorry for him. There was a distinct midline abdominal swelling below the umbilicus – a grossly over-filled bladder. I then realised that I had no anaesthetic gel in my bag, just an unopened tube of KY jelly. Trenton barked – 'just get on with it, never mind the jungle juice.'

It was with huge relief – not least to me – that the catheter passed easily and a torrent of urine flowed into the bucket conjured up by Marjorie. Five minutes later we were all drinking tea and Trenton agreed to be referred, urgently, to the urology team at the local hospital. In fact, he walked me to the front door, thanked my profoundly, patted me on the back, and said that my wife and I – 'you are married, aren't you?' – should soon come round for a drink. I had obviously passed some sort of test, a rite of passage.

Three days after our late evening drama, Marjorie rang to tell me that Trenton had indeed been found to be anaemic on admission to hospital – anaemia secondary to mild renal failure. It was no surprise, then, that he'd been drowsy every day and not eating. She sounded relieved that circumstances had, at last, forced her husband into a situation where the issues might be resolved. Marjorie's next call to me was not so optimistic – Trenton had had a stroke on the ward. He had been treated with the 'clot-buster' drugs and was recovering but she was concerned about the appearance of new bigotries. Now he was demanding that the ward team bring in his 'excellent' GP who would look after him much better than they were currently managing. He couldn't seem to abide the fact that those dealing with him were an ever-changing stream of people he never saw twice, however kind they were. It was not hospital medicine as he remembered it. How the worm had turned.

The pace of change didn't ease up and Trenton went rapidly downhill. He developed uncontrollable diarrhoea that proved to be an infection with Clostridium difficile. His body chemistry spiralled out of control and in 36 hours he was dead. When I called to console Marjorie, she pointed out, as a retired microbiologist, some sick symmetry. A man who had been so difficult to cultivate was killed by a germ which is also difficult to cultivate, and hence its name.

~

Dorrie

Older couples who have been married many decades have learnt, mostly, to share their lives' contents. And they often share their illnesses. Harry Buxton was nearly 90 and Enid, his wife, 85. Together since the year of the General Strike, they had never had children but had acquired a heavy responsibility.

Enid was one of twins – undiagnosed until their mother went into labour. Her sister, Doris, always known as 'Dorrie' within the family, was the second-born. Her delivery was delayed and she had presented as a breech – a bottom-first birth. The midwife had done her best to prevent the baby's head bursting into the world like a cork from a bottle but was not wholly successful. The brain damage was significant.

Dorrie developed way in arrears of normal milestones, she never mastered reading and writing, her speech was permanently slurred, she drooled, and she hobbled on spastic legs. She might have progressed further but was cruelly teased at school as 'dim Doris' and she became school phobic. She was sheltered and, perhaps, pampered by her ever-patient parents who always tried, nonetheless, to give at least some of their attention to Enid. No other children came along and by their teens, the two girls were so different that people couldn't believe that they were twins. Dorrie's parents devoted themselves to her care well into her adult years but there was an inevitable crisis as they aged. Eventually, after both parents had died, Dorrie was taken in by Harry and Enid.

When I first met them, all three were very old. It was a curious threesome in which Dorrie had always been a passenger. She contributed nothing to the running of the home and showed no interest in learning to cook or clean. She would push the trolley around the supermarket for Enid but never decide on its contents. She would, however, always make sure that Enid took her to the cigarette counter – she was a life-long chain smoker. She would spend her days sitting and smoking in the yellowing conservatory at the back of the house. But she also smoked in the house itself and in bed. Harry and Enid were passive smokers – heavy passive smokers.

My knowledge of Harry, Enid and Dorrie had been absorbed piecemeal. Winter never seemed to pass without a visit to their Edwardian semi. Sometimes the 'bronchitis' patient was Harry, sometimes Enid, but never Dorrie. My advice that she should stop smoking for all their sakes fell on deaf ears – not literally so because I think Dorrie's hearing was the one

131

faculty that worked well. Then, last winter Harry developed another 'bad chest.' I found him abed. He was hot, cyanosed and breathing heavily. He had a significant pneumonia, and I was worried. He insisted on staying at home and to make life easier for her I helped Enid set up a single bed downstairs, promising a commode from our store. Dorrie was fumigating the conservatory as usual.

48 hours later Harry had improved but Enid now also had a chest infection and had taken to the downstairs bed, evicting Harry to a recliner by the fire. Neither of them were now fit enough to look after each other or cater for Dorrie. We had a crisis on our hands. I was using the phone in the hall to try to speak to a social worker when Dorrie tapped me on the shoulder. She was mouthing something, but I couldn't understand. We went into the 'sick room' so that Enid could translate. Apparently Dorrie was saying that she would look after Harry and Enid. She would cook the meals, keep the house clean, 'see to' the boiler and take on the nursing chores. Harry and Enid were looking at each other and shaking their heads in unison. Knowing, however, that any official help would take at least a day or so to set up I could do no more that suggest that we at least give Dorrie a chance. I could feel the anxiety spinning round the room as Harry and Enid looked blankly at each other. 'Well, I suppose so' was the response from Enid but I felt that neither 'patient' had the strength to object, in any case.

Both Harry and Enid recovered and Dorrie was a revelation. She coped perfectly well with all the demands suddenly imposed on her. She had provided her 'charges' with hot drinks and simple meals, had found them clean clothes, given Enid a bed-bath, hoovered through the house, kept the boiler charged with solid fuel, put the dustbin out on the right day and, Harry thought, smoked far less.

~

4
MORE BRIEF ENCOUNTERS

Black and blue

Some patients will refuse the offer of a seat when they arrive in the consulting room. It usually means that they have back trouble or something wrong 'where the sun don't shine.' But, on occasion, it's wrong to jump to conclusions. Ryan was the eldest son of Jim Mansfield, a gentry farmer with acres running to four figures. At 28, Ryan was a tall, muscular figure. He worked on the farm that would, one day, be his and rarely came to the surgery.

'I need to show you something and ask your advice, doc.'

He proceeded to drop his trousers and lift his shirt. I was taken aback for a moment. He had several large and very intense bruises – on the backs of his legs, his thighs and there was one extending up under his underpants on his left buttock.

'How on earth did this happen, Ryan?'

'We were taking some heifers down the lane to our 30-acre yesterday. One of them bolted and panicked the others. I wasn't quick enough and was pushed over and trampled. I could have been killed.'

'Well, although these are spectacular bruises and must be very sore, I think you may be OK.'

'But could you have a look at the one on my spine?'

Further up under the check linen shirt that farmers always wear, I found a further injury where, over the spinous processes of his backbone, the skin had been broken and snow-ploughed up into a heap.

'Ah, right. Yes, with broken skin we'd better protect you against infection and also give you a tetanus booster. I'll ring sister and if you'll go up and wait in her side-room she'll put a dressing on and give you the jab. That top bruise is, by the way, near where your left kidney lives and I'll ask her to test your urine for blood. You're not allergic to penicillin, are you? Come back and see me at the end of the week.'

The following afternoon our practice nurse tapped on the door immediately after a patient left.

'Hi, you haven't sent for the next one yet, have you?'

'No.'

'Good. I thought I should tell you about someone I've just seen – Stella Roberts. You know who I mean?'

'Yes.'

'She came to ask my advice. She has a very large, swollen bruise on her inner right thigh. It shows all the colours of the rainbow and must be very sore. She slipped when getting over a gate at the Mansfields, she said. You probably don't know, but she's engaged to Ryan.'

'No, I didn't know that, should I?'

'Well, no, not really, but it is relevant. I didn't consciously react to the gate story but somehow Stella sensed that I didn't believe her. Just on leaving she told me the truth.'

'Oh, good. I like the truth.'

'She and Ryan, for want of privacy, have been riding out on their horses and meeting at the very top of Blisset Down to have sex. On Sunday it was such a nice warm afternoon they decided to strip right off and have a completely naked session.'

'Au naturel, eh?'

'No, naked. Towards the end they got rather over-excited and noisy and one of the horses slipped his halter and jumped on them, trying to join in. The injuries we've been dealing with are from horse kicks. I think they were lucky not to be more seriously hurt.'

'I'll say. And I thought that coitus interruptus was old hat.'

'Yes, I suppose that's what it was really. Anyway, don't challenge Ryan's version of the story when he comes back in. I want Stella to go on trusting me – it'll be very necessary soon. We're probably in for dealing with a different kind of bump – they've never used any other form of contraception. I've given the obvious advice but, of course, the horse has already bolted. Ba – boom.'

~

Grandstand

There was a substantial brass ball within a surrounding brass assembly but no visible doorbell. The ball could be gripped and, by pulling it, I presumed that an ancient linkage rang a bell somewhere in the house. I heard nothing and nothing happened. The large Regency villa was set in what looked like several acres of parkland and was approached down a long, winding drive onto gravel. I'd been asked to call and see a two-year old who was very hot, fractious and vomiting. After a minute or two and after hauling on the brass pull again, twice, I tried the door. This time the lever – more polished brass – moved sideways and I was into a tiled lobby. I knocked on the inner door but although I could hear noises somewhere within the house, no-one came. The inner door was also unlocked. From the immense hall I could hear activity more clearly. A male voice was saying, shouting almost, 'yes, yes, come on, keep going, yes, yes yes.' I wondered what orgiastic activity I had come upon and whether I should, discretely, back out onto the gravel. But I could also hear something familiar – broadcast commentary that I recognised to be of a horse race. BBC Grandstand perhaps. A few paces forward and I was looking into a panelled sitting room. Sure enough, there was a large colour television and, in front of it, a middle-aged man in jodhpurs sitting astride the rounded arm of a very large sofa. He had a riding crop in one hand and was getting excited again 'yes, go on, yes, yes, ooh no.' Then he saw me.

'Sorry, old man, but it's the 3.30 at Doncaster. Did you put anything on any of the runners? Me, I've just lost 20 quid.'

'No, I'm afraid I didn't. I'm the doctor – I've come to see uh, Robin isn't it?'

'Oh, yes, my son. He'll be upstairs in the nursery with his mother or maybe with his nanny. Anyway, go on up, old man – end door along the balcony to the right.'

Robin was being cuddled by a woman I took to be his mother. The history of his illness was reiterated, and I explained that I would need to examine him. The mother said she was 'really no good at this sort of thing' and wouldn't be able to hold him. She placed the child down in a cot and left, saying that she was going to fetch their nanny. Robin and I looked at each other: he in obvious pain and me discomfited by the odd circumstances. Nanny appeared to be very young and oriental. However, she knew exactly what to do and was a considerable help, especially in bracing the little boy while I examined his throat and ears. Robin, I was quite convinced, had an otitis media, a middle-ear infection. I gave the customary advice, prescribed some Calpol and a Penicillin and made to leave. Mother stood at the doorway.

'We're back in London tomorrow evening, doctor. Shall we take Robin to see an ear specialist next week? We know a very good one, married to my cousin.'

I explained that if Robin improved, as I would fully expect him to do in a couple of days, there was no need for a specialist intervention.

'But I think I'd be happier to know that there'd not been any permanent damage doctor, and I'm sure my husband would agree.'

'Well, I'm not banning you from seeing an ENT colleague but simply advising that it's not normally considered necessary.'

'OK, doctor, bless you for coming out. Now does the medicine contain any products derived from animals? We're all strict vegetarians. Well, most of the time, in the case of my husband.'

'I'm pretty sure not, but it is the best antibiotic in this situation and ought to be started without any delay.'

'And what about Penicillin allergy, doctor?'

'Well, you told me that Robin had no history of allergies.'

'Yes, but suppose it starts with this medicine?'

'Oh, I'm pretty sure it won't but if it does we'll have to try an alternative. I think the airlines have the right phrase – if, in the unlikely event.'

All this time nanny had been rocking the little boy and humming him a tune. He'd gone to sleep, and I made to leave.

Coming down the cantilevered staircase I began to hear more vocal encouragement. The boy's father was still astride the sofa arm and whipping it vigorously. He was engrossed in what I took to be the next race at Doncaster.

'Oh, sorry doc. Is the lad OK – nothing serious?'

I shook my head and kept moving. I didn't want to be drawn into a further inquisition. I needn't have worried. Robin was not the focus here.

'Hey, doc, do you want a red-hot tip for the 4.30? I've put a bullseye on it.'

~

Uncle Bert

Just listening to patients knowing that you're not going to have to make a professional response can be pure pleasure. This Utopia is rare but does sometimes happen while one performs minor surgery under local anaesthetic. Once the offending tissues are fully numbed the patient, buoyed up by relief that the procedure isn't torture after all, will often relax enough to embark on a series of jokes or a story. Many of them are not repeatable, some are difficult to believe, some are just seedy gossip, but some of them are valuable currency.

Bill Woods had been booked in for a minor surgery session for about a month. He had a nuisance-value sebaceous cyst – a wen – on the top of his head. It would eventually have grown big enough to peep above his hair, but he didn't have any. Well, not much. His grandchildren had been teasing him that his brains were trying to get out and, in any case, his youngest daughter's marriage was imminent, the photographer already booked. Bill lay down comfortably on a pillow under his arms and chest and positioned his head to best surgical advantage. There was the usual tense silence as I infiltrated some lignocaine and a palpable sigh when he heard me drop the syringe back in the kidney dish.

'Did you ever meet my uncle, doc? Uncle Bert.'

'No, I don't think so.'

'Well, he's gone on now. He was stationmaster at Otter Halt. You know, the private station belonging to Lord Wickstead's family. Trains only stop there if one of the family or an important visitor are travelling. It was a deal done, I think, in the 1850s. His Lordship's great grandfather would only allow our branch line to cross his land if he could have a private station. You must know Otter Halt?'

'Yes, of course. I've walked past the old buildings. I presume it was axed by Beeching?

'Yes, and what a mistake that was. Anyway, Uncle Bert was stationmaster from somewhen near 1930 until the line was taken up in 1965. My cousins grew up there – they were always known as 'the railway children' long before the TV series. Uncle Bert was very upset at the end but actually due to retire anyway. He'd always taken great pride in keeping the station immaculate. Someone once told me they'd seen him at the top of a ladder polishing the signals. I think that's a porker. But he did always have flower beds on the platform and hanging baskets at the waiting room in summer. And he always kept the paintwork gleaming and free of smuts. He was something of a hero with his Lordship, but he could also be very naughty. He and the signalman got up to pranks during the war. Have you heard the story of the unscheduled stop, doc?'

'No, I haven't. By the way, Bill, are you still comfortable. I've freed the cyst from your skin and I'm just trying to get underneath it to be able to lift it out whole. There's a bit of bleeding – let me know if any runs down into your eyes or your mouth.'

'OK, doc. Anyway, the branch line was very busy during the war and very popular with the RAF oiks from the base at Broad Langley. Each new batch of recruits coming to the radio school, when they had a few hours leave, usually on a Saturday evening, found they could get a bus into town here. They could then get the train to Eastbury, to the pubs, the cinema, the dances and, of course, the 'skirt.' The last train back here on a Saturday night would always be packed and many of the passengers worse for wear. Otter Halt was not a public stop of course and trains would usually steam straight through. But late at night, especially if it was raining, with all station signs removed, and in the blackout, one stop looked like any other to strangers.

Uncle Bert and the signalman on duty, would prime the driver and the guard of the last train back up from Eastbury to make an unscheduled stop at Otter. They would then walk rapidly down the platform shouting 'terminus, all change; terminus, all change' and then run and lock themselves in the signal box. The passengers would pile out onto the platform and begin to look around them. They would then watch, with confusion, the doors all being closed by the guard and the train pull away, the guard jumping on at the last second. Old hands would stay on the train of course. They weren't going to be caught twice. But they didn't give the game away – they enjoyed it as much as Uncle Bert. There would be no bus waiting, of course, and the hapless passengers now had a five-mile walk, most of it uphill, to the RAF base. When they eventually arrived there they were usually in awful trouble for overstaying their leave permits. Uncle Bert said that hiding in the signal box was an education. They learnt a whole new dictionary of unrepeatable words.'

'So, all those poor young men were stitched up, good and proper?'

'Yes, they were. Actually, it seems a bit cruel now. But I suppose people were desperate for amusement during the war.'

'Yes, I suppose that's true. Anyway, you're the one that's stitched up today. I've finished. Ask at the desk on your way out for an appointment with sister in a week's time. She'll take out the stitches for you.'

~

HWB

The message came in from the warden of the sheltered flats. Doris was wetting the bed and would the doctor visit? Angus, our handsome young trainee – who was, for some inexplicable reason, very popular with the receptionists – had been 'sitting in' for over a month. Here was something 'into which he could get his teeth'. A simplistic clinical approach to this problem was never going to solve all the issues. Antibiotics for a urinary infection might well be needed, according to the textbook, but were far from holistic medicine. Here was a golden opportunity for a novice to learn how to use 'the team' – to discover the invaluable skills of the district nurses, the health visitor, the social worker and perhaps the geriatrician. And, anyway, it was a winter Monday morning and all the partners had visits enough that a proper lunch break was a remote possibility for any of them without tangling with wet sheets.

Angus was surprised to find Doris on good form. She was up and about and fully dressed. She denied any symptoms and asked him 'not to let on' but she thought that the warden was 'making a fuss'. No, she wasn't off her food. She had no nausea, shivering or backache and was only up at night once as usual. Angus noted that her answers were prompt and appropriate and found nothing wrong on an examination. Doris seemed baffled, however, by the instructions for performing a mid-stream urine specimen and was glad to know that a nurse could call in and organise it. She seemed to understand why she needed to take an antibiotic for her 'bladder infection' once the sample had been sent away and, yes, her son would be able to fetch the prescription from the chemist. Angus forgot to make up some pretext for checking the rest of the flat for signs of confusion or neglect but was able to see into the bedroom where there was some bedding drying over a chair.

The 'team' moved in and Angus called back a week later armed with the urine report. The nurses had reported further wet beds but the test result was unhelpful – a mixed growth of bacteria that normally live, harmlessly, on the skin. Angus had been prompted to organise a joint visit with one of the nurses and explore further – did Doris have a uterine prolapse affecting bladder drainage? There was only one way to find out – difficult on a low, damp, spongy bed but he and the nurse managed it. They agreed - Doris's 'undercarriage' seemed entirely intact and remained dry, even on coughing.

A week later the nursing team thought that Doris's bedding was far less damp and perhaps things were improving. At the same time, they realised that they might be 'clutching at straws'. Another week passed. The warden left a familiar message – 'Doris's bed is very wet again and would the doctor call.' Angus was away at 'playschool' – at one of the regional formal training sessions for wannabe GPs. The senior partner - me, the 'trainer' who 'knew' all about the case anyway, was the obvious candidate to visit. Doris remembered me and we had quite a chat reminiscing about her late husband, a panel beater who had, twice, taken untoward creases out of my car and expertly resprayed it. The chatter was not entirely idle - it struck me that Doris was 'as bright as a button'. I suggested the bedroom so that I could examine her. But something wasn't right. It took a few minutes of more idle banter before I suddenly realised – there was no smell of urine despite the sheets drying over a chair, exactly as Angus had described them. And there, on the draining board of the kitchenette was a hot-water bottle. It appeared to be half full. I picked it up. A fine jet of cold water hit me in the face, and I had to remove my spectacles to dry them. Here was the problem and the true diagnosis.

Doris's son was invoked to make another trip to the Chemist – to buy mum a new 'hottie'.

I think I'll just pop in and see . . . .

'Ancilla' is Latin for handmaiden. Hence the term 'ancillary'. Quite a few fellow practitioners in medicine are customarily classified as 'ancillary' in what is, really, a false dichotomy with the word 'essential'. There are, of course, the hot pebble merchants and the foot ticklers who prey on the gullible but properly trained and fully qualified 'therapists' can provide great service. Chiropractors are a good example. They use their upper body strength to treat muscular and joint problems in patients who, for the bulk of their workload, are suffering backache. They are virtually always independent of the NHS and charge patients directly. Working from their own premises they never visit patients at home and though they may well acquire a loyal clientele they carry no long-term responsibility for their patients.

My patient, Edgar Russell, was a smallholder at a village nearly ten miles out of town, one of the satellite markers of our practice boundary. He had a few sheep, some geese, some chickens and a couple of paddocks that he rented out to horse-owners. He also had a huge vegetable and fruit garden. Kath, his wife, had half a dozen hives of bees in a nearby copse. They sold their popular produce at various farmers' markets and from the cottage. Edgar had frequent back problems that were, I guess, occupational. Having such unremitting commitments in the way he earned a living he had taken to going to a chiropractor in Swindon the moment his back played up. A very busy winter Tuesday in the practice was one such occasion. Edgar had bent down to pick up a bucket of feed for his geese and his back had 'gone'. He couldn't straighten up and it took him some time to get back to the cottage, crabbing sideways along various fences for support. Kath rang 'their back clinic' and got her husband to the car in time for a two o'clock appointment.

Unfortunately, as I was about to discover, the manipulations of his back were unsuccessful on this occasion. Edgar could barely get off the couch and there were several crises even getting back to their car. All this was related to me by Kath on the phone after they had struggled home. I was just embarking on a fully booked surgery of 18 patients. Kath demanded an immediate house call: 'Edgar can't go on like this.' I gave what I thought was appropriate advice and said I would happily see Edgar as an extra in surgery or call in after seeing all my waiting patients. This wasn't good enough. I was put in the dock as negligent because the chiropractor had told them, explicitly, that on getting home they should 'get the GP out immediately'.

Edgar had travelled to and from Swindon, albeit uncomfortably, but there was 'no way', apparently, that he could get to the surgery. Rightly or wrongly, I persisted. I repeated the advice on posture, on taking some simple painkillers, and that I would be along the moment my surgery was finished. The phone was put down abruptly but I could easily imagine the invective.

Shortly after seven that evening, 'The Archers' were under way on the car radio, I was being hissed at by geese somewhere out there in the darkness as I knocked on the low door of the Russell cottage. I was greeted warmly and thanked profusely, the altercation of a few hours earlier seemingly forgotten. Edgar was, in fact, better. He was sitting up in a chair and Kath was hurriedly trying to hide the evidence of a hearty supper that they had just eaten in front of the television and a roaring fire. I examined Edgar very carefully. This was not the occasion to miss something catastrophic. But there was no reason to be guarded about the prognosis – I was quite sure that Edgar's muscle strain would be better in a few days. As I wrote a prescription for some stronger analgesics, Kath scuttled off. She reappeared with a jar of honey – 'for your children, doctor'. I thanked her and returned to the car in a good mood. More hissing.

As I drove to the main road it occurred to me that I would be back up to the village in the morning to revisit an old friend, Phyllis Slee. I was so euphoric that I decided to visit her now and save some time tomorrow. Phyllis lived in one of the post-war council houses past the church. She was the lone survivor in the property after she and her late husband had brought up five children. I'd been treating her for trigeminal neuralgia, a very nasty facial pain that's not so rare in the elderly. The medication needs careful and regular titration to get full effect without the dangers of drowsiness. There was no response to my knocking at the front door. The downstairs curtains were open and there were lights on. Side-stepping across the frosted garden to the front window I could see Phyllis in her chair. She seemed to be asleep and tapping the glass had no effect. I went to the back and found my way through the kitchen. I felt a strange urge to cough. As I entered the front room I could barely breath. My throat was immediately dry and hot. Phyllis was unresponsive, her chin on her chest. She was breathing but looked strangely pink. I suddenly realised we were both breathing in carbon monoxide. I threw open the windows, the front and back doors. My eyes moved to the Rayburn stove. It was hot but giving off visible smoke at the base of the flue. I opened it – the coke was smouldering anoxically and then burst into healthy flames. After a few minutes Phyllis revived and although surprised to see me and a little more confused than usual, she seemed fine otherwise. I rang her eldest son and arranged for him to fetch his mother to his house for a day or two until the boiler had been serviced and the flue thoroughly swept.

I later thought to myself, in a very lateral way, that this was probably the only time in medical history that a chiropractor had saved someone from a fatal carbon monoxide poisoning.

~

Hump

'Sorry to bother you but the optician said I should bring you this letter. She said I was going blind, but it was nothing to feel guilty about.'

I'd met 'Hump' professionally before but only knew his nickname from his sister, our cleaning lady. 'Hump' because he was reckoned to be 'not quite straight' – the sort of character who, on finding a lost purse, would hand it in to the police station without question, any money included, but having lifted the green shield stamps.

The brief note related that he was developing cataracts and a quick glance through the ophthalmoscope confirmed it. While I was thinking about how best to organise a urine test for diabetes Hump launched into his worries. He was very anxious about having to 'hand in' his driving licence. He had been a driver since his teens, had never taken a test – being that old – and had never had an accident. Driving was one of his 'pleasures in life' but also essential where he and his wife lived. In fact, he continued, he had been a professional driver in latter years. He had been the chauffeur for Lady Duckett at Palmerston House.

'Was she not been pretty much a recluse' I asked? The job sounded like a sinecure.

'Well', he admitted, 'I was also her odd job man, dog walker and errand boy. And there were always jobs in the gardens. But she did get out and needed the Rolls once a week. Being very old-fashioned she insisted on paying all her staff weekly in cash and always paid a visit to the bank every Thursday morning.'

It was obvious that Hump was coming to some end point in the story, so I let him carry on.

'It was only after some years,' he giggled, 'that I twigged. Her ladyship always left the house through the front door, came down the steps, and got into the back seat of the car on the nearside. Outside the bank – right outside mind – she would get out the same side, go straight into the building and return the same way. Back at home she always headed straight indoors, anxious to lock up the cash.'

'It suddenly occurred to me', he said, 'that as long as I always drove up to the house clockwise, parked exactly opposite the door and likewise at the bank, I could save myself some work. When cleaning the "roller" – a very big car after all – I really only needed to wash and polish the roof, the bonnet, and the left side. OK, I'd do the whole car from time to time but only the tops and near side needed the weekly attention she insisted on'.

The story was entertaining, and I congratulated him on his cunning. But to return to the medical matter in hand, I told him that he was going to need cataract surgery. I had, however, seen the opportunity for something irresistible – for a harmless wind-up. I explained that having a cataract extraction was by way of having the front compartment of the eye flushed clear and a new lens put in. There was, though, a stringent NHS ruling that only one eye could be done – so which side did he want cleaned? Unfortunately, Hump saw my poorly suppressed smile. It then took some time to convince him of the real circumstance - that he certainly couldn't have both eyes done at the same time.

~

Gan

Bob Mullins was nearly 60, ex-RAF. Like a lot of men in our practice, 'nights on the town' from the local RAF base during their Service years had introduced them to girls from the community. The resulting 'entanglements' led to them settling in the neighbourhood.

Bob had a question: 'but first I'd better explain.'

'You'll have heard about Gan, doc – in the Indian Ocean. In my time it was one of our bases, built during the war by the boys in dark blue. After the war we took over the airfield. The RAF used it as a refuelling stopover on the way to Singapore and Honkers. At first sight it looked to be a great posting – a year in the Maldives – who wouldn't jump at it. But it was less popular than you'd expect. Older 'wise birds' used all manner of dodges to avoid it.'

'You see, it was men only – there were no women on the island; and strictly none allowed. After all the island is only an overgrown coral atoll and billets were pretty primitive. With only one brief leave granted about half-way through the year's posting, the top brass was very uptight about our trouser department. For the footloose there was absolutely no chance of any horizontal exercise, if you'll pardon the expression. I was sent there a year after I married Marjorie. We were not best pleased about it, especially with our first child on the way, but that's Service life.'

'We all knew, of course. It was in the tea. You could taste it. And we used to think it was even in the beer. But the 'high ups' were desperate and devious. I suppose they were terrified that discipline would break down in what was more a bloody monastery than an airbase. Sorry. But it didn't work, you know. Not a jot. I can vouch for that or, rather, it didn't work --- until now.'

'My question is this: is there an antidote?'

I just wasn't sure if Bob was joking or whether he genuinely wanted to broach the subject of recent erectile failure. I took him on head-first. I explained that this predicament was very common in his age group and that it had nothing to do with Bromide – even if it once happened to be in his tea. He would have to let me do some tests – for raised blood sugar for instance. And he would have to cut back on the beers and the gins at the golf club. There was an 'antidote', as he put it, - Viagra - but it could be dangerous for him – because of his heart condition (he'd had coronary artery stents inserted).

'Do you mean the straightening of the kinks in my fuel pipes?' he asked, in his groundcrew, garage-mechanic way.

The answer was yes but his highfalutin military analogies were not finished.

'So, doc, you're saying that I could stand to attention more if I drank less? That the hydraulics would work again if I took less booze on board?'

~

Daylight Robbery

We were only in the middle of a lunch-time practice meeting and already all the sandwiches had gone; it's easier to eat than take decisions. We were held up in a debate. Should we close the surgery for an hour at lunchtime as did the other practice in town? Those in favour were anxious to curtail our having to act as a 'de facto' casualty clearing station for the town, even for patients registered with our opposition. Those against were unhappy 'without being altruistic' – that breaking with a long tradition would inconvenience patients 'popping in' to deliver prescription requests during their own lunch breaks and also create yet another time stricture in the working day. Then the phone rang. It was passed to the duty doctor. With immaculate timing someone had just been brought into the building in a state of collapse.

A middle-aged woman had responded to screaming and shouts of 'help me' when walking home from shopping. The victim had been found partly entangled on a newly pruned shrub in a front garden. She was unable to talk and was sobbing violently. To half carry her, half push her, to our surgery – just round the corner - seemed the obvious answer to the dilemma. The 'good Samaritan' now needed to sit and compose herself and the victim – now patient – had flopped to the floor and was now over-breathing in a fetal position amongst scattered chairs in our waiting room.

The duty doctor didn't recognise his 'case' and neither did the two receptionists on duty. Asking the customary questions to establish identity only increased the sobbing and trying to get the patient up onto a chair only caused passive resistance. The muddy backside and gaping empty handbag were hardly useful clinical clues and a glass of water was pushed away. The woman who had brought in the patient was unable to help beyond describing, again, what she had happened upon and there was something of a stalemate while the patient continued to over-breathe. The situation was saved by the arrival of the afternoon shift of receptionists. Among them was Margaret. She immediately recognised the patient and was able to talk to her as a friend and things calmed down. The patient's name was June Remnant, we were told, and she and Margaret played bingo together every Friday. And now, out came the story, as she allowed Margaret to help her up and into a side-room.

Mrs. Remnant had also returned from town with some shopping. Nearing her house she'd noticed an old white van parked outside and people putting things into the back of it. Then she had realised that some of the items of furniture were hers. The front door of the house was open and two more youngsters were carrying out a settee. She had shouted at them and they hastily closed the van on the contents, ran forward to the driving compartment and sounded the horn. She was now on her path to the front door and several more 'yobbos' came running out of her house and pushed past her. Now she broke down again. It took some time before the rest of the story emerged - in fits and starts. Next out of the house came her own daughter. June hadn't seen her for some months after throwing her out of the house for smoking cannabis, bringing obvious drug addicts into the house and being abusive. Her daughter had been carrying a cigar box

– which June kept hidden for storing spare cash 'for rainy days'. Then came the awful shock of having to fight off the daughter who was now trying to steal her mother's handbag. It had turned into a screaming tug of war and when the handbag fell open the daughter had snatched all the contents and ran to the van, pushing her mother into the shrubbery. The vehicle had roared away in a cloud of diesel fumes.

The glass of water reappeared and so did Mrs. Remnant's medical records. Her own doctor was called down from the meeting but in effect the necessary treatment was given by Margaret once we had established that there were no serious physical injuries and the danger of syncope from hyperventilation had subsided. June's daughter, it appeared, had become a drug addict now living some miles away – 'but not far enough' - according to Margaret.

The meeting resumed - the topic now being the value of our receptionists and how we would prefer, in the end, that they were around at lunchtime.

~

BTM

'Morning, Doc.'

'As I'm sure you know, Janet and I have always been very keen on personal hygiene and all that, but we've been suffering, for some time, with an embarrassing problem – so embarrassing that Janet won't come and see you.'

I'd known the Smythes for some years. They had joined the practice – onto my list – just after myself and I'd seen Janet through her three pregnancies and the children through the usual spectrum of childhood complaints. Their home was always spotless, pressed top-quality towels always put out for me to dry my hands. In fact, the latest of our trainees, after visiting one of the children, had commented, with admiration, how immaculately clean the home was when we were having a de-brief over coffee.

'If you want my advice' the senior partner interrupted 'always have a list of patients who don't mind the odd cobweb.'

Anyway, James ('Janet won't let anyone call me Jim') Smythe continued his story.

'You see, both of us have had very itchy bottoms for many months. Janet changed the loo paper to something more cushioned but that didn't work. She thinks there are chemicals in all the bumf, actually. We then tried wet wipes – again no good and it was beginning to get to Janet. So, after Christmas, we decided to upgrade our ensuite bathroom, install brand new earthenware and include a bidet. Neither of us had ever used one before and it was an odd experience. But it did seem to work and we thought it money well-spent – at least for a while. Neither of us was itching so much and certainly not scratching ourselves raw. We were even able to sit still through the sermon on a Sunday morning. I'm sorry it's a long and boring saga and thank you for listening. I have, though, come to ask your advice. Perhaps you could recommend a good dermatologist. For the last fortnight things have been just as bad as ever and Janet is even tearful.'

The story was not an unusual one but most patients consulted earlier for this symptom. I'd never before known people first send for a plumber. James wasn't at all surprised – or, at least, he showed no reaction – when I invited him up onto the examination couch and into the left lateral position bereft of his trousers. With his underpants down and in a strong light I parted his buttocks. Certainly the skin adjacent to the anus was reddened and slightly swollen but I couldn't see what I was looking for.

'Yes,' he said 'he'd had a bowel movement about an hour before.'

He dismounted and, as he was dressing, I asked him if any of the children had complained of sore or itchy bottoms.

'Well, funny you should ask' he said 'because Oliver, our eldest, overheard Janet and I talking about the problem a couple of weeks ago and said that he, too, was itching down below, especially at night.'

I asked James to make an appointment for Oliver and bring him in as soon as convenient. He screwed up one side of his face as I launched into my working diagnosis and explanation. I suggested that the whole family likely had threadworms.

'Worms! No, you can't be serious. Janet will be devastated. She is always so careful with what we eat and with keeping the home spotless. No, you must be wrong. You know that we have BUPA for the whole family. We could see a skin specialist privately. Please don't be offended but Janet said that I wasn't just to come home with yet another cream or ointment to try.'

I held my ground.

'No, please believe me. I could be wrong but I don't think so. If you could just bring Oliver in there's every chance I could prove the diagnosis to you.'

OK, doctor but I think Janet will be very upset and what, exactly, do you propose to do to Oliver?'

'It will be an inspection just like yours today – purely external.'

James Smythe brought Oliver in three days later after picking him up from school. I explained, in very simple terms, to the boy, the purpose of our meeting. He happily got ready and his father and I peered at his bottom under the light. There they were – three or four little thread-like glistening white worms on the skin immediately adjacent to Oliver's anus. They were writhing, unaccustomed to the light.

We all sat down and I explained about the microscopic eggs of these little beasts and how easily they spread among schoolchildren and then among family members, even when every hygiene rule is followed to the letter. And that the eggs themselves, which the worms lay on the moist, warm perianal skin, usually at night, provoke intense itching. I then explained that the whole family would need simultaneous treatment with a vermicide, for it to be repeated in ten days, and that they should expect itching to stop only after about three weeks.

'I'm sorry, Doctor, so sorry, not to have trusted you and to have been such a pain in the ass.'

James then suddenly remembered that Oliver was in the room. He turned to him, making him promise, on oath, not to tell his mother what he'd just heard.

~

Number Fourteen

The surgery rang me while I was driving in dense traffic and it was some minutes before I could pull over and ring back. There had been a desperate call for a doctor to go to Oaks Crescent where a man had collapsed in the street. An emergency ambulance had also been summoned. The Crescent was only a few hundred yards distant and I was there in no time. I could find no patient but someone recognised my car and came running towards me. The patient had been taken into no. 14 and I parked outside leaving my lights flashing to guide the ambulance.

The front door was open and several people were crowded around a recumbent figure on the floor. The bystanders parted when they saw me and I could now see someone giving cardiac massage. I recognised the patient – it was a Mr. Janes – someone on my list and whom I knew to have had angina relieved by cardiac stents. I checked the airway for false teeth and then took over the cardiac compression. No-one seemed at all sure how long resuscitation had been going on but the pupils were still small and I noted the time to be exactly midday. The patient, I was told, had been conscious but grey and struggling for breath when found in the street and had demanded to be taken into no. 14 – the lady owner was apparently a friend. She was currently in the kitchen next door being consoled by a neighbour.

Four minutes later the ambulance arrived and one of the crew took over the massage and his colleague applied some ECG leads while I primed their defibrillator. There was no hint of cardiac activity on the trace and I thought the pupils were now more dilated. In desperation perhaps, we agreed to try the defibrillator but had it no effect and we returned to chest compression. At ten minutes past twelve, with still no response to our resuscitation and with the pupils now widely dilated, I gave the patient one last shock with the voltage turned up to maximum. There was no discernible change in his condition and the ECG trace was still flat-lining. I took the inevitable decision to stop all treatment and declared my patient dead. The room was silent, and we could now hear sobbing in the kitchen. I went and spoke to the lady of the house and explained that we had done all we possibly could but, sadly, with no effect and that her friend had died.

'I was sorry', I added, 'about the massive intrusion into her home' and she just shook her head.

The ambulance crew were loading their equipment into their vehicle as I went across to thank them.

'Would you like us to contact the police on our radio – it'll be a Coroner's case, won't it?'

'Yes, almost certainly. Thank you'.

Even though I knew the patient well I wouldn't be in a position to issue a death certificate without discussing the circumstances with the Coroner and the police would have to be involved.

'However,' I heard myself say 'I'll pop round and see his wife. I know her well and it might be better to give her the awful news myself rather than she find a couple of policemen on her doorstep. Tell the officers that I'll be back in a few minutes to give them a statement.'

I drove the short distance to the patient's home, an address I knew well. Mrs. Janes answered the door and was obviously surprised to see me. And I was equally surprised – shocked even – when, on hearing the terrible news – she asked, in a very challenging way – 'where was he, doctor? In all innocence I gave her the address and she let out a loud long scream, turned and ran into a room at the back of the house and slammed the door. I could hear her shouting – 'No, No, No, not there.'

For some seconds I froze, wondering what best to do next. Then, thankfully, one of the Janes' daughters came up the drive. She was weeping. She had been phoned at work to be told about her father and had rushed home to comfort her mother. She, too, could now hear the tirade from within the house.

She explained. 'Dad had a very long affair with that 'bitch on heat' at 14, Oaks Crescent. Sorry Doctor. But he swore, to all of us, after his heart operation, that it had ended. Now he's been caught out and if he's collapsed and died after a 'session' with his fancy lady then, well, if I don't say it, Mum certainly will.'

'Serve him right.'

~

Lakeside

There are about half a million caravan owners in the UK; almost double that number if you include motorhomes. A very small proportion of them ever come to our practice area but there are a few. We have a caravan site that is incorporated with a fishing lake. Many of our caravanners are therefore anglers – men, usually in small groups, having a fishing holiday. However, some couples do check in – again often fishermen with their very tolerant, long-suffering wives, human floats that bob up and down at mealtimes. Our caravanning visitors generally have no impact on our practice workload: angling is meant to be relaxing and recuperative after all. But occasionally we will be asked to visit someone at 'Lakeside.'

A recent call to the site, over Easter weekend, could have been easier. It came in just as we were settling down for bed. It was a very dark night and it was raining heavily. Nevertheless, the call sounded reasonable. A Mr. Priestley who had a strong northern accent was worried about his wife. She had suffered colicky abdominal pain all day, had lost her appetite and had now vomited. The pain had become very severe. She was normally in robust health and, as if it confirmed her normal vigour, he told me they came from Leeds.

Lakeside is a large site, mostly grass. The one metalled road splits into two spurs, one each side of the lake. The reception and toilet blocks are just inside the entrance. When I arrived, the barrier was down and locked. There were no signs of life in the buildings – no surprise at midnight. I had instructed the caller to meet me at the barrier but there was no-one around. I left the car, skirted the barrier and resolved the dilemma of going to left or right by going right. I was wrong and it was still raining heavily. I reached the end of the road having passed a dozen or so vans, none of them showing any light. Back to the barrier. The third van along the left-hand road was the one – there were lights on. I knocked the door. After a long silence I knocked again. There were muffled voices inside and then a gruff shout: 'who is it, what do you want?' I said I was the doctor. Voice said 'pull the other one matey, there's no way we're opening the door to a stranger at this hour.' I backed off. This was obviously not the right van.

It was still bucketing down. A hundred yards further on I found another van with lights on. As I approached, someone shone a strong torch in my face. 'Ah, thank goodness you've come, doctor. Thank you so much.' It was obviously Mr. P who was blinding me. I was rather fed up and I was most certainly very wet.

'I thought I asked you to meet me at the barrier?'

'Yes, doctor, you did but, you see, the wife is very upset and didn't want to be left alone. She's been sick again and is in terrible pain.'

I left my umbrella in the awning, a canvas construction that seemed to be very wet even on the inside. Inside the van Mrs. P was lying on the bed with her knees up and groaning. In the very confined space I narrowly avoided putting my foot into a bowl pebble-dashed with vomit. The focus of the pain was in the upper right abdomen where she was very tender just under the ribcage. She had suffered 'niggles' before, she told me, but nothing like this. It appeared to be a case of biliary colic: pain from an infected gall bladder that might very well contain one or more stones. In the feeble, alien light of the van I was hesitant, but I didn't think Mrs. P was jaundiced.

At medical school we were given the mnemonic that gall bladder 'customers' would be female, fair, fat, flatulent, and fertile. Mrs. P scored three out of five – maybe four – I hadn't asked about 'wind' and she could hardly be fertile at 56. She would need to seriously restrict her diet, have some antacid and begin an antibiotic. My colleagues in the north would have to take it from there. Her immediate need, though, was for some pain relief – a wet walk for me back to the car. Mr. P kindly lent me his torch but it did nothing to protect me from the elements.

On my return, duty done, I made to leave. Mr. P followed me out into the awning, pointedly closing the van door. The torchlight reflected from the canvas revealed his fishing tackle but also exaggerated his slight tremor. Rather falteringly, he asked: 'can I stop you a minute, doctor?'

'Sure.'

'You don't think, do you, that my wife's problem has been brought on by intimacy? You see, she usually gives me a 'treat' when we're on holiday. I've been so worried that I might have injured her is some way. I'm sure you understand.' He put a tremulous hand on my sleeve.

I was able to be genuinely reassuring and I hope I covered my astonishment by stepping out into the rain to open my umbrella.

Back in surgery, after the Easter break, we were having coffee and signing prescriptions when a local police sergeant phoned, asking for the senior partner. A caravanner at Lakeside had reported a worrying incident, around midnight on Saturday, to the owner of the site. Some sort of pervert had been going around the site knocking on van doors saying he was a doctor and asking to be admitted. The proprietor had phoned the police – he thought they ought to know. And, in turn, the police thought the practice ought to know. We knew already.

~

On my way home

Two weeks before Easter. The worst of the hibernal surge of colds and 'flu was over whilst the A303 was not yet a car park. For once, afternoon surgery had not overrun, but there was a call waiting.

A man I took to be elderly was ringing on behalf of his wife. She had been suffering 'tummy pains' all night and all day. There were no ramifications to the story and a wafer-thin set of case-records was put into my hand by a receptionist. The patient had been registered for 20 years and never been seen: a sure sign of serious pathology. The home address was between me and my supper and, perhaps too cheerily, I said that I would visit shortly. I was somewhat surprised when the caller repeated that, actually, he only wanted some advice.

'I don't want you to come out, doctor, there's really no need.'

I remember using some sort of platitude - 'no, it's really no trouble' - whilst thinking that not laying a hand on an angry abdomen was always to invite a negligence rap.

It was a pleasant evening and not yet dark. Driving out to the village I could see still the white horse and I knew that Stonehenge was over the horizon. I was still eyeing the view when jolted out of my reverie. The door was being noisily unlatched. I was admitted rather than welcomed. I recognised the timbre of the voice from the earlier telephone call. 'Front bedroom' was all he said before turning away smartly and shrinking along the dim passage. Perhaps the couple didn't get on – nothing unusual there.

I found my way up the stairs and along to the front. Once in the bedroom I recognised the odour - there was fresh vomit lurking somewhere. My patient was submerged under traditionally bulky bedding. She appeared older than her recorded age and her hair was thin and receded - the early stages of male baldness that some post-menopausal women suffer, I thought. It was difficult to make other judgements under the 60-watt bulb. She was grimacing in pain, more so when I asked a few obvious questions. There seemed little point in not getting on with a physical examination.

She was fully dressed but didn't protest as I pulled up dress and petticoat. Something made me take the pink satin bloomers right down over the stocking tops. Into view came an obvious and strangulated left inguinal hernia, and a full complement of male genitalia.

Autopilot to 'off'. This was a rupture that had two dimensions – surgical and social. The latter would probably be the one that caused most turbulence.

~

Morbilli

The reason for the requested house call was a cryptic one-worder – 'rash'. There was no medical record envelope. The family had just registered having moved from Bristol, I was told. The house was in turmoil – unopened boxes and furniture stacked all in the wrong places but at least the heating was working. Two cats were draped across the back of a sofa fronting a radiator.

There were two little girls – mother had one in arms and she was grizzling and fractious. But it was the four-year old, the older one who had the rash. She allowed me to lift her little dress and vest and there, across the abdomen, was a discrete red rash to match her red cheeks. She wasn't hot and there had been, apparently, no other problems. She distractedly scratched her belly and I couldn't see how this wasn't some sort of allergic rash – an urticaria. After all, with the family chattels all in dusty disorder and in a family with pets, the list of possible allergens would be endless. I issued a prescription for piriton syrup and gave expansive reassurances.

The next morning my visiting list included the same address and the same reason – 'rash'. This time it was the younger child – the mother had organised a same-day appointment but rang back later to report that the child now had diarrhoea and was very hot.

The younger child had the same rash as her sister but was more obviously ill. Mother, quite rightly, wanted to know how many allergic rashes were contagious and caused a high fever? I hid behind procedure. Putting thermometer, torch, tongue-depressor, auriscope, stethoscope and my sense organs into action gave me time to think and, thankfully, a clue. Inside the child's cheeks were areas that looked like small, cream, bacterial colonies on an agar plate – Koplik's spots – the child had measles (Morbilli). It was a diagnosis I had not made for some twenty years.

My embarrassing discomfort transferred itself to the mother. No, she had decided not to have her girls immunised in view of all the recent publicity. The media had been full of warnings that the MMR (Measles, Mumps and Rubella) vaccine could cause chronic bowel diseases. This was the work of Andrew Wakefield, the middle-ranking doctor son of our local neurologist. In the surgery we had discussed this scare-story several times over coffee. It was bad news all round. Most authorities had rejected the conclusions of the Wakefield paper even though it had been published in The Lancet. But even so, the widespread negative headlines across the media had spoiled our practice immunisation targets. More importantly, national vaccination rates against measles were continuing to drop well below herd immunity levels and measles cases were reappearing after years of being a rarity. Here, being cuddled in front of me, was the sad outcome of unwarranted scaremongering and media hype.

The Piriton went back to Boots, replaced by Calpol and thankfully both children recovered without any serious consequences, the horrors of which I was personally very well aware: my own mother had been partly blinded in one eye after childhood measles.

~

Gardening

Rosemary – 'call me Ro' – came in with her mother. She was an 'extra' fitted in to morning surgery because of her urgent symptoms. For most of the night the family had been disturbed by her 'belly ache'. Once or twice the pain had been bad enough to make her scream out and she had, from about seven a.m. been retching and, now, vomiting. With Ro being 17 it was appropriate to slip in some questions about her menstrual history. This was straightforward – her last period had begun and ended a week before.

With mother in the room, I held back my reservations that this might not be the untarnished truth, especially in a patient who had bright green hair, luminous warpaint around the eyes, pins in her nose and a ring through her lower lip. When I asked where the pain was at its worst, Ro pointed to the right side of the lower abdomen.

'It is now' she groaned and retched again.

A low-grade temperature, the vomiting, the right-sided pain (and tenderness when I pressed) and the 'innocent' menstrual history all led me to think that Ro could have acute appendicitis and that I should refer her, very promptly, to the duty surgeon. I like to think that I'd managed to suppress any visible reaction when I'd found a further ring in the navel and that an exposed margin of pubic hair was also a lurid green. Mother asked if the referral could be to the local military hospital as 'Dad, as you well know Doctor, was in the RAF.' I was happy to oblige but couldn't take any credit for making a special effort. As it happened, RAF Wrington Hospital was on 'take' for surgical emergencies that day anyway.

A week later Ro and her mother reappeared in my surgery. Mother sat down full of praise for the way I had seized control of the situation and 'got Ro under a surgeon' so quickly. But Ro remained standing, having limped into the room. She was obviously still very uncomfortable. Mother passed me a letter from the surgeon; there had been complications.

Acute appendicitis had remained the working diagnosis at the hospital after various standard tests and Ro had been taken for appendicectomy during the evening of her admission. However, the operation had been more complex than usual. The surgeon had been unable to reach the inflamed appendix through the customary small incision. The offending organ was 'retrocaecal' – in an unusual position, lurking deep to the large bowel and, being inflamed, now stuck to surrounding tissues. Removal had required more skin prep and shaving in order to extend the wound to the 'south' and the larger breach in the abdominal wall had become infected. I was asked, in the letter, to best judge when and which stitches should be removed and to continue the antibiotic cover as necessary. I noticed, on examining the wound, that the ring through the navel had been removed and that the surrounding tissue there was also inflamed. I noticed, also, the faintly green stubble where the pubic hair had been shaved.

Mother then said that she thought I might like to see what Ro had found tied to her wrist when she came round from the anaesthetic. She handed me a manilla label with the string still attached. It was stamped 'Ministry of Defence' on one side and on the other was written:

'Sorry, love, but we had to mow the lawn.'

5
SCRAPES AND TRAGEDIES

Just a check-up

Patients turning up in a GP's surgery 'just for a check-up' can be a nightmare in the making. It may be appropriate in private medicine, and a money spinner, that the annual premium confers the 'bonus' of a 'free' screening medical including certain tests and lasting up to an hour. But even here there are pitfalls. Very few sinister medical conditions present detectable warning signs months, or even weeks, in advance and a 'clean bill of health' conferred at New Year can look absurd by Easter.

In general practice it can be more productive to spend some time winkling out why the patient has decided that he or she needs to be 'checked.' A covert anxiety can then orchestrate the session and expose a treatable condition; if there is one. This is more valuable for the patient and less frustrating for the doctor. But even this gambit can fail. The only compromise then possible in an average 500 second consultation is a cursory check of some simple parameters which, unfortunately, the patient may take to be superficial and uncaring. But even a grateful patient can be left in jeopardy and fail to absorb your warnings that many illnesses can appear extremely suddenly, totally out of the blue.

Les Warren was a case in point. He showed up in the middle of a busy morning – 'just popped in for a check-up, doc. Hope you don't mind. I've never had one and I retired last week.' My quizzical expression was the prelude to some tentative probing. Les denied any recent problems and it simply seemed that the end of his working life was the stimulus. He wasn't a smoker, wasn't much overweight, drank little and his personal life seemed very settled. Unsurprisingly, I found nothing to worry either of us on examination. I pronounced him fit, hoping I was right. I trusted he would enjoy his retirement as much as I was looking forward to mine. We parted with a handshake.

At 5 pm the same day I was interrupted by one of our receptionists – a Mrs. Warren was on the phone and was extremely distressed. She was at home. Her husband wasn't breathing. There seemed little point in talking to her and I rushed round to their address – only a few hundred yards from the surgery. Les was splayed across a fireside chair, propped on one arm. He was cyanosed, mouth agape, eyes open, pupils widely dilated, looking very surprised and obviously dead. It looked as though he had, in the last few seconds of his life, tried to get up from the chair and then flopped backwards. Mrs. Warren was sitting opposite, pale and frightened. She had been out to see a sick relative and had come home expecting Les to be pottering about in the garden or preparing their tea.

'He was anxious to do more about the home now he's retired' she said, weeping.

Here I was, in the snake pit. I took Mrs. Warren into her dining room and we sat across the table.

'Les said you found him absolutely fit this morning, doctor. He said you wished him a long and happy retirement. It only lasted six hours.'

This was true. This was painful. But at least she was more traumatised than angry. Anything I was about to say would sound defensive and my condolences insincere. How does one avoid weasel words? I couldn't possibly expect someone in a state of such profound shock to grasp the nuances of why medical check-ups are untrustworthy. I stumbled on, trying to sound professional but was interrupted.

'Did Les mention his bad attack of indigestion last week? I told him to tell you, but he said it was only because he'd been out drinking with his workmates – one of his best friends was also retiring'

'No, honestly, he didn't.'

Here was the clue to what had happened. Les had almost certainly had a heart attack the previous week – not 'silent' as they can be - but signalled by a less than common symptom which he had misinterpreted. Now, this afternoon, something further, and this time fatal, had happened to his heart. I think Mrs Warren understood my explanation, but I was sure it would need shoring up. An ambulance drew up outside. I explained the circumstances to the crew, and excused myself to go back to my waiting patients and to phone the police. This was, most certainly, an unexpected death and destined for the Coroner.

I went back to see Mrs. Warren after surgery. Les had been discretely removed and some of her relatives had arrived. We went over the events of the day again and I felt more reassured that no-one was blaming me for the death, at least not to my face. Mrs. Warren asked me if I could help her claim money back on a holiday she and Les had planned – a week in a smart Bournemouth hotel. It would obviously have to be cancelled but thought she might go later in the year taking along her mother-in-law. Les's mother was in her mid-eighties and 'still full of beans.' Les had been her favourite son – the only child of her first marriage, her first love. Les's father had been killed, aged only 30, in a works accident. Mrs. Warren was a remarkable woman – widowed less than two hours, she was already thinking of others.

Mid-evening, a week later I'm on call. Wilf, our local undertaker is on the phone.

159

'Evening, Norman. Sorry to bother you but we've got a dead body here.'

I made the only possible reply, not realising that he wasn't being facetious.

'Well, that's a surprise, Wilf.'

'No, really, – a fresh one.'

'Wilf, what *do* you mean?'

A shocking story unfolded. Les Warren's body had been released by the Coroner earlier in the day and Wilf had brought him back to town. Some of his relatives, including his mother, had been anxious to say their goodbyes and Wilf had prepared the body for a viewing in his Chapel of Rest. He had left the family to their privacy and then, after a few minutes, one of Les's stepbrothers had burst into his office, red in the face and shaking. His mother, in the middle of remarking how much Les, in death, resembled his father, had suddenly dropped to the floor. They had assumed that she had fainted but then froze with horror when they couldn't rouse her. They thought she might have died. Wilf was sure they were right.

'Norman, could you possibly attend to confirm the death and do all the necessaries. As you know, I can't just pop her in the fridge, although I do have a couple of empty drawers.' He was going to make his visitors a cup of tea.

At least I hadn't given the poor old lady a clean bill of health earlier in the day.

~

Spy in the sky

Our senior nurse popped her head round the door between my patients and held the door shut in a rather threatening manner. She half-whispered:

'Sorry about this, I know you're running way behind this morning, but I've had to put Mr. Proudfoot in your side-room. He's in a dreadful state emotionally, having very dark thoughts and wondering how many of his anticoagulants would be fatal. I didn't dare send him away, he might do something stupid. His warfarin dose, by the way, is spot on.'

Most of my surgery sessions run into quicksand at some point but occasionally one is confronted by one very time-consuming problem after another. I looked at my watch. I was almost an hour behind schedule already but, in a strange way, lapsing into two hours late doesn't feel any worse. Hopefully, the staff would highlight my predicament to my partners and offload some of my house calls. They will know that I have school medicals at 1.30 pm.

I knew Ken Proudfoot – professionally and, slightly, socially. Now retired, he'd been the finance officer at a factory in the next town. He'd come to see me, about three months ago, complaining of tiredness and swollen ankles. There was a loud murmur entangled with his heart sounds that even I could hear. He was found, as I suspected, to have a leaking aortic heart valve: some of the blood being pumped off around his body was leaking back into the heart. His need for surgery was seen as very urgent and he had a new heart valve put in place a few weeks back. However, there were major complications during the operation. The stitches tethering his new valve in place wouldn't hold – his tissues were too friable. Eventually, though, the surgeons were confident that things would hold in place and they restored his circulation. The heart surgeon went off in search of Mary, Ken's wife, who had waited many, many hours at the hospital. She had wondered why the operation was taking far longer than predicted and was glad to have the surgeons' explanation and to know that Ken was in recovery and now doing well. It was only when she got home that she found a message on her phone that Ken was back in theatre. The team worked on him all night, desperately trying to secure the new valve in place – it had partly dislodged about an hour after Ken had come round from the first anaesthetic.

Understandably, Ken's recovery was very slow. It was nearly three weeks before Mary was able to collect a very thin and weak husband from the hospital. We took over his management, and in particular, his anticoagulation, monitoring the blood-thinning with weekly blood tests. This was why he had been in to see Sister this morning.

Ken was sitting in my examination room, his fists clenched and looking very anxious. I sat up on the couch and told him that Sister had spoken to me.

'I understand, Ken, that there are some problems over and above your heart.'

There was a significant silence, then: 'Doctor, you've not got time for all this – I don't even have an appointment with you.'

'Ken, leave my clock problems to me – just put me in the picture.'

'I've been a silly bugger' he said. 'When I knew I was going to have major surgery, and that I might well not survive, I got it into my head that I didn't want to die without confessing something to Mary. It didn't last long, but some years ago I had an affair. When the girls were in their teens and then off to university, Mary and I rather drifted apart – physically - if you take my meaning. It didn't cause any stress between us and everything else seemed as good as ever. Look, doctor, this is just tittle-tattle. You have sick people waiting to see you. Let's just leave it at that.'

'Ken – you've begun to tell me something that I think could have a massive impact on your recovery. I think you should go on.'

'Well, I suppose I got a bit frustrated and, to be honest, a bit resentful. Mary had begun to go off to look after her ailing mother – for weeks sometimes. I'd known Irene – one of the account clerks in my department, a divorcee and actually a friend of Mary's – for a long time and somehow, out of the blue, we became closer. Then it became physical. We would go up onto the downs during our lunch times or, if Mary was away, drive over to our house – as you know it's not overlooked by any neighbours. So, just before going into hospital, I confessed all this to Mary. To my amazement she was very understanding, said she still loved me, told me to forget the whole thing and concentrate on getting ready for my operation. I couldn't believe it and felt even more guilty. I began to think it would be a good thing if I died on the table.'

'Do you still feel guilty, Ken?'

'Worse, much worse. When I finally came round after the op and discovered how long I'd been under, that the surgeons had spent fourteen hours working to save me and that Mary had gone through all those hours of terrible anxiety I could think of nothing except how worthless I was. Why on earth did all these saintly people do so much for me? Mary caught me, yesterday, lining up and counting my warfarin pills. She guessed what I was thinking – how many would it take to finish me off? After all, they're rat poison aren't they? She saw how miserable I was and, perhaps desperate to help me, she also made a confession. She told me she had always known about the affair but had decided to overlook it. One afternoon – it must have been during the times while Irene and I were, well, you know . . . a salesman had come to the door of our house. Mary answered – I was at work. He was selling aerial photographs and had one of our house and garden. The print was stamped with date and time. It was the middle of a week when Mary had been with her mother. And although she had the wit not to buy the photo, there in the drive parked next to mine, she saw Irene's car.'

Ken now broke down and I took the opportunity to dash off to try to reorganise my day. When I returned he had composed himself. He told me that learning how Mary had known he was a cheat for such a long time and still been such a marvellous wife and mother had actually made him feel even more guilty. Her loving attempt to try to help him had made him worse – so much so that he hadn't been able to disguise it from Sister this morning.

I tried to reassure Ken that his self-loathing was not just because of the affair. He had the familiar 'guilt of survival' – of pulling through when others maybe didn't and that he was far from unique in this respect. I also suggested that talking through his feelings and reactions was the best therapy in this situation. Perhaps he might consider me referring him to a counsellor, but privately. We could then get him seen very quickly. He should certainly take Mary fully into his confidence and tell her that we've had this long conversation this morning. I suggested, perhaps on rather shaky ground, that his having been able to tell me everything this morning was a good indicator that he would pick up psychologically and soon. Ken nodded, reached out to shake my hand, and thanked me for my time again and again.

Ken did, in fact, improve emotionally. He made an appointment to see me a week later and Mary came with him. It was really only to thank me and cancel the counselling. The gloom had gone, and Sister told me a few weekly blood tests later that Ken was very much better, and his anticoagulation still spot on.

It was such a shock when he died in his sleep. The post-mortem showed that his flimsy aorta had ruptured. A broken heart?

~

Unwanted tan

Conveniently, there was always somewhere to park, and it was on my way home. It became a pleasant chore to stop at 'Halfway House' at the end of each working week. I had always picked up the local paper there but it became something of a social call when a very nice couple took over the shop cum post office and joined my list. John had worked in commercial property law, making a heap of money but he had come to yearn for life in the slow lane. Mary had shared his dream of running a small shop - as long as it was many miles from London. 'Halfway House' ticked all the boxes for them when it came up for sale. Their obvious charm and enterprise proved more and more popular and the bell over the shop door now clattered ever more frequently. I became used to having to queue, even more so when they became an outlet for a new local bakery. We began to get all our bread from them, and woe betide me if I arrived home on Friday evenings without cake.

One morning I spotted John's name on the appointments list. This was most unusual. I never remember medical matters invading our banter while I was in the shop. The couple always seemed to exude good health and cheery optimism. When he came in, I was on alert.

'Good morning, Doctor. Sorry to bother you but have you heard about the new Post Office computerised accounting scheme?'

I hadn't.

'Well, all sub-postmasters are now obliged to install the system and for the first time since taking over the office I've been accused of accounting errors. I've had to put some of our own money in the till to make up the daily balances. We just don't understand how this has happened but, anyway, the point is that the worry has been putting me off my food and I'm not sleeping too well either. I'm sorry about this but I also have to tell you, Mary said, that my poo has gone a funny, pale colour now that I'm not eating so much. Oh, and she insisted I tell you that she thinks I have lost some weight but that doesn't bother me – it's all around the middle.'

My heart was sinking – slowly but surely. It was obvious that John, even across the width of my desk, was jaundiced. I presumed he hadn't noticed that his eyeballs were yellow and perhaps Mary had also missed the fact, being with him all day every day. I invited him up onto the couch and pummelled his abdomen. I could feel nothing abnormal but he had now sensed my discomfiture. I tried to let him down gently.

I explained that he was 'slightly' jaundiced and that the likely explanation was that something was blocking the normal outflow of bile from his liver. His bile pigments were therefore damming back into his bloodstream and turning him yellow rather than colouring his faeces. What did I mean by 'something' was difficult to bat away but I reverted to the formulaic. Tests were needed before a diagnosis could be made and these could only be done by a specialist. We agreed that it would be helpful to call on his BUPA membership and I gave him the name of a local gastroenterologist. I knew that John knew what I was thinking but he was kind enough not to push me into being painfully frank.

Half an hour later, in the reception area, I found the staff tucking into cakes. John had brought them in from the shop and presented them. Some people are so kind.

In the next six weeks – before he succumbed to complications of what turned out to be extremely difficult surgery – John was served with a demand for an external audit by the Post Office. They were alleging false accounting and that they could, potentially, cancel his contract to run the post office. Mary desperately tried to keep it from her husband and asked the management to hold their fire until John was better. But the authorities were very hard-hearted about it. After they had ignored her own pleading for a delay, she asked me to write a letter to the Post Office prosecutors explaining that John, officially the sub-postmaster, was very seriously ill. I was quite disgusted by their attitude but happy enough to write the letter. It was probably the most therapeutic thing I was able to do for my patient before he died.

To me, John's precipitate demise was a perfect instance of the old medical saw – that the nicest people get the nastiest diseases.

~

Lynchet Farm

Lynchet Farm had been in the hands of the Carrs since before Waterloo. When I first met the family, near neighbours, Edmund Carr, the owner, was a burly man in his late fifties. His only son, Jack, worked with him on the farm. Jack and his wife, Melanie, had been given the keys to a new bungalow at the bottom of the hill as a wedding present. Father and son rubbed along. Ivy, matriarch, book-keeper and peacemaker, would moderate the frequent 'discussions' between father and son about how best to run the farm. Jack (two years at agricultural college) was keen to modernise but his father (learnt on the job) was very conservative. It was a classic hierarchy/succession dilemma. Of course, we don't have such problems in general practices (fake news).

The Carrs were very sociable and I had learned of the family dynamics on occasions such as pre-Christmas drinks rather than in any rare professional encounters in surgery. In fact, it was at a summer drinks party on their lawn to raise money for the village hall that I learned of something rather worrying. Perhaps because of the sunny euphoria of the occasion or because of the wine that was flowing, Jack was rather indiscrete. He told our little cluster of guests a story that he found rather amusing. 'Father' had got up at five, as usual, a few mornings ago. After the usual cup of tea, he had gone to the milking parlour and pulled on his wellies – but on the wrong feet. He later insisted that he hadn't felt any discomfort and had, 'after all, got the milking done.' However, his feet had tingled for the rest of that day and through that night. We all laughed, but I had a gut feeling that Edmund might soon be coming my way.

Sure enough, Edmund was brought in to surgery by an apologetic Ivy about six weeks after the party. He was limping and seemed distant. Ivy spoke for him. He had fallen in the milking parlour – twice, and on the second occasion he couldn't get up. He was losing weight, had had more tinglings in his feet and, now, also in his hands. He was having trouble with buttons. Ivy now had to get up with him every morning to get him into his green boiler suit. Not people to make a fuss, the two of them had agreed to keep 'buggering on – as Churchill used to do in the war' she said. But yesterday, at lunchtime, Edmund had nearly choked on some roast lamb. Jack and Melanie were at the table and the whole story then surfaced. Melanie had insisted on, and arranged, an appointment for them to see me. Something told me this was all rather sinister - some sort of neurological syndrome. To me, Edmund was normal on examination, but I suggested referral to a neurologist.

'We'll go private' Ivy said. 'We've paid into BUPA for years and never used it, as you know.'

We learned that Edmund had Motor Neurone Disease within a week. The neurologist had found a pretext to talk to Ivy and Jack alone. It was a solemn and devastating conversation.

Edmund deteriorated quite rapidly. Before long he was in a wheelchair, displaying out-of-kilter emotions, drooling, relying on semi-solid foods and desperately depressed. Jack took over the running of the farm completely and, out of delicacy and to please his mother, he resisted the temptation to bring in any significant changes. Despite the heroic efforts of our district nurses, Edmund finally had to be admitted to a hospice. He died there, trapped in a wasted, disorganised body but with real and agonising awareness, much of the time, of his coming demise.

After all the erstwhile arguments about the future of the farm, sometimes fractious, Jack discovered that his reactionary father had been plotting improvements all along. He had discussed his Will with Ivy long before getting ill and besides ensuring that she would be 'well taken care of' should he die before her, he had won her approval that a generous sum of money be left to Jack with the proviso that it be spent on modernising the business. And at her own suggestion, Ivy moved down to the bungalow so that Jack and Melanie could take over the farmhouse. After some eighteen months of contractors coming up and down the lane, the crumbling silage clamp walls had been demolished to make way for a new rotary milking parlour. And a gigantic silo, so symbolically modern to Jack, was erected to replace the unsightly piles of silage held down by polythene and hundreds of old car tyres. Jack also expanded the herd and engaged a full-time cowman, Ivan.

It was late May of the next spring that the accident happened. At the top of the silo Jack was supervising the loading of fresh grass. Somehow, he fell in. Ivan heard a single shout of 'help' but then there was only the sound of the blower. Eventually Jack's body was found some feet down in the fresh mowings. His body appeared unharmed except for the deep cyanosis but the pathologist did remark on the fragments of grass under his fingernails. Jack had obviously tried to claw his way back to the surface but failed and suffocated.

I called at the farm the day after Jack's funeral. I was beckoned into the big kitchen. The two widows were sitting opposite each other in silence. They said they couldn't cry any more. They were waiting for their solicitor, their financial adviser and a man from the estate agency. Melanie said the meeting was needed but the real decision had already been taken. The farm would be put up for sale. There was no way she could live within sight of 'that bloody silo' and more tears flowed.

~

A Motspur

Sometime in the mid-1980s – I can't remember exactly when – Douglas Adams ('Hitchhiker's Guide to the Galaxy') and John Lloyd ('Q.I.') published a little gem of a book called 'The Meaning of Liff'. It was full of their one-word definitions of a host of everyday life experiences. My particular favourite was the 'Motspur' and I quote – 'the fourth wheel of a supermarket trolley which looks identical to the other three but which renders the trolley completely uncontrollable.' I don't expect to be unique but, to me, this concept matched, exactly, any day in general practice – mostly it rolls along smoothly only to be upended by something totally unexpected and unavoidable.

88-year-old Bob Farley was a long-retired motor mechanic. I'd had cause to visit him a few times over the years. I always associated the home with the smell of pipe tobacco. Bob had always smoked a pipe. I don't think his wife did, but I couldn't be sure. Bob even smoked his pipe in bed – at least I assumed so from the ashtray and pipe-smokers accoutrements that lived on his bedside table. This time I was called to see him, at home, with 'cough and breathlessness.' When I arrived, he had just been to the toilet with the help of his wife. He was sitting on the edge of his bed, hands on knees, having to use his arms to pump his chest up and down to get some air aboard. At least he wasn't blue but there was clearly something wrong with his bellows. I found obvious signs of a right lower zone chest infection and put him on antibiotics. I could detect no serious problems with his heart and circulation and thought it reasonable to treat him at home. I was strongly advising him not to smoke when his wife interrupted:

'Oh, he won't, doctor. He hasn't wanted to for several days – that's how I knew he was not well. He hasn't even been at the snuff.'

'Well, anyway, stay off the baccy, Bob, until I check you over. I'll come and see you again before the end of the week.'

I spoke furtively to his wife on the doorstep, and she assured me that she would ring if Bob didn't seem to improve.

Three days later Bob felt better though still abed and still coughing sputum. I thought the chest sounded clearer and he was now able to talk in long sentences – mostly grumbles about the amount of electronic 'crap' in modern cars. I took the antagonism to be a good clinical sign but still banned the pipe.

The Wednesday following was my half day: morning surgery, paperwork and then any house calls. After that the day was mine. It was also my wife's birthday and we'd invited her sister and husband to join us for fizz and lunch. The morning went well and I finished surgery only 20 minutes behind schedule. There was only one new house call and I therefore thought I had ample time to pop in on Bob Farley again. He was a lot better, sitting downstairs, dressed and chipper. His chest sounds were now normal and he'd stopped coughing. His wife was pleased that he was eating well again – she set great store by his appetite – and Bob asked permission to take up his pipe again.

'You know, Doctor, thanks to you I could fancy a pinch of baccy again.'

Perhaps with my morning's work virtually finished and with a pleasant afternoon in store I was too euphoric. I forgot to beware the Motspur. I happily agreed to let Bob smoke again once I'd checked that his chest was clear. It was. When I arrived home a few minutes later our guests had arrived and, after greetings and hugs, I strode straight to the fridge for the birthday champagne. I was peeling the foil from the cap when the phone rang. It was the surgery.

'Could you please visit Mr. Farley.'

I laughed. 'You're too late, Janet, I've just driven away from his house.'

'Well, I'm afraid you're going to have to go back there. His wife has just phoned. She thinks he's died.'

I hurriedly passed the bottle to my wife, passed my apologies to everyone and explained that I was having to go back to a patient immediately.

'Please carry on with the drinks and food. I'll be back as soon as humanly possible. Something totally unexpected has just happened.' The shoulder shrugging response was a familiar family routine, road-tested on many such occasions though few as socially disruptive as this one. This was a Motspur for sure.

Bob was still sitting in the chair where I'd left him. He was certainly dead. His wife, understandably upset, flopped onto the sofa. She described going to the kitchen to prepare lunch just after I'd left. She'd shouted to Bob to ask if he would like some soup, but he didn't reply. She went back to the sitting room thinking he hadn't heard her but could still get no response. It took her a minute or two to realise that he was dead. Bob's pipe was on the carpet in front of him but there was still a plug of tobacco in his right hand. He was going to have to light it elsewhere.

~

Going up

It said K TILEE ROOFING CONTRACTOR on the sides of his vans. K TILER would have been ideal but life's not like that. Ken was a large man with a large personality. On the other hand, he had very little fear of heights. A well-known local figure, he and his family were patients I'd inherited from my predecessor. He was very friendly – and entertaining – when he came to tile our home extension. It was my chance to observe his work schedule. On site by seven a.m., he and his men would work non-stop until about one or one-thirty and then go for lunch. This was liquid – at the nearest pub. Irrespective of blood alcohol levels they would then roll on to Ken's yard to load up materials and tools for the next day's work. At sea their songs would have been called shanties.

While I admired the work ethic and wallowed in the bonhomie and banter whenever I was at home during our build, Ken's chain smoking was something I felt I should tackle. He brushed me off with a laugh and, without meaning to offend, began rolling another 'fag.' It was rare to see him working without a 'tab' in his mouth.

Then, some years later and with a sobering predictability, Ken had a heart attack. Fortunately, he was at ground level and when his chaps saw him clutching his chest and describing the pain as 'f . . . ing terrible' they bundled him into the van and whisked him to hospital. He was 57. Of course, he was told, as many times before, to stop smoking and drinking. But he didn't. I saw his married daughter in ante-natal clinic and she told me how angry were all his family but 'you know, doctor, that he's a brick wall and it's just like talking to one.' He'd even taken on more work having won the contract for roofing at the new development at Farrow Cross. 'You know, he even works Saturdays now and Mum's getting very fed up, especially with all the new paperwork.'

Three years on it happened again. Ken had another heart attack. This time he was on a roof but collapsed forwards onto the ridge and with the tiles being dry he was saved by friction. Somehow his team managed to manhandle him down to the ground by which time he was semi-conscious. Once again he was revived. The cardiology department could now perform angiography and visualise the state of his coronary arteries. They were pipe-stems and it wasn't clear how blood was actually getting through. He urgently needed a quadruple by-pass. Able to fund it at the private hospital, he was done only days later and was home a week after that.

This time the opposition to his smoking was so strong that he accepted that he must give up. In any case, he hadn't been able to smoke, now, for almost a month. But nothing was going to stop him working, however much money was left in the bank. He promised everyone that he would stay on 'mother earth' but, to general dismay, he was up and down ladders and scaffolding within a week or two. And then, less than a year later I one day saw him, from the car, up on a roof with a tab in his mouth. Should I have stopped and remonstrated? Perhaps yes, but the moment passed. I was to feel more guilty after only a few days.

Late on a Saturday afternoon on duty I answered a phone call long waiting in the wings. Ken's unmarried daughter, who still lived at home, was in tears. Her father had come in from work, had a beer from the fridge and then taken the dog for a walk. The dog had returned with his lead attached but there was no sign of 'Dad'.

'Mum's gone up the lane behind the yard to look for him – that's usually where he goes. Can you come over quickly – please!'

Sure enough, Ken was found about a hundred yards up the old drove road, lying face down in a muddy gateway. His wife had returned home with the bad news by the time I arrived and said she wanted to come up the lane with me. I guessed she wanted to say something in confidence. I had the difficult duty to confirm the death and try to console her. She seemed strangely unmoved, even when we spotted that Ken had started to write his name in the mud with a finger before he passed out. The letters K and E were clearly visible. I began to talk about the stages of grief but she interrupted me.

'We've been grieving for weeks already, doctor. We've all known that this was going to happen. He was such a stubborn man and I even challenged him that he was really committing suicide. And do you know, he agreed with me. That was the worst thing – much worse than this but I don't want the girls to know.'

The dam then burst and she sobbed deeply as I helped her back to the house. I'd learned about so-called 'anticipatory grieving' as a student but had always associated it with terminal cancer cases. How naïve.

~

Poorly Pauline

Pauline was one of those middle-aged statistics that we all fear. Just short of her 54th birthday she became increasingly tired. She assumed it was the menopause. A divorcee, she very much valued her full-time job. But it became more and more difficult to drag herself through each working day. When, one morning, she passed out at the office printer, hitting her head, she was taken, against her will, to Accident and Emergency. After a long wait and having made several attempts to leave (resisted by her work colleague), she was seen by an alert junior doctor who spotted signs of anaemia. Subsequent tests showed that she was losing more red blood cells than she was making – she was bleeding internally. After a couple of false trails Pauline was found to have an extensive colon cancer and, tragically, secondary deposits in her liver. After surgery to remove the tumour and chemotherapy for the liver she recovered well and was soon back at work. But, of course, the 'sword of Damocles' was hanging over her.

It was around the time of her next birthday that Pauline began, once again, to feel listless. She lost her appetite and visibly lost weight. She suspected, correctly, what it meant and couldn't face the thought of further operations and certainly not more chemotherapy. Her daughter persuaded her to check the diagnosis, at least. The cancer in the liver had returned however, and the oncologists were honest enough to admit that any further attempt at curative treatment was unlikely to extend her life. Pauline and her daughter cried together in a side-room of the out-patient department. Knowing there was a wedding in the offing, Pauline set herself a target – to be alive when her daughter walked down the aisle.

Frantic efforts were made, successfully, to bring forward the date of the wedding. Meanwhile Pauline deteriorated with frightening speed. She was very grateful for the palliative care given by our team and we were, in turn, very grateful for the support of the local Macmillan nurse. After a spell in a hospice to stabilise her medication, Pauline returned home to where her older sister had now moved in to help look after her. Pauline had mastered the use of the subcutaneous morphine pump to control her pain, but it still creased her at times and she would wince and sometimes retch.

The family now saw it as race against time. Distant relatives, friends and neighbours, most of whom had not watched the downhill progress with any regularity, were now shocked by Pauline's appearance. She was deeply jaundiced and extremely thin with gaunt facial features. But she had an enormously bloated abdomen. 'Cocktail sticks in an orange' was how one rather insensitive visitor described her on leaving. Somehow, Pauline fought on. It was a fortnight to the wedding. Then it was a week, then only days. It was obvious that Pauline would not be able to attend the service, even by wheelchair, and arrangements were made to video proceedings for her.

The day of the wedding dawned and Pauline's daughter, in her bridal finery, sat with her mother before the car came. There were tears, but Pauline was almost euphoric that she had survived long enough to 'be around'.

No-one spoke about it, but everyone assumed that Pauline would now 'let go' and die. Even the clinical team thought it already a miracle that she had survived, that she had stubbornly resisted her fate, for so long. But Pauline held on and on. It was ten days after the wedding that her new ambition was unveiled. She didn't want to die while her daughter was on honeymoon and spoil the couple's happiness. And, once again, she made it to her selfless target – well, almost. The day before her daughter was due to return the nursing team were surprised to find her almost free of pain and using much less morphine. She was in an upbeat mood and freely talking, some of it gossip she wasn't supposed to have overheard and there was laughter. She asked to see the wedding video once more and propped herself up in bed to watch it. Mendelssohn's wedding march and Pauline faded away together.

~

No smoke without fire

The Mount family had joined the practice – on to my list – six months before I met any of them. Shirley was the mother of twin girls aged eight. First, she brought one of them in with a verruca. Then the other one with a very mild cold. Then back to the other one – dandruff. The consultations were all in quick succession and, on the face of it, unnecessary. But sometimes consultations only make sense as part of a sequence. Along the way I'd learned that Dad was a fireman in our nearest city, working funny shifts.

When Shirley next appeared with the twins – again with something seemingly trivial – I inadvertently opened a door to a secret cupboard. In what was a facile remark I said to the little girls: 'I bet your Daddy is so proud of you.' Tears welled up in Shirley's eyes – enough that she couldn't disguise them and she saw that I'd noticed. She quickly thanked me, her voice breaking, and shooed the girls out ahead of her. 'Mm', I thought, 'I wonder what sore point I've touched on there?'

A couple of weeks later Shirley came to see me mid-morning – when I knew the twins would be in school. She started to thank me for being so kind to her twins and then tears started. I waited, wondering whether all our previous meetings had been her means, really, of weighing up my likely tolerance levels, my empathy score. I put out a few feelers and when I asked her about her relationship with her husband the tears became loud sobbing and her hands went to her face. But I could get no further other than she wasn't sleeping at night. Whatever was going on was currently too painful to explore. I needed a barbed hook to pull her back – and soon. She accepted a prescription for seven Mogadon together with my indication that they were very much a stopgap. After she'd gone, I made a diary note to be sure she returned.

It was ten days before Shirley made another appointment – I'd been on the point of chasing her. She apologised. She'd waited until her husband had gone back onto day shift. She didn't want him to know that she was 'under' the doctor. She hadn't taken any of the sleeping tablets. In fact, she hadn't 'cashed in' the prescription and put it on the desk in front of me. Now, in what was, effectively, consultation number six, we got to the real problem. What had been a very happy marriage, crowned by the birth of the twins, had recently gone sour. Shane, her husband, had been made redundant, two years before, from the factory job that he had held since leaving school. But he'd stayed positive and worked hard to meet all the rigours of the recruitment process to join the Fire Service as a full-time fireman. Shirley and all his family were very proud of him – he'd been such a slouch at school.

Shirley hesitated. She was obviously conflicted. Telling me more was, I guessed, going to mean being disloyal to her husband.

'At first it really didn't matter, doctor.'

I waited.

'But Shane's demands for more and more weird sex began to upset me. He would come home from the night shifts and as soon as the girls had gone to school, he would start. It was if he'd been winding himself up to a state all night. And once, when I challenged him, he admitted that the firemen – they're all men – would spend hours looking at porn once all their jobs were done. Once, he hurt me so much that I was bleeding from my bum (sorry, doctor) for days and having a poo was agony. In the end I refused everything point blank and he said that in that case he'd go elsewhere.'

Shirley sat staring ahead, breathing very deliberately.

I waited.

'I don't know if he has or not, but the last three months have been misery. The twins are beginning to sense that something is really wrong.'

Having said that I was so sorry to know of her awful predicament, I asked if she thought the marriage was at an end. Her breaking into sobs and searching her pockets for a tissue was the answer.

'But, doctor, how can you help me without Shane getting to know. The way he is he frightens me. He's not the man I married. Anyway, it's not a medical problem is it? I'm so sorry to take up your time. But I don't have anyone else to turn to, certainly not in Shane's family and mine live so far away.'

I took the line that the obvious physical danger that she was in should take priority. That she should move, very quickly, via Social Services, to get a place for she and the twins in a women's refuge – though not in the city where Shane worked. How did she feel about that as a plan?

'You're right, doctor. I don't really have a choice.'

Shirley's sudden flush of rationality surprised me, but I was relieved. I promised to speak to our attached social worker, before the end of the day if I could track her down, or, certainly, as soon as possible. Shirley left and I felt chilled. I had no idea why. I would know soon enough.

Half the town was woken, in the small hours, three days later by sirens, bells and arc lights. The Mount's end of terrace house, ironically built on spare land right next to the town's Volunteer Fire Station, was on fire.

Neighbours beat down the front door and found Shirley and the twins, blinded and choking in thick smoke, trying to find their way out. They'd been pulled clear of danger and into fresh air when Shirley broke free and dashed down the side of the house to the back shouting that she must get her handbag from the kitchen. There was an explosion and Shirley didn't reappear. Everyone heard the first floor collapse. Two neighbours tried to distract the twins who were screaming for their mother.

On duty overnight, I was phoned at quarter to six by the police. Living out of town I was unaware of the fire or that there'd been a fatality. 'Would you please attend to confirm a death?' On learning the address, I froze.

The house had collapsed inwards but the rear extension was still standing. I was guided through the black slush to where a body lay, on its side, in a fetal position. A lot of the flesh had gone from the upper part exposing some skull, jaw and teeth. Identity would need forensics and dental records but I knew it must be Shirley and kept thinking if only, if only, if only . . . . A policeman put a hand on my shoulder: 'are you OK, doc?' and I followed him outside. Back at home, breakfast was on the table. I wasn't hungry.

The police treated the incident as arson and Shane a likely suspect. Questioning the duty chief officer of the night shift at the city fire station soon revealed that Shane had left early that night on the pretext that Shirley had phoned to report serious illness in one of the twins. And CCTV at an all-night filling station had caught Shane filling a petrol can, still in his fireman's uniform. He was soon arrested, sitting in his car in a layby, as if waiting for the inevitable.

To my huge relief, Shane pleaded guilty to murder and I wasn't called on as a witness. I was able to avoid any dilemmas of confidentiality. The twins, who had had their whole lives blighted in an indescribable way were scooped up by their maternal grandparents from Cumbria, an amazing couple. For my part I was never again disgruntled when consulted about a verruca – as long as it was just that!

~

Brave little Imran

It will surprise most people to know that the first Indian restaurant in London opened in 1812. Indeed, it was possible to order 'curry and rice' in some coffee houses nearly a century earlier. But the subcontinental cuisine nostalgically pursued by retired Indian civil servants became a regular attraction for the whole British population from the 1950s onwards. The phrase 'going for an Indian' has come to mean visiting an Indian restaurant where, in fact, the food is often not truly authentic. No matter, popularity trumps validity.

With the evolution of our eating preferences came hard-working immigrant families, mostly from Bangladesh, to open 'curry houses' all over the country. Such signs as 'Mogul Grill' or 'Tandoori Takeaway' now feature even in many of our smaller communities and by the 1980s there were two such establishments in our Wiltshire backwater. A whole new lexicon has been absorbed. Diners now appreciate the differences between 'biryani' and 'korma', between 'saag' and 'Madras', 'naan' and 'papadums' and know to ask for mango chutney or lime pickle. Most striking, perhaps, is that we now understand that rice need not be white, cloying and masquerading as a pudding. But while we dip and dive into the array of dishes, we should remember that for every exotically dressed waiter who brings you the menu, numbered or not, there will be two or three beleaguered cooks in the kitchen preparing your amazingly varied food.

A row of shops and food outlets along part of our high street was a 1970s replacement of much older terraces, some erected shortly after the Civil War. And above the modern, commercial premises there are two storeys of flats. Access to these is up steel stairs from the rear delivery yard where there is, at least, usually somewhere to park. The industrial bins, the stacks of used pallets and the randomly parked vans were all familiar sights when we visited patients in the flats. The tenants were far from affluent and not the healthiest. The familiar diseases of deprivation therefore drew us to this part of town relatively often.

Late one routine morning I was climbing the stairs to the flats when someone shouted: 'good morning doctor.' It was one of the Bangladeshi waiters from their restaurant. I waved and shouted back. I'd been recognised, I guessed, because I had had recent cause to visit their establishment. It was not to eat but to attend to a drunk who had fallen in the toilet and cut his forehead, someone who was in no fit state to tell the difference between a chapati and his handkerchief. I think I was probably wasting NHS resources when I used local anaesthetic before stitching him up.

My late-night embroidery was a couple of weeks ago. Now my humdrum day was about to turn into something extraordinary. In an instant. I was just about to walk back down to the car park when someone came charging up the stairs up at a threatening speed. I stood back to let him through but it was me he was looking for. It was the waiter who had greeted me earlier. He was breathless and desperate.

'Come quickly, doctor. Come quickly. Come now. Something bad. Something very bad.'

He virtually pushed me down the steps and across the yard to the rear of his restaurant, all the time repeating 'something very, very bad.' The rear door was wide open. In the corridor a chef was supporting another man who was slowly shaking his head. I was ushered past, into the kitchen. It was one of those occasions when time stood still, seconds felt like minutes. The first sensation was the attractive smell of spicy cooking. A chef at the large stove indicated with his eyes that I should look to my left. What I then saw dried up my saliva and put my upper bowel into reverse. Another cook was holding up a little boy behind a large electric mincing machine. I tried to deny to myself what I could see. I couldn't. The boy's right arm had disappeared into the mincer. He must have been helping to put chunks of meat into the hopper and pushed too hard. The feeder screw had taken his fingers down into the spiral. Then, before the machine could be switched off, his hand, his wrist, his forearm, his elbow and part of his upper arm had all been dragged down into the works on a one-way journey. He must have screamed and screamed with indescribable suffering but now he was silently sobbing, shivering coarsely with distress. His endorphins had kicked in but adrenaline would be putting his life in danger. Young children can collapse and die in shock. Transfixed as if in a tableau at a waxworks, everyone in the room was looking at me. My palms were tacky and I felt very lonely. I heard myself barking demands.

'What's the boy's name?'
'Imran, doctor. Imran Azad.'
'How old is he?'
'Eight.'
'Is his father here?'

The man whom I'd seen being supported in the corridor was brought in but couldn't look at the child. I stepped closer to the mincer and its tortured human attachment. It was clamped to the table. Thankfully there wasn't much bleeding from the crushed arm – presumably the machine was itself acting as a tourniquet. I couldn't help, though, spotting two little fingernails among the minced flesh, skin and spicules of bone that had emerged. I took a deep breath.

'OK, unplug the mincer and start to undo the clamps holding it to the table. I'm just going out to my car to fetch a painkilling injection for Imran. You have a van?'

Nodding.

'OK, bring it up to the back door and empty the back of it – quickly.' There seemed little alternative than to take Imran to hospital and immediately. There was no time to wait for an ambulance.

When I returned, Imran's mother was being comforted by her husband. Imran was breathing more heavily and was clammy. It was time to free up the machine and lie him down. I was still trying to use my own adrenaline to some useful purpose. As I was giving Imran a fairly hefty dose of Pethidine (for his age) I asked about the van. It was ready. I demanded a blanket for Imran and then supervised he and the machine both being carried outside, into the back of the van. Imran screamed each time we failed to hold him and the mincer in exact juxtaposition. Once in the van I knelt alongside the little boy and demanded his father join me. Two cooks came with us. One of them drove us, as smoothly as possible, to our nearest Accident and Emergency – a journey of 21 miles. Each time the van vibrated or rocked on a corner Imran suffered a stab of pain. His father spent most of the journey comforting him in what I took to be Bengali. I was terrified of an uncontrollable haemorrhage. Thankfully it didn't happen. I was also grateful that no-one asked me the question I was dreading. It was only too obvious, though, that Imran was going to lose nearly all of his right arm.

The staff at A and E, when I rushed in and announced the arrival of an inevitable limb amputation, took over very smoothly. A nurse and a young doctor brought a wheeled trolley out to the van. They tried to swallow their shock. I wrote down the dose and time of the Pethidine I'd given as Imran and the mincer were transferred. I also introduced the doctor to Imran's father. One of the cooks said he would stay with Mr. Azad. The other cook and I were suddenly redundant as Imran was whisked away to theatre. I rang the surgery to let them know where I was and why. On the way home in the van neither the cook nor I spoke much. He was crying and I was desperate for a pee. We each had more than enough private thoughts to occupy the journey.

It may or may not be consequential, but the Azad family closed their business and moved away from our community a few months later. But being right-handed, I still think of little Imran every time I fork some curry up to my mouth.

Highs and Lows

There are some diseases where a diagnosis is made only with the passage of time. There are others where the diagnosis is instantaneous. And there are times when the clues offered by nature fall somewhere between these two extremes.

Shelley Burgess was listed fourth on my Monday morning visiting list. 'Fever and headache' it said. 'Just home from university.' For reasons of local geography, I saw her as second patient on my round. Her mother proudly told me that she had 'got' her degree in law from the University of the West of England and was joining a local firm of solicitors to 'get her articles.' I offered my congratulations but tried to be diplomatic in moving the conversation on to her health. Shelley was in bed, obviously hot, flushed and the curtains were drawn. She had had a sore throat on arrival home the day before. Her other symptoms, including the headache, had developed overnight. Among other signs I looked for was neck stiffness and I was relieved to find none. I also searched very carefully for any rash having let in the daylight and mother remarked how thoroughly I was looking. I don't know if she had suspicions of my motive for so extensively exposing her daughter. 'No rash' I pronounced, and I think she sensed my relief. 'Some sort of virus infection' was my next pronouncement and I gave all the obvious advice. I also indicated to mother, back downstairs, that 'we' were always available to see Shelley again if she didn't recover promptly.

'Well, it'll be a relief if she is better quickly, doctor. She's going to be very busy for the next few weeks – she's getting married in September.'

I returned to my car, but I'd been spotted by a neighbour. He came across the road as I opened the car door.

'Sorry to stop you, doctor, but just to thank you for what you did for my brother, Frank. Frank Lewis. You see so many people you might have forgotten, but you cleverly spotted that he had sepsis in his shoulder and sent him straight to hospital.'

I nodded – 'yes, I do remember Frank. Is he fully recovered now?' I tried not to be cagey, but some people are totally fascinated by illness in others, relatives or not, and can't resist mining for medical details that will be valuable currency in the gossip shop. In fact, I think Mr. Lewis was genuine and simply wanting to express gratitude. Even so I had to keep moving. I opened the car door to its full extent and reached across to put my diagnostic bag on the passenger seat, all the time paying attention to what he was saying. Then, suddenly, we were interrupted by Mrs. Burgess.

'Hello Mr. Lewis. Doctor, I'm so glad I've caught you.' She came closer to me. Mr. Lewis took the hint and sloped off.

'Shelley asked to go to the toilet just after you left and I helped her – she was feeling very shaky. I know you were looking for a rash and I suddenly saw one on her shins while she was sitting on the toilet.'

I retrieved my black bag, locked the car and followed Mrs. Burgess back into the house.

Sure enough, there was a pinpoint red to purple rash on Shelley's legs. This was meningococcal meningitis until proven otherwise and I had missed it only by bad timing. I rushed out to the car to fetch a vial of penicillin having told Shelley's mother to ring 999 for an ambulance and that I would speak to them.

It was great news, three days later, when Mrs. Burgess rang to say that Shelley was fully recovered from what had indeed been meningitis and to thank me for my prompt action. I told her the prompt action had been as much hers and that she should take all the credit for saving her daughter's life.

The next month, two weekends before the wedding, Shelley and her fiancé were both killed in a head-on collision on the A4. I visited the Burgess home on the Monday afternoon after the crash, only seven weeks from my previous Monday call. Mr. Burgess let me in, thanked me for coming, and we went along the corridor to the dining room at the back of the house where his wife was sitting at the table. I had a strong feeling that other family members had been scooped up and ushered into the front room. The table was strewn with family photographs that they had all been looking at. Mr. Burgess took up station at the French doors, looking out. He was crying.

Whatever I said – and I can't remember – it was totally, totally inadequate. I had saved a life from infection only that it could be taken away in a millisecond of extreme violence. But I do remember what Mrs. Burgess said. I can see her now, sitting with a large turquoise hat in her hands, dripping tears all over it.

'I know, I ruining my hat. But who cares? I won't need it any more. I can't wear it to a funeral.'

~

Although it swims and quacks it may not be a duck

Some nights on duty were eerily quiet, others non-stop activity. After several calls one Sunday evening reporting 'creasing tummy pains' and 'torrential' diarrhoea, I began to wonder what had poisoned our population. Not everyone was content with my advice that there was little I could do; that they should drink water only and that they could only be in serious jeopardy if the symptoms didn't settle after 12 hours or so. If they had other, long-standing illness it was wise, perhaps, for me to visit but of those that I did go to see none were in any danger, they simply had 'the trots' or whatever euphemism was current in their household.

By midnight I'd advised more than a dozen patients or relatives. There was certainly something highly infectious in the community. Was the weekend's carnival and hog roast in the frame? This might be one for the public health boys tomorrow. After advising four more 'I'm ever so loose, doctor' callers between midnight and three o'clock I saw no point in staying in bed, my wife repeatedly disturbed. I unplugged the bedside phone, threw on some clothes and went downstairs. Just after four a Mrs. St. Clair rang about her eighteen-year-old daughter. Not only did she have very watery diarrhoea and severe 'belly cramps' she had actually 'lost control' of her bowel and the watery contents were 'all in the bed.' 'Surely, doctor, there's something you can do to stem the tide?' I carefully explained, once again, the realities after having checked that the girl was normally fit.'

'Well, she is very overweight, doctor, I have to admit. She's been comfort eating for several months. She's trying to get a job and finding it very stressful.' The girl's emotional state was not for now and I simply explained, over again, the immediate first aid requirements and to ring again if things didn't settle down during the morrow.

At five-forty five I was dozing in a chair. The phone – yet again. It was one of the butchers from the factory slaughterhouse. He, too, had diarrhoea and was seeking authority not to start his shift at six. It was very obvious that he shouldn't, but he wanted to be able to quote me and, if the management 'got heavy', could he get a 'sustificate' from me? He was followed by two of his mates, each, effectively, with the same request. Any more, I thought, and there would be a significant number of pigs given a stay of execution. Then, immediately on putting down the phone it rang once more. It was Mrs. St. Clair. She was in a very emotional state. 'Doctor. At last. I've been trying to get through. It's a boy.'

'What *do* you mean?'

'My daughter, doctor. She's had a baby boy. I've just helped him into the world. I don't know what to do now. What do I do with the cord? Oh, and I think you should know – she's bleeding a bit.'

I was more wide-awake that I'd been for a week. Her diarrhoea must have been the waters breaking and the pains those of uterine contractions.

'OK, Mrs. St. Clair, is the baby breathing?' In fact, I could now hear a baby crying.

'He's on the bed, doctor – he's all wet and sticky.'

'OK, well, just wrap him up in a dry bath towel leaving his face clear and lie him on one side. I can be with you in about five minutes. In the meantime leave the cord and boil some water for me. Can I just check your address again?'

I rushed upstairs and apologised for waking my wife. 'Have to fly. We've just had an unexpected delivery and I don't mean from Amazon.' I reconnected the upstairs phone and dashed. Seven minutes later (I timed it) I was at the bungalow. The front door was open. The baby still crying. The cord was well contracted and pale. The new mother was bleeding, but not significantly. She had a small tear at the introitus. The placenta was still undelivered, the uterus well contracted and the baby warm; he looked like a term baby – I thought about seven pounds. It was time for a deep breath. I found some locking forceps, clamped the cord and cut it. I asked grandmother to put the baby on mother's chest. Nature did the rest. Slight tension on the dangling cord delivered the placenta. It was healthy-looking and whole. We put it in a glass trifle bowl – the least appetising dessert for many a year.

We all relaxed; flopped backwards into a chair in the case of Mrs. St. Clair. 'What a night' she gasped. 'Thank you for coming so quickly, doctor. I can't believe it. What on earth is my husband going to say. He's on nights this week. When he went to work at 10 he was a dad. When he gets in he'll be a granddad. Just as well he likes children.'

It was time for the cavalry. I rang the duty midwife and explained that none of us had known of this pregnancy except the new mother. It was a booking that hadn't been booked! She said she could be with us in about 15 minutes. The good news – as I announced to everyone – was that she hadn't been to the hog roast.

~

Cows that go mad: a Tale in three parts

PART 1: CHATTING OVER A DRINK IN THE MID-EIGHTIES

We were guests at the annual Mayor-Making, the newly elected incumbent being a good friend. We'd never had a cross word by dint of never talking politics. We were introduced to Angus, the agricultural correspondent of the main regional newspaper, the Western Daily Doings (or something like that, I didn't quite catch it). Since I couldn't, ethically, talk in detail about my job, we learned a lot about his.

Angus had spent the last few weeks visiting dairy farms across the area and had a fascinating tale to tell. Panicky farmers had been phoning their vets for urgent help. Among their herds they had noticed that some cows were losing weight, and their milk yields dropping off. The same animals also seemed disorientated, no longer knowing the herdsman, unwilling to follow the herd to the farm for milking and then losing their way in the milking parlour. They could be aggressive and, most alarmingly, could stagger and slip as if on (non-existent) ice. If they fell, they were unable to get back up. Angus had written a long article for his paper entitled 'Cows that go mad'. I remember saying, rashly, that whatever the cause of this bizarre neurological complaint in these cattle, it was surely unlikely to spread across species and certainly not to humans. Angus frowned:

'Well, I don't know about you, Norman, but I take milk in my tea and on my cereal and I love a juicy steak. Perhaps our vegan friends are on to something after all.'

PART 2: READING OVER COFFEE IN THE EARLY NINETIES

Although it may be widely assumed that doctors regularly read scientific journals it is probably exceptional behaviour, certainly among general practitioners. But occasionally a journalistic article, second-hand perhaps, but more user-friendly, will grab the attention. I remember being engrossed by just such an item. It reported on growing evidence that 'mad cow disease', as it was now called, had spread to humans. I suppose this was about five or six years after talking to Angus. I was horrified – perhaps he'd been right to be pessimistic. The testimony was convincing – recycling bovine meat and bone meal into cattle feed had been policy from the early

1980s. Such cannibalistic practice resulted in cattle consuming food that contained bovine neurological tissue. It had been fed to beasts with more regard to economics than to risk of disease for it could be contaminated with something called a prion protein. This renegade molecule, that distorts and effectively destroys other proteins was, by now, known to be the causal agent in mad cow disease.

Then somewhat slack abattoir routines (allowing cattle brain and spinal cord – despite their prohibition - into processed meats) had allowed these pesky prions to piggy-back into the human food chain, hiding in burgers and the like. Cases of what were called 'new-variant Creutzfeld-Jacob Disease' (human version of mad cow disease) appeared during 1986. And by 1996 there was even clinching experimental evidence: contaminated cattle nerve tissue fed to Macaque monkeys (primates like us) resulted in a simian version of the disease.

PART 3: DEALING WITH A TRAGEDY IN THE LATE NINETIES

One of my partners – Celia – was about to take her main annual holiday. As customary, she had prepared a brief hand-over list so that the rest of us could carry on the active care of her seriously ill patients as seamlessly as possible. But she came to see me, personally, about Julian.

I already knew something of Julian's unique tragedy. He was 21 and, if he hadn't become ill, this would have been the summer of his graduation from Oxford University. But during the long vacation from his studies, the previous summer, his parents had watched, aghast, as he began to display very odd quirks in his behaviour and lapses in his memory. Among other peculiarities, he would forget to put shoes on when going out, omit to lift the lid on the toilet when peeing, repeatedly confuse knife and fork at the table and get very angry when reminded to undress when going to bed. At first his parents suspected that Julian was abusing some drug or other – after all he was a student and a chemist to boot but when, to their horror they tracked down an awful smell to a dollop of faeces in his coat pocket, they sought Celia's advice.

At first, Celia could hardly believe that someone of such high intellect and barely out of their teens could be dementing. But that's what it seemed to be. An urgent referral to a neurologist brought no immediate result. But after a month of very obvious further decline in Julian's health – he now had a Parkinsonian tremor and gait - a personal call to the Neurology Registrar on call produced a next-day out-patient appointment. An MRI scan shocked the radiologists. Julian's brain was grossly disordered and full of holes like a worn sponge. He had Creutzfeld-Jacob disease. Probably, they felt, the new variant, the colonizing prion proteins originating in contaminated meat containing (as it shouldn't) neurological tissue from slaughtered cattle. Now humans were 'going mad'.

Celia told me all this in quite a troubled state. She was almost upset to be going on holiday at this point. She had developed a deep relationship with Julian's parents and I thought she was helped, personally, by being able to tell me the story in such detail – a kind of abreaction. Most distressing was the fact that Julian was now very close to death – in the nursing home in town. He had pneumonia and since he'd been in a coma for some weeks, it was not being treated specifically. Did I mind taking over? I would inevitably meet his parents – they were constantly at the bedside - and they already understood that Julian's death would need to be reported to the Coroner and that there would probably be an inquest.

'Finally,' Celia added 'I've also left a message that the undertakers must follow the present government guidelines on the handling of bodies such as Julian's. Oh, and lastly, your friend who is Mayor again has been extremely helpful and you might thank him from me when you next see him. He banged heads together at Social Services and at the hospital so that Julian could be brought back to die in the community. That, at least, has made it easier for his poor parents.'

~

En Passant

If a weekend on duty for the practice was a long, dark tunnel, the gloomiest time was surely teatime on Sunday afternoon; 30 hours in but 30 more to go. Arthur didn't have this perspective but for some reason it was always the time he chose to ring.

'Is that the doctor?'

'Yes.'

'I've decided to kill myself. I think you know me, and you know I mean it.'

This was the typical opening gambit in what, to me, always felt like a game of psychiatric chess.

'I'm going to finish it all today. I'm 55 next week and there's no point in living any more.'

1.   *White: King's Pawn to E4*

'Is this a sudden decision because of something that has happened?'

2.   *Black: King's Pawn to E5*

'No, but today's the day.'

3.   *White: Queen's Knight to C3*

'Have you spoken to anyone in your family about this?'

4.   *Black: Queen's Pawn to D6*

'I don't have any family – none that will speak to me.'

5.   *White: King's Bishop Pawn to F3*

'Well, it's difficult for me, on call for many patients, to talk to you at any length. Have you thought of calling The Samaritans?'

6.   *Black: King's Bishop Pawn to F5*

'I've done that – they're useless.'

7.   *White: Pawn E4 X black Pawn F5*

'I think you've told me before, though, that you have a community psychiatric nurse.'

8.   *Black: Queen's Bishop X white Pawn F5*

'He's not around today and anyway he always tells me there's no point in making gestures, in crying wolf – but this time I mean it.'
9. *White: King's Knight Pawn to G4*

'And there's no-one else you can talk to – no friends or neighbours for instance?'
10. *Black: Queen to F6*

'No. No-one. You sound as though you'd rather I just went away and got on with taking my life.'
11. *White: Knight C3 to D5*

'Well, that's not really fair, but I don't think I can do very much except explore with you how you might get some human support. Do you want me to come and see you briefly?'
12. *Black: Queen to E6*

'I'm not at home.'
13. *White: Knight D5 X Pawn C7. CHECK*

'Well, where are you?'
14. *Black: King to D8*

'That's no business of yours.'
15. *White: Knight C7 X black Queen E6*

'Are you taking any medication – are you taking it properly?'
16. *Black: Bishop F5 X white Knight E6*

'Yes, all sorts – and they're all useless.'
17. *White: Queen's Pawn to D3*

'Do you know any of the drug names?'
18. *Black: King's Knight to F6*

'If you're thinking of telling me to take more bloody pills, forget it.'
19. *White: Pawn F3 to F4*

'You seem to be quite aggressive. Perhaps you're less depressed than you think. There must be some purpose in your life, some sort of ambition?'
20. *Black: Knight F6 X white Pawn G4*

'No. Nothing. My life's no use to me or to anyone else.'
21.   *White: King's Bishop to E2*

'Well, I really can't stop you harming yourself under these circumstances and we're blocking the emergency phone line. Who is your community nurse – I can talk to him tomorrow and make him aware of your crisis.'
22.   *Black: Pawn E5 X white Pawn F4*

'So, I have a crisis but I'm not an emergency. Thanks, pal.'
23.   *White: Queen's Bishop X black Pawn F4*

'Look, I'll ring your nurse tomorrow – there must be a contact number in your notes.'
24.   *Black: Queen's Knight to C6*

'I've told you, time and again, I won't be around tomorrow.'
25.   *White: Bishop E2 X black Knight G4*

The phone clicked off. Sooner or later it usually did. I sat down to make some summary notes that could be copied into Arthur's medical record the next day and stuck on a post-it to remind me to ring his nurse. This verbal Fischer/Kasparov duel repeated itself during odd duty weekends over a year or two. My partners had similar experiences. We began to assume that Arthur also saw it as a kind of game if not chess. Although we all knew that late middle age is a high-risk time for suicide in men, we settled on the opinion that each of his calls was a 'crie de coeur' made when he knew we would be pretty much unable to help. One partner saw the behaviour as a form of sadism, of doctor-baiting. Another saw it as severe 'crying wolf' syndrome and that Arthur would come to regret it. But, finally, the 'coffee cups consensus' was to do nothing skilfully – to be physicians.

In fact, we found the frequency of Arthur's Sunday teatime calls abated. For some months his name did not appear on the weekend incidents board. It therefore came as something of a shock to hear that he had, on a fine Sunday afternoon, gone to Bristol; to Clifton. He had walked out onto the Suspension Bridge, clambered up the railings and protective grid, and jumped.

Checkmate

Not a one-act play

I was the junior in the room when we interviewed Jonas, our then senior partner having decided to retire early. Jonas was an obvious winner for our short-list having finally decided against a career in paediatrics and with a very impressive curriculum vitae. But there was also an elephant in the room. He was 32 and still single. He himself broke the tension. He had, in fact, been engaged to be married. It was while he was doing his 'obs and gyny' house job that his fiancée had called off the wedding, the near-impossible demands of his career finally convincing her that she could not be a medical wife. We listened to his story in deepest silence. We had all been through the dark tunnel where medical reality pulled relationships to near breaking point. And perhaps our joint sympathies gave Jonas the edge and a unanimous 'thumbs-up'. We took it for granted that we'd be able to find Jonas a suitable lodging with some kind soul who wouldn't mind answering the telephone evenings and nights, perhaps several times, up to three times a week and throughout every fourth weekend. After all, our wives did.

Jonas threw himself into the practice, side-stepping with slick diplomacy all the idiosyncrasies of his predecessor without upsetting too many of the long-standing and demanding 'list' that he inherited. He coped well with the introverts, entertained the elderly and had enviable skills with children. By a coincidence that no-one really noticed at the time, the practice was also endowed with a new health visitor. We had the pleasure of getting to know someone who was affable, knowledgeable, efficient and popular. What's more she stayed. Pam, like Jonas, was a significant asset to the practice. The sad fact that she had been a polio victim in childhood and wore a knee-ankle leg brace seemed to be no drawback whatsoever. In fact, the more psychologically orientated among us mused, over coffee, that it gave her a massive edge in empathy.

Three years later, Jonas went, on a bank holiday afternoon, to meet his parents off a train at Chippenham. And there he bumped into Pam – waiting for her widowed mother off the same train. Just as they acknowledged each other there was a tinny announcement that the train was 15 minutes late. It was greeted by an audible groan and Pam and Jonas, in their mutual disappointment, fell into conversation. Into a conversation that didn't, for the first time ever, involve patients, drugs, development issues or social disadvantage. The chat bounced along and they found they had much in common over and above a late train. Jonas hadn't known that Pam was a bellringer (as he had been before going to medical school). As she said, 'it's the one physical activity where a withered leg is irrelevant' and they laughed together. A further ten-minute delay – 'works on the line' – shot by and ended with Jonas, much to his own surprise, inviting Pam to join him for a meal. He had in mind a country pub – 'it's a great place and miles from the practice.' Pam happily accepted – not too 'eagerly' she hoped. As everyone at the surgery and a host of busybodies were to say, later, it was 'Brief Encounter' but with a happy ending.

Pam and Jonas became engaged – to everyone's delight – and the whole practice including the caretaker and his wife (who did phone duty for Jonas) was invited to the wedding. We closed the surgery for the big day. The other practice very kindly covered us for emergencies (for a 'reasonable' price). The marriage and the reception were a wonderfully enjoyable occasion. 'Confirmed bachelor' Jonas and 'totally dedicated' Pam seemed blissfully happy as we saw them off on honeymoon – at Chippenham Station. Of course.

It took only a few months before Jonas sheepishly announced to us across our early morning post that Pam was expecting. Letters flew up in the air. There hadn't been a 'practice' pregnancy for several years and this would cause such excitement. Someone said, 'yea, a bonus for Jonas' and we all squealed. All went well in the pregnancy and there was cake and bubbly at teatime on the afternoon that Pam had her section and was delivered of a little girl. In a different era there would have been cigars. Jonas seemed to cope well with more sleepless nights than usual but was glad to report that, at six months, baby Clare was now only waking once at night – for a feed. She was developing normally and there was much joyous cooing in the office when Pam brought her in for her immunisations. The 'practice' union had produced the 'practice' baby.

A dark, wet, early morning a few weeks later Jonas was out 'on a call.' It was sevenish and just getting light as he drove home. Turning into the drive he lurched to a halt. Pam was standing in the rain, in her nightdress, rocking the baby. He leapt out of the car.

'What on earth are you doing, dear?'

'She's gone, Jonas. She's gone.'

The wet baby was cold to the touch. Jonas couldn't speak. They stood in the rain holding each other, the dead baby between them. Then something remotely rational took over. Jonas pushed Pam into the house and wrenched Clare from her. He lay her on the kitchen table and began to remove the wet clothes. Pam was right. There were absolutely no signs of life. The pupils were widely dilated and fixed.

'It's no good Jonas. She's gone. Her voice was breaking. 'I went to her when I got up and I knew she was dead the moment I saw her. You couldn't have done anything even if you'd been here. Did you check her on the way out?'

'No, I didn't. I didn't want to wake her.'

'Well, you couldn't have anyway, could you?'

They both collapsed into kitchen chairs, sobbing uncontrollably, the little body between them on the table. Pam was first to speak. 'We've had a cot death, haven't we? Us, of all people.'

Jonas just nodded. The phone rang and they both flinched. They just looked at each other while the insistent noise continued. Jonas couldn't face answering it and it eventually stopped. Silently and slowly, Jonas went to the receiver and Pam heard him trying to talk coherently to Bob, the senior partner. Bob was with them within ten minutes and all his many years of toughening experiences were hardly enough for him to cope with this close-to-home disaster.

The shock wave of that morning's discovery was devastating. The staff spent all day drying their tears and when word got out into the community a surprising number of patients cancelled their appointments. A tragedy such as this may not have cured their ills, but it certainly put them into a different perspective.

If Jonas and Pam's wedding had been an impossibly happy occasion, Clare's funeral was just impossible. Tiny coffins give colossal grief. Jonas returned to work after a fortnight but he couldn't cope. He could break off in the middle of consultations and just stare out of the window in a fugue. His appointment schedules drifted. Patients realised, at the pharmacy, that he hadn't completed their prescriptions and he even overlooked some hospital referrals. One patient asked to see our practice manager and said that, in his opinion as an HR executive, Jonas should not be at work. It got worse. Jonas began failing to turn up for work and finally, and very distressingly, resigned from the partnership. Pam had never returned to her job. She knew she would find it impossible to face working with babies and children and we all understood.

Jonas and Pam moved away. News got back to us that they were running a nursing home in Norfolk – anything removed from children one heartless wag commented. Contact was maintained only by reassuring Christmas cards – we would recognise Jonas' handwriting and there was usually some cheering anecdote. Then, one year the Norwich postmark was joined to Pam's hand. Sinister? It was. Jonas had been diagnosed with male breast cancer just after New Year. There were already secondary deposits of tumour when he had realised that there was something amiss. He had died in November aged only 48. 'Brief Encounter' did have a sad ending after all.

∼

6
PERSONAL PERSPECTIVE

Miss Harris and Miss Harries

I hadn't been in the practice for more than a few weeks, a neophyte trying to find my feet. I remember the visiting list I was given that morning because of its peculiarity. Would I visit Miss Harris at 14, The Glebe. She was giddy. And would I visit a Miss Harries about her feet – at the same address. No, the receptionist told me, there was no spelling mistake, the two names were different. Miss Harries let me in. The Welsh lilt was immediately apparent.

Miss Harris (of the same cadence) had been suffering from a spinning sensation, on and off, for about three days and had been nauseous at times. She had learned, very quickly, not to turn her head other than very slowly. She'd never had such trouble before and had a blameless health history otherwise. She knew what I meant by tinnitus and hadn't experienced it. I thought she probably had benign positional vertigo, usually a self-limiting condition. But being anxious not to miss anything I performed a very detailed neurological examination including tickling the bottoms of her feet to assess the Babinski reflex. I think she found my thoroughness slightly irritating and pointedly moved my patella hammer off a pile of ironing when I parked it there. Finally, I thought it safe to advise her that her symptoms would all settle down – that she hadn't suffered any sort of stroke. She seemed more alarmed than reassured. Perhaps it would have been more diplomatic not to have verbalised what she probably dreaded. When I offered to prescribe some tablets that would help her symptoms although they might make her drowsy, she declined.

'Thank you, but no, doctor, thank you.' in what I took to be Welsh syntax.

I turned to Miss Harries. I didn't like to comment on the similarity in their names – the staff at the surgery would be sure to know more. She apologised for bothering me but thought that I would be glad not to have her clogging up my surgery with minor problems. She sat and took off her shoes. Two of the toes on her right foot showed severe hammer deformity – they were bent up to a right angle in the middle and fixed. There were nasty corns on their peaks. They certainly must have been very painful at times.

'You see, I can only just get into my right shoe and I would hate to have to wear those bulbous orthopaedic boots that one sees.'

She denied ever wearing high-heeled or sharply pointed shoes – 'Oh, doctor, would I ever?'

I promised to refer her to an orthopaedic surgeon. At least only one of my two patients had taken an inordinate amount of time.

Back at the surgery in early afternoon the first person I bumped into, in the corridor from the car park, was the senior partner.

'Well, how's it going young man?'

He apologised for asking and hoped that, without breaking any ethical boundaries, I could put him in the picture regards the health of Gwyneth Harris, a very old friend. I reassured him that there was nothing wrong that might carry any long-term significance.

'Thank goodness' he said 'she's more than a family friend, really. She and her sister do all our ironing.'

'Oh, the pile of ironing was yours, then. Ah, in fact I should have recognised that shirt on the top – I've seen you wearing it. Why didn't I think at the time?'

'Well, you were being a GP and not a journalist or private detective. As time goes by your antennae with sharpen up.'

'You say they're sisters? But their surnames are different. To be honest I wondered if they were . . . '

'No, certainly not. They're not Offa's dykes if that's what you were suspecting. No, they're not even ladies who lunch. They really are sisters. Gwyneth dropped the 'e' in the family name many years ago. When the two of them bought their bungalow and began living together they found it annoying and sometimes embarrassing not knowing whose post was whose. Gwyn was a junior schoolteacher and Gwen the needlework mistress at the Secondary Modern. They both enjoy taking in ironing and any clothing repairs or adjustments. You should remember that as your waistline gets bigger – which it will!'

'OK, thanks for the gen, it's good to know. I suppose that in thirty years' time I'll be passing on equally useful information to the latest greenhorn?'

'Well, that's something to look forward to. Incidentally, to give you yet more background, Gwyn and Gwen are sad examples of a whole generation of women who, during their youth, in the thirties, suffered from a serious shortage of manhood – all killed in the Great War. And on top of that they're from Aberfan and lost two great nephews in the terrible disaster there.'

'Wow – sociology and history.'

'No, just good general practice, young man.'

~

195

Sidelined

A day of machine-gun medicine was nearing its end on what had been a hot, sultry afternoon, even with the window open. Bill Dorman was an old friend who was having three monthly hormone implants into his abdominal wall after surgery for prostate cancer. He handed me the Zoladex box; the chemical pellet and hefty trochar in its sealed package. He knew the routine and, almost before I invited him to, he was heading for the examination side-room where he would undress and lie down, waiting for me to fetch some swabs, skin cleanser and local anaesthetic. But just as he was leaving the room my phone rang. Bill signalled that he would go next door as bidden and I nodded, the phone receiver in my hand. The call was reasonably urgent but ended with my only having to give advice. I then, by reflex almost, pressed the bell for the next patient and found myself Swiss-rolled into a tortuous consultation that sent the minute hand of the clock spinning. Then, as the patient left, my trainee, Mike, appeared in the threshold, asking if I would mind looking at a mysterious skin rash. We took off in the direction of his patient, conferring, in the corridor, on the history and his findings. On examining his patient I was able to diagnose a 'tinea versicolor' and Mike and I discussed the necessary treatment, a shampoo to kill the harmless skin fungus, and put the patient in the picture with some reassurance. Mike said he would re-read his I-Spy book of rashes that evening and I agreed to show him any similar cases that I might find. I returned to my room and, resuming autopilot, pressed the buzzer for the next patient. It was someone with a simple enough administrative matter requiring my signature that could well have been left at the desk for my attention but never mind. It allowed me to chase the clock and I sent for my last patient almost eagerly. Last consultation over, I strolled up to the office and, having checked the phone log, sat down to sign some prescriptions and sort some letters for filing. Then one of the receptionists came across and asked what had happened to Mr. Dorman – he normally called at the desk on his way out to arrange his next appointment. I leapt in the chair like someone stung by a wasp.

'My goodness, he's still in my side-room' I spluttered. How on earth was I going to apologise sufficiently – how was he going to take my stupid neglect? There was nothing for it – I would have to play this one with a very straight bat and be entirely honest and hope that he took it in good heart. All this was racing through my mind as I virtually ran down the corridor, kidney bowl of necessities in my hand.

Bill was fast asleep on the couch, snoring softly. In fact it took a couple of shakes to wake him.

'Oh' he said 'I'm so sorry, Doc, I must have nodded off. I hope I haven't kept you waiting?'

My gaffe had the staff quietly amused for some days. I didn't mind, in the least, them referring to me as 'Dr. Dement' but I had to issue a gentle rebuff when I discovered that Bill had been nicknamed 'Mr. Dormouse.' In our small, tightly knit community such a moniker would always, somehow, go public and eventually cause offence, however apt and harmless.

~

Terrorists

Whenever Dawn Packer brought her children to the surgery, we were on a war footing. Aged six, four, three and a babe in arms (there was always a babe in arms) they created mayhem. They would charge up and down the waiting room, swerving in and out of the chairs, bang on the aquarium, pull magazines onto the floor and disrupt any 'how long have you been waiting' conversations by shouting and shrieking to each other. Dawn would sit with the baby, seemingly oblivious to the anarchy and few patients felt it their job to discipline the kids although they might protest on any impact. None of the staff could remember anyone complaining if it was suggested that Dawn be sent ahead of her turn.

More worrying was the havoc the children could create in the consulting room. If the tribal name appeared on the appointments list it was time to put things away – and not in any drawer the children could access. Last time one of them was unwell – and Dawn brought them all with her as usual – the disposable paper sheet on the exam couch was dragged onto the floor and the older boy rolled himself up in it. His brother tried to join in and I listened to the baby's chest to the accompaniment of tearing paper and screeching sibling rivalry. The other child, meanwhile, had crawled to the far side of my desk and was pulling on wires. I watched as my phone shimmied across the desk and cascaded into the wastepaper basket. I had suggested to Dawn, on previous occasions, that she leave at least some of her brood with relatives or friends when coming to the surgery but she said they were too busy. I suspect they made sure they were.

On this occasion it was clear enough that the baby had only a mild upper respiratory infection. No specific treatment was needed and Dawn said she had some infant Calpol. I was relieved not to have to issue medication. Handing over a prescription to her was a test of one's reflexes. The two older boys had invented a new sport – prescription grabbing. The flimsy usually became torn as we, and they, fought over it. I once had to issue three forms in succession before Dawn had managed to secrete one, whole, in her handbag. Admonishing the children obeyed the law of diminishing returns – on skates. Their transient look of astonishment rapidly turned into no reaction at all. The only tactic that really helped was to get through the consultation with express speed – maintaining some order was a function of time, just as in the waiting room.

Perhaps the most serious trouble came when the practice was computerised. Now the children had a keyboard to molest. Keeping them away from it and being a mouse guardian was vaguely amusing the first couple of times but then palled. And with only primitive knowledge of 'Windows', if they did manage to reach the keys and tabs, restoring the program could require an unscheduled coffee break while the practice manager performed the magic. On the last occasion that Dawn brought in the children she herself was unwell 'down below.' The practice nurse came in to be a chaperone but her more vital function was to babysit. It was an impossible task. After I'd examined Dawn I threw back the curtain to see her three-year old daughter ramming a used rubber glove into her mouth – 'jelly' she said. 'Oh, no,' we said in unison.

Now, today, the familiar name was on the list again. I spent some time hiding everything that wasn't bolted down, clearing the exam couch, taking out the clinical bin and the wastepaper basket and tying up high the strings on the venetian blind (just waiting to be yanked, I always thought). The door opened and Dawn's three older children came in. They stood against the wall and watched their mother come through the door. She was followed by a young man I'd never seen before. Introduced as 'Bob, my new friend' he took the second chair on my bidding. I watched, open-mouthed, as the three older children gathered round him. He opened a book and began whispering a story to them as I took a history from Dawn and examined her baby in virtual silence. The clinical needs were soon met and I sat back in my chair, still amazed by the profound changes in the children's behaviour.

'The kids love Bob more than me' Dawn said.

'He takes an interest in them.'

∼

Moving Day

Occasionally, in the life of a general practice there will be a red-letter day – a move to new premises. Usually positive, the upheaval will be worth the effort; particularly if the new home has been purpose-built and immediately eliminates the everyday frustrations of working in an outdated or overcrowded building. Such fundamental reorganisations do not come about spontaneously. It will have taken a great deal of time and effort to get to this point and moving day, of itself, presents massive obstacles.

Our practice decided to move – it was only about 400 yards by a drone flight to our new premises – on a Friday before a non-bank holiday weekend. We would hold no surgeries or clinics that day while one partner would man an emergency phone line, initially at the old premises and then, from about midday, from the new surgery. BT confirmed the feasibility of the plan and would redirect the line on our instruction. We all hoped that the information leaflet that we sent out to every practice household would lead patients to understand that any true emergencies would be attended to should they arise – rather like the back-up arrangements on a regular Sunday. We specified that we would not be able to issue repeat prescriptions, make formal appointments or handle any bureaucratic paperwork that day.

The random feedback – mostly comments to our receptionists – was totally positive. Our patients, it seemed, were as excited by the move as we were. However, all general practitioners will tell you that a minority of patients regard 'their' doctor as forever available, absolutely certain that he or she will be wholly fascinated by their current distress and delighted to issue immediate advice or a prescription whether he or she be shopping, stuck in traffic, standing at a urinal, attending a Nativity Play, digging potatoes, or fishing from a boat on a lake.

John and Derek, two of the partners in the practice, had volunteered to take charge of moving all the patient records; it was thought best not to leave these to the professional removers. It was as they were carrying out the third heavy box of notes early that morning that they were accosted. A Mrs. Gardner, one of John's 'regulars' appeared from nowhere and said she wanted to talk about her husband. He was having one of his 'bad chest' days and she really wanted him visited at home as soon as possible. John was supremely diplomatic and, even while supporting a loaded box, listened her out. He then moved his head in a way that indicated that he was hardly in a position to help her and pointed out that one of the other doctors was seeing all patients during the day. It was as if she didn't understand the situation; she appeared unresponsive to body language, verbal communication or any such combination. She repeated her request, adding that she was sure that John 'wouldn't mind' having a 'break' from moving the surgery to see her 'very sick' husband. In turn, Derek then tried explaining the circumstances to her and that they had to finish the moving exercise within the day but to no purpose. Mrs. Gardner followed them out to the car park where there was a stand-off but eventually John said that he, himself, would go and speak to the duty doctor and arrange for him see her, take a proper medical history and give considered advice. She just stared straight ahead, obviously very unhappy to be rebuffed.

Eventually the van was fully loaded and John and Derek headed off to the new surgery. It was in the new car park and as they were unloading the boxes that Mrs. Gardner reappeared – like a persistent wasp. Again she accosted John – standing very close to him to be sure of his attention. The duty doctor had been prepared, it seems, to visit Mr. Gardner but had seen no need to rush immediately to his bedside.

'But then', she said, 'he doesn't know my husband's condition as you do, doctor.'

John, with exemplary patience, allowed her to repeat, specifically, her husband's current symptoms and said that, on the face of it, the duty doctor had made a very reasonable assessment – that it really wasn't an impelling emergency.

'But the duty doctor did say that he would visit sometime today, did he not?'

Mrs. Gardner just pulled a face and shrugged. The two doctors were now carrying boxes into the new reception area – the two of them doing the heavy lifting and Mrs. Gardner following, backwards and forwards, like a diligent sheep dog, trying gambit after gambit to extend the conversation. Eventually Derek felt that he should intervene once more and put it bluntly that a house call during the day would definitely be made and, for the moment, that was that. He then turned to lift yet another box from the van.

'Well,' Mrs. Gardner said, 'could it at least be before two o'clock? I want to go out this afternoon – there's bingo at the Conservative Club.'

The two partners held their breath long enough for Mrs. Gardner to be out of hearing, put down the boxes, and then let out a joint stifled scream.

~

Itadob?

The motive may be entirely selfish, but I have always ensured that the title 'doctor' does not appear on my passport. Being consulted ardently across the dinner table on a cruise is not a welcome experience if you're not the ship's doctor. And, even then, it could hardly be the time and place. However, some people think that you'll be fascinated by the boil on their kneecap. They may even bare their leg and plonk it on the table. Not that any of us in the caring professions wouldn't do their utmost to help someone in dire difficulty. In essence, I think it perfectly reasonable that as immediate threat to life goes down our professional reticence should go up. But being an airline passenger puts one on the spot. When the dreaded plea is announced – 'is there a doctor on board (ITADOB?)' – medic passengers have a heartsink moment. You can't know what you're letting yourself in for. Even if one is a superspecialist of the most esoteric liver disease, you're going to have to be a GP.

We were on our way to Singapore, halfway house to New Zealand. A long-planned holiday for our nuclear family of four. It was an overnight flight. We were towards the front of the economy class cabin. Dinner had been served with a drink or two and the detritus cleared away. Some of us had managed to find a half-decent film but by midnight (UK time) lights were going out and the roar of the engines was the only noise. Some passengers seem to manage it easily, but most of us find going to sleep sitting up unnatural and difficult. If and when success comes, it's its own reward.

ITADOB woke us all. I pretended not to hear it. I didn't want to hear it. Surely, I had dreamt it? But my conscience was strapped into the seat next to me and, quite rightly, she nudged me in the ribs. I released my safety strap and stood up. I did not feel like, nor, I'm sure, look like a knight in shining armour but several crew appeared as if from nowhere. I looked across the cabin. No other doctors – at least no honest ones. I was on my own. Escorted to the very back of the cabin I found other crew looking at a form on the floor behind the rearmost row of seats. Two of them were kneeling alongside a large male passenger who appeared to be unconscious. A male steward whispered the story to me. He and other crew – working in the rear galley – had seen the man staggering down the aisle and then trying to access one of the toilets. He didn't seem to be able to open the door, not realising that one pushes centrally and that it folds open. He then tried another door and then gave up. He turned into the corner by the emergency door and in the words of the steward, 'opened himself up' and began to pee on the floor. Before any crew could stop him he then just folded and fell backwards, unconscious.

The man was lying in a sizeable wet patch which had spread beyond the blanket someone had thrown over his exposed private part. I asked for someone to go to try to find any accompanying passenger or family for us to know more about him as I checked him over. He was supine and snorting. I didn't have a torch, but I thought his pupils were normal. He stank of alcohol. When I pressed hard on his shin he made a positive withdraw and moaned. He was not out very deeply. When I tried to turn him over he reacted and I realised he was about to vomit. Two crew helped me when I gesticulated and we just about got him onto his side before his stomach contents spewed out onto the carpet. The vomitus was probably 30% proof. A steward in a different uniform that I took to symbolise seniority now knelt alongside me to tell me that he had spoken to the patient's wife. She hadn't been worried about her missing husband and he thought she, too, was drunk. But she was able to tell him that Ian was a plasterer, usually in good health. They were from Tewkesbury in the UK. They were emigrating to Australia and had been to a party with all his workmates at the airport terminal. The whole shebang had travelled to Heathrow in a works van to give the couple a proper send off. You couldn't make it up – a plastered plasterer. Now there was some turbulence to add to our difficulties and in one violent lurch I reached down to steady myself and put my hand in the puke. At least it was still warm.

After a further check on life signs, I was happy to suggest that the crew leave Ian to sleep off his toxins lying on his left side on the floor, even with the turbulence. Perhaps after an hour or so, or if he became belligerent, then to take him back to his seat, make sure he was belted in and allow him nothing but water. They took me back to the galley, helped me clean up and gave me a welcome cold orange juice. They were a lot happier than when I'd first arrived on scene.

Back at my seat my wife lifted her mask: 'anything serious?'

'No, just a drunk from Pukesbury. Sorry, Tewkesbury. No, pukesbury is better. All pee and vomit.'

'Well, I hope you can get some sleep now. Aren't you glad that you've such a glamorous job. That decade of training was really worthwhile after all. Good night, dear.'

I couldn't sleep for, perhaps, half an hour. Then I drifted off. Some minutes later someone was gently shaking my shoulder. I opened my eyes on a three-crew delegation. The leader was in a very resplendent uniform. I guessed he was chief steward and from the first class cabin. One of the girls with him handed him a six-inch cubic box that was garishly decorated. Signalling me not to stand up he presented it to me and they all bowed. He then indicated that I should open it.

'On behalf of Singapore Airlines' he whispered 'in gratitude for your excellent care of our unfortunate passenger.'

The box contained four little bottles. They were essential oils.

'If you try that one, doctor. It's very good for helping you get to sleep. Just rub a little on your face.'

I almost pointed out that I had actually been asleep, but held my tongue. After the presentation party had dispersed, I tried the lavender oil that they had suggested. It didn't work. However, the strong scent woke my wife and we were both still awake when the lights went up for breakfast.

~

We've got one

It was Bastille Day in France and it was hot; very hot. Temperature records were being broken in Southern England by mid-morning. Poorly protected flesh was being exposed on a massive scale. But not everyone was storing up health problems for the future. Some were happening today, a Sunday. As duty doctor I was already driving to a village on the periphery of the practice. An acute asthma attack was relieved by a nebuliser session, which was interrupted by my bleep. I rang home. A garbled message had come in – an elderly man had 'passed out' in his cottage on the edge of town. I made my way there without delay, juggling with the hot steering wheel.

Several people were waiting for me at the address, among them Barbara, our retired (and revered) practice manager. 'It's Reg Paige', she told me – 'my gardener. A widower and a delightful man.' When he hadn't appeared that morning – he liked to water all her pot plants on a Sunday and then share a cup of tea – she had gone across to his cottage and tried to find him. She had no reply to her knocking, front or back, and he didn't answer his phone. Another neighbour had a key and they had found Reg – to some embarrassment – naked in his bath. He was unconscious.

He was certainly in the bath, he was just as nature had intended, and he was unrousable. The water was cold and clear. The soap was still in the tray and was dry. Reg must have had some sort of stroke while bathing early morning. There was no indication that he had slipped and hit his head. He must have passed out during his first indulgent soak. Fortunately, his head and therefore his airway was above the plimsoll line. But he was otherwise fully immersed. His pupils were small, he was breathing, albeit slowly, and his pulse was 60. I hunted down my low-reading thermometer. His body temperature (armpit) was 33 degrees centigrade. His core temperature would probably have been somewhat higher but he was certainly hypothermic.

I dialled for an urgent ambulance and, armed with his recent copy prescription, I rang the hospital. Midday was chiming somewhere in the cottage. Even in the old chalkstone structure it was distressingly hot and I found myself holding a clammy phone. I introduced myself and asked to speak to the duty house physician for medical admissions. The receptionist asked me the nature of the problem – quite standard practice. Without thinking I said 'hypothermia.' The receptionist presumably flicked a switch or put a hand over the mouthpiece but I distinctly heard her say, presumably to a colleague at the switchboard:

'We've got one – a hoax call. What shall I do with it? It's someone saying he's a doctor and he has a case of hypothermia.'

'What!'

'Yes, hypothermia, that's what he said.'

'What – today of all days! It can't be true.'

'Yes, I know, it's even hot in here with two fans going flat out.'

The receptionist returned to me without the inadequate muffling and asked me to repeat the details – 'did you really say hypothermia, doctor?'

This time there was a long silence. I began to think the line had been cut, that I'd been abandoned as a nuisance caller. Eventually, though, another female voice came on the phone. She asked me my full name, the name of our practice and the names of any two of my partners. I was in some sort of identity parade while my patient was freezing to death. As I explained the circumstances in detail I could almost hear a sigh of relief. She now introduced herself – she was the medical registrar on call. I was advised, quite rightly, not to attempt to warm up my patient too quickly and to transfer him as soon as was humanly possible – lightly wrapped and in the left lateral position. All this was second nature to me and rather condescending, but I thought it not the time to make a sarcastic remark. Barbara and I saw Reg into the ambulance and off down the road; bells and lights.

Sadly, Reg died at the end of the week. It was still exceptionally hot and I thought my partners would have tired of teasing me after the story had first unfurled. Fat chance. Even Barbara, I could imagine, was still smiling to herself as she watered her own plants.

~

When the weather closes in

Most winters in England are just dark and dank, the gloom occasionally interrupted by frost and, sometimes, flurries of bright snow. But even these rapidly turn to slush most times. But one winter in my mid-career brought, in the first weeks of a new year, heavy snow that fell for a long weekend while ambient temperature was well below 'brass monkey'. The snow was at least thigh-deep as the new working week approached. And up on the Downs a strong east wind blew the flakes hard against any obstacle – hedges, embankments, houses and any hapless farm animals left out.

On Monday morning the senior partner rang round proposing that we were to take no risks in trying to drive to the surgery – rather to walk in if it were feasible. And that house calls would be allocated geographically never mind personal lists or patient preferences. Living in a village only two miles from town and along a road that was being snowploughed and gritted, I did walk in to work – in wellies and skiing suit. In the event, few patients turned up at the surgery – everyone was snowed in. I therefore left the practice around 2.30 to be absolutely sure of being home before dark.

Soon after arriving the phone rang. It was the surgery. Ruth, a farmer's wife, had pleaded that someone try to get to their downland farm. Her husband had slipped in the yard and, she thought, dislocated his right shoulder. There was no way they could get him to accident and emergency in Swindon. If a tractor met the doctor at the main road, it should be possible to carry him and his bags across the fields to the farm. The lane, usually ensconced between high hedges was now a massive rampart of packed snow that would swallow up any vehicle. The senior receptionist saw me as the nearest 'Titus Oates' and was perfectly confident that I could reduce a simple dislocation! It was a very rash assessment. In a man in his late fifties the diagnosis could very easily be a fractured neck of humerus. Nonetheless I accepted the 'commission' and the telephone number.

I rang the farm after assessing the current state of the main road past our house. It appeared that I could, just about, get down our drive and that I might get up the hill to the lane junction. Mrs. Bye answered. 'It's so good of you to try to get to us, doctor. My husband is in so much pain. John, our son, thinks he can get across the fields to the main road junction in our big tractor and meet you there.'

'OK, Mrs. Bye, but you should know that I don't have snow chains or four-wheel drive. It's now 5.30 and John and I should agree that if we're not both at the junction by 6 we should head home. In which case I'll ring you as soon as its light in the morning.'

'Thanks again, doctor. I think that's a good idea. I hope you have a shovel and a blanket in the car?'

'Yes, I do. And my wife's making me some sandwiches and a flask of tea in case I get stuck but hopefully I'll be with you soon. Has your husband taken any painkillers?'

'No, but he had a very large brandy about an hour ago – he usually does at this time of day.'

'OK, but do you have any analgesic tablets there, of any sort?'

'Just a minute, doctor. Yes, I've found some Panadol Extras.'

'Right, give your husband three of them now, assuming he's no known allergies. They'll then be working at their peak if and when I get to you. But don't allow him any more brandy.'

There was only light snow as I set off into the darkness. I reached the junction of main road and farm track without incident but then made a big mistake. I braked too violently with the two near-side wheels on virgin snow and the offside pair on salted highway. I performed a handbrake turn without touching the handbrake. The steering wheel was wrenched out of my hands. Thankfully the vehicle came rest without hitting any obstruction or glissading into any deep drift. The adrenaline slowly subsided. A figure appeared alongside me and opened the car door.

'Smart driving, there, doc. You're facing the right way to get home now. I'm John, from the farm. Thanks for coming to see our casualty; Austin, our father.'

A large tractor was parked in a nearby field, its lights showing the way after we'd helped each other over a half-submerged gate. John put my medical bags in the tractor cabin and helped me up to stand on the drawbar and hang on to the mudguards. He insisted on me having his fur-lined gloves. I rang home on arrival at the farm so they knew that I was safe and warm and how to reach me. Now for the emergency farm kitchen orthopaedics. Normally when a human shoulder dislocates the knob on the top end of the upper arm bone slips backwards from its shallow socket which is on the outer aspect of the shoulder blade. One would think this would be easy enough to pull back into place, allowing for the momentary agony of the owner. But strong muscle spasm can make the manoeuvre very difficult especially without proper anaesthesia and I was secretly aware that I had failed on both my attempts as a junior casualty officer. Austin did have the features of a simple dislocation and he was adamant that I should 'try your darndest to pull the bugger back.' John braced his father's trunk against the back of a big Windsor chair and I put my right foot on the seat between his legs. I took his limp right arm at the elbow and yanked it forward horizontally. Austin let out a blood-curdling yell and then we both drew breath.

'Thanks, doc. You did it. I'll be able to salute you now whenever I see you.'

I tried to mask my surprise while folding his arm across his chest and supporting it by a crepe bandage around his neck. The euphoria was crowned by the appearance of brandy and glasses but I thought it wise to refuse. Just as well, for Mrs. Bye now began to tell me, apologetically, that there might be another patient. The wife of one of their labourers – not a patient of our practice – was expecting twins in her first pregnancy. She was 'something like six months gone' and had been unable to get to her ante-natal clinic because of the weather. The midwife had stressed that it was an important check-up and not to be missed.

'Would you mind, ever so much, doctor, popping across to the cottage and just checking that all's well?'

There was, of course, no question of refusal. Bad weather trumps any ethical niceties.

'As long as mother is willing to see me and can produce some urine, of course I'll look in while I'm here.'

Mrs. Goodson had all her ante-natal documents – what an asset in the circumstances. She was actually 32 weeks into the pregnancy and clearly carrying twins. Thankfully all was well and I updated her records. She herself had planned to phone the midwife the next day and I stressed that this was vital – if the weather didn't soon improve she might have to be hospitalised lest she develop a complication or go into premature labour so far from help.

Back to the farm. Mrs. Bye offered me a brandy 'just for the journey'. Again I refused. 'We thought you would, doctor, so here's a bottle for later. No, Austin insists – and so do I. John will look after it until you get to your car.'

I tried to drive home with full concentration but was distracted by the recollection that I was 'on call' overnight. Could be difficult. But on getting home there was good news. The senior partner had phoned to announce that since he lived at the 'bull's eye of the practice area' he would take any calls overnight.

'Ah, isn't that considerate. He's a born leader.'

'Yes' said my wife 'but he also said that you could make redress at your regular rota planning meeting.'

We both sank a large brandy with the sandwiches I'd brought home.

~

Party time

Despite only a minority of our nation professing to be active Christians, Christmas is now a time of universal revelry and over-indulgence; more Dionysus than Dickens. We would never be forgiven, as a medical practice, if we didn't arrange a Christmas party for our staff and they certainly deserve one. Traditionally – for us – invitations extended to family members, close friends and partners and, following the tradition in the military, the party is an opportunity for the partners to wait on and spoil the staff. On a Friday evening every December the partners descend on the waiting room as soon as clear of 'customers' and convert it to an outpost of bedlam. In come decorations, a tree, a sound system with massive speakers, trestle tables, chairs, table cloths, crockery, cutlery, serviettes and glasses and all is organised to leave a central space for the dreaded disco dancing. Festive food and drink arrives in huge quantities and we tidy ourselves up to greet our glad-ragged guests.

Notwithstanding the drum rolls, the bread rolls and the lager spills one sad individual in the partnership has to remain Salvation Army sober. He or she – the duty dog – may even be lucky enough to be thrown the odd morsel of food and passed a warm soft drink while they hover near the out-of-hours phone in order to hear it. Bring on the flaky feeling of being the only clear-headed clod within a hundred-yard circumference, all the time watching the accelerating evaporation of inhibitions and ballooning of egos. In rotation that dutiful canine was me. One Christmas party evening on duty was difficult to forget. Before things became too rampageous the phone rang. It was the wife of one of the local publicans. There was obviously also a loud shindig at her end and although I missed some of the conversation, I gathered that 'mein host' was not well. It didn't sound like 'brewer's measles'. He had collapsed onto the floor in the snug. He had 'heavy' chest pain and was a weird colour. He was someone we all knew – no, professionally – and a heart attack was, to be honest, overdue. I was on my way.

Tony was on the floor in the very narrow space behind the snug bar. His significant bulk made it difficult to move him and I was immediately concerned that the narrow confines would make any attempt at CPR completely impossible let alone be able to examine him properly. Eventually we manhandled him into the corridor between the lounge bar and the kitchens. Desperate guests in reindeer hats from the whoopee works outing in the restaurant were stepping over us to get to the toilets and plates of hot food were passing us the other way. In this friendly mayhem it was difficult to examine Tony effectively, but he did seem more comfortable sitting up and his pulse rate certainly dropped when I gave him some diamorphine. He was glad to see the ambulance crew arriving but not as pleased as I was. All the time, Tony's dedication to his calling was exemplary. He never stopped issuing orders to passing staff and cajoling his wife that the party must not be interrupted, nor the beer pumps allowed to run dry.

Back at the surgery there was some transient sympathy and another tepid drink. Then, shortly before eleven, I was dragged, kicking and screaming would be an exaggeration, but dragged certainly, onto the dance floor - to jive with the practice manager. She and I were of a generation that knew the movements, but our limbs were no longer up to it. There was cynical applause, non-rhythmic stamping of feet and jeering. Someone threw glitter over us. Thank goodness the phone rang again, and that someone heard it.

Once again, the caller was having to shout at me above saturnine noises off. Was the whole world having a party, I wondered? He seemed confused. There was an unconscious woman in his stairwell. He had phoned for an ambulance, but they had advised him to ring for a doctor – they were frantically busy and there would be a delay; surprise, surprise. When I asked for patient details there weren't any. No-one at the party knew her. Just the same, could I please come quickly. At least I had an address that made sense. As I drew up it was obvious that the party extended over two conjoined semi-detached houses. Here's one way to avoid your immediate neighbour complaining, I thought. The front door was wide open. I walked in. Someone blew a party horn in my face but not before I'd spotted an inert body at the foot of the stairs. I looked around for any familiar face, but no-one was interested in me or my function.

When I knelt over the unconscious woman, I realised who it was. It was a bit disconcerting to think that I could be the only person in the house (or houses I suppose) who knew her identity. Then someone tapped me on the shoulder – it was the man who had phoned me – the owner of the house. As I started to make some attempt at a neurological examination he explained. The woman had come to the party with one of his friends. They had had a very high decibel row and he'd left. She'd resorted to drinking spirits and had been seen coming down the stairs like a rag doll. We were then pushed aside by a couple trying to go up the stairs. As they climbed up 'he' was stroking 'her' bottom and they were giggling. I tried to concentrate.

I told the party host that at least I knew the patient's identity. She was called Helen, a single parent, and she would have to be hospitalised for observations. There was a large and worrying bruise over the rear of her skull. There could therefore be internal bleeding and her drunkenness was making any clinical observations unreliable. I also said I would call at Helen's home address on my way back across town – my best guess was that Helen's mother would be baby-sitting her two young girls. She needed to know what had happened and make arrangements to stay the night (general practice as social work). Then the ambulance arrived. I collected my things together and made to leave.

'Well, you can go back to your own party, now, doc.'

'Oh, I wasn't really at a party.'

'No? Not with all that glitter in your hair?'

~

Madge on a Monday

I'm very fond of the partners desk that used to be in my consulting room and which is now in our study at home. It was a generous good-luck gift from my practice predecessor. In oak, it has a gilt tooled leather top and ample drawer space. The only slight drawback when I was working was the overall size. It left only a narrow gap between the patient sitting to my right, at the side of the desk, and the examination couch. Getting past required a balletic sideways movement. The geographic consequence – that I was effectively trapped in my consulting room - never occurred to me until one gloomy Monday in mid-career. I can specify midway now, but it was nearly otherwise.

Madge Cunningham was the next patient listed on my evening surgery list. Tony, her husband, had recently died, in his mid-fifties, from an aggressive brain tumour. At the end, his deterioration was very rapid and in hospital. My condolence visit to the home the day before the funeral had not been easy. I didn't expect it to be. The grown-up children were there and though I'd never met them it was they who made conversation. I remember Madge being very reticent and I wasn't altogether surprised. I began to wonder what might have brought her in today. She was not someone who frequented the surgery. However, it's well known that new widows and widowers are at high risk of serious health problems during the early grieving period.

I press the bell. Madge comes in, sits down and says nothing. She is carrying a large shopping bag. I begin to offer my sympathies again but tail off as I watch her reach into the bag and pull out a 12-inch carving knife.

'I've come in to kill you' she says. 'I don't see why you should be alive and my husband dead.'

She delicately places the knife on top of the desk, the blade pointing towards me. It looks as though it has been very regularly sharpened but the surface of the metal seems dull. I really don't know why I remember such detail. More important is the fact that she has placed it well within her grasp but beyond mine. In fact, as I push back my chair as a reflex, she grabs the knife hurriedly before putting it down again. My mouth is very dry and my heart thumping. I try not to shake or show signs of panic.

'Whatever you do' she says, 'don't lift the phone or make any loud noise. It won't help you – it'll only take seconds to stab you and one stab will do the trick. I've smeared my shit over the blade this morning so you'll die of blood poisoning even if I only wound you.'

Something tells me to try to keep talking.

'I'm really so sorry about your husband, Madge. Do you think, then, that I'm to blame for his death?'

'Yes, you. And your partners. None of you cared twopence when Tony came to the surgery. All of you put down his character change to depression and gave him stupid tablets. You even said his nodding off all the time was just the bloody pills you gave him. If he hadn't had that fit at work, you'd have gone on conning us that he was alright. The blood tests you kept doing were all a waste of time. No, your time is up doctor.'

I'm struggling to be coherent. 'But harming me won't bring Tony back, Madge. Have you thought about what it would mean for you? You're bound to be held to account and probably be sent to prison.'

'Why should I care, and in any case, after I've killed you, I'm going to kill myself.'

Silence. We are looking hard at each other. I am trying not to glance at the knife, even momentarily.

'But your children, what would they think? And don't you have some grandchildren, Madge?'

More silent staring. Then, slowly and deliberately, Madge folds forwards and puts her head in her hands. She begins to sob. I wait for some long seconds and then roll my chair forwards. No reaction. I reach across the desk and pick up the knife by the handle and, passing it from right hand to left, put it in a bottom drawer and lock it away. Madge hasn't looked up. She is rocking in the chair, still sobbing. Her bag is on the floor on her far side. I have to hope that it's now empty.

Madge suddenly sits bolt upright and I'm afraid I twitch violently. She then stands up, reaches down for her bag and walks to the door.

'You can keep the knife. You won't be seeing me any more. I'm going to Slough to live with my son.'

For well-known reasons to do with adrenaline excess, I take a break from surgery and go to the toilet. On passing back through reception I add 'personal security/panic buttons' to 'any other business' for the next practice meeting. Fortunately, it's tomorrow.

I like to think that I managed to avoid any post-traumatic stress even when sitting at that desk but life can creep up on you and fork over old ground. About six months later I was called to see a butcher who had suffered a penetrating wound of the abdomen. He had slipped on an abattoir floor. Luckily for him his knife was not heavily contaminated and he survived his exploratory laparotomy. I might not have been so fortunate.

~

On being a corkscrew

Late in the day and still plenty of last-minute customers, customers increasingly likely to be acutely unwell.

Ken Gale came in and sat down - very gingerly.

'Evening, doc. Sorry about this.'

'Well, we rarely see you, Ken. What's the problem?'

'I been and fell off the horse.'

'I didn't know you owned a horse, Ken, or are you in a syndicate, perhaps?'

'No, doc. The horse. The white horse on the Down. I'm in the team from the village. We're re-chalking it – I 'spect you've noticed.' Course, it's bloody steep up there. I let go the rope for a second and slipped. I fell on my arm and there's a bad pain in my side. My arm's OK though.'

'When did this happen, Ken?'

'Two days ago, doc. I thought it would go but it's worse and I couldn't face work today – all that bending over engines.'

'Well, let's see what's amiss. What happens, Ken, if you take a deep breath?'

'No thanks.'

'And if you cough?'

'You're joking.'

'OK. I get the message. Just gently lift out your shirt for me and stand up. Is the pain about here?'

That he flinched would be the understatement of the day.

'Ken, you've broken some ribs – probably the largest two or three of them I should think. You haven't coughed up any blood have you? He shook his head. He was managing to string sentences together without gasping so I thought it unlikely that he had any lung damage. Ken's breath sounds were normal and his trachea central – all good news.

'What's the bad news, doc?'

'Well, broken ribs always heal themselves unless the chest is completely stove in, say, after a car crash.'

'But?'

'I'm afraid the pain gets worse before it gets better – most people say the end of the first week is the worst.'

'So I won't be able to get back to work this week, then?'

'I take it you're still a full-time mechanic at Harpers? You've not been promoted to the office or reception?'

'No way. Give me engines over people any day. I don't know how you do your job.'

'Well, Ken, maybe that makes two of us. I suggest I give you a certificate off work until middle of next week. If you're not ready then, give me a ring. How's that seem to you?' A nod. 'Even so you'll need some powerful painkillers on prescription. Take two of these up to four times a day but do all the obvious things to avoid getting constipated.'

Ken picked up the chitties from the desk forgetting to bend the knees and not the trunk and let out a loud groan. 'Sorry, doc. Thanks very much.'

'Cheers, Ken. I had noticed the horse – it's already looking so much better thanks to you chaps.'

'Yep, but I won't be going up there this weekend, that's for sure. Still, it'll get done. Everybody's dead keen to finish it now that we've started and we've plenty of good chalk. Thanks again.'

I didn't expect a coda at the door and there wasn't one. Ken did ring me four days later, though. 'Hi, doc. Pleased to say the ribcage is getting better but those pills you gave me have made me very constipated. I haven't been able to do a proper job in the lav for three days now and I'm feeling very full.'

I shouldn't have glossed over the need to prevent the constipation. Tears and spilt milk came to mind. 'Well, Ken, you'll need to increase, by a lot, the amount of fluids you drink and I'll prescribe for you what we call a bulk laxative. And you need to use some glycerol suppositories – do you know what I mean? Good. And, in fact, it will be cheaper for you to buy them over the counter. Ask at Boots for Glycerol – g-l-y-c - that's it.'

'So, just to be sure, I put them up my bum, doc, that's right isn't it?'

'Yes, you've got it – into your back passage – what we call the rectum – we're not talking about the corridor to the coal store.' It was obvious that Ken wasn't in the mood for banter and there was a pronounced silence on the line. 'Put two in every morning, Ken.'

'Thanks again, doc. Do you know, I don't think I'm going to be ready for work on Thursday. Could I have another week?'

'Certainly. I'll put another certificate at the desk – will someone be able to collect it?'

'Yea, the wife will do it for me. She can see how uncomfortable I am.'

In fact, it was Ken's wife who next made contact – late on Saturday evening. I was on call. Ken was in great distress – his bowel still hadn't moved and his 'tummy' was now very distended. The very thought of more laxative drinks was making him feel sick.

'He's in more pain now, doctor, than he was with his broken ribs. Can you possible do something tonight? He's not far from tears and he's such a tough nut usually.'

I began to describe how our district nurses would call and give Ken an enema – I didn't dare embark on the details of a manual clearance.

'But will the nurse come tonight, doctor?'

'Well, honestly, I'm afraid not, Mrs. Gale.'

'Then couldn't you yourself come and help Ken, somehow, tonight, doctor? You can probably hear him moaning in pain. He's really desperate.'

Knowing what I might have to do, I hesitated. But there was no escape. 'OK, Mrs. Gale. Tell him to put two of the suppositories in and I'll be there shortly. Which number is it? Exactly opposite the school gate – OK, I know.'

Ken was pale and haggard, leaning on the back of the family sofa, both hands gripping tightly. 'Sorry again, doc. My exhaust is completely blocked. Those things you told me to put up just seem to fall into my pants.'

'Well, Ken, if you want me to try to get things moving mechanically, shall we say, let's take you up and lie you on the bed. You OK to lie on your left side now? Do you have a large old towel, Mrs. Gale?'

Double-gloved and rather fearful, I felt the material in Ken's rectum. It was probably as impacted as the chalk he'd been laying on the white horse. Ken groaned but let me hook some of the fecal matter out onto the towel. The smell of constipated stool was intense but I persevered until Ken pleaded for a break. I'd managed to deliver about a fist-full of poo and we both took a grateful breather. A second attempt was less successful – the matter was now beyond my probing finger but there was, at least, now room for a couple of suppositories. Ken was only too grateful to stay lying on the bed and watch me go back downstairs. Mrs. Gale had been hovering. She had ready a large, new bar of soap and a very crisp white towel, indicating the downstairs washroom. I carefully handed her the old towel and its contents. After cleaning up we fell into conversation. I apologised for how one medical problem can so often lead to another one but that falling from a Wiltshire white horse was, at least, unique.

'I was born in the village', she told me, 'and I've known the monument all my life. I'm so proud of Ken and his mates that they kept it so clean. Mind you it was covered up by turf in the war to that Jerry pilots couldn't use it as a map reference.' I hadn't known that. 'Oh, yes. Uncovering our white horse was the way we really celebrated the end of the war here. We were so pleased to see it again.'

Just then Ken reappeared from the stairwell, grinning from ear to ear. 'You've done the trick, doc. You're a miracle worker. I've just damn-near filled the pan. It's going to be a lot of flushes to clear it but never mind that. It must have been bloody awful for you doing what you had to do. Thanks again. If ever you have a car that won't go, get hold of me. I'll get it going if it's the last thing I do.'

~

My life on crutches

My partners were perceptibly anxious when my wife and I decided to take up skiing in our early fifties. 'I hear that waiting times in casualty are not too bad at the moment' was one not so veiled comment. They had a point. After careering around out of control and falling over each other and the rest of the Tyrol tyros for two days we were checking our travel insurance documents. But we survived the week intact and proudly lined up with our new friends to be photographed holding our 'survived against the odds' certificates.

We flew back to Bristol airport in self-congratulatory euphoria and our bags even appeared early on the conveyor belt. In the car park I lifted the first bag into the boot of the car and 'wham' – there was a mouth-gaping explosion of pain in my back. I screamed silently. Squirming in the passenger seat on the way home we discussed the consequences. How on earth was I supposed to work when my back was locked and unlikely to be better for several days? Would I even be able to get out of the car once home? On a whim that it might help we stopped at the surgery: I knew where to put my hands on a pair of elbow crutches recently abandoned by a lucky Lazarus.

Next morning, tanked up with analgesics and at the surgery early to have time to read a week's post and messages before surgery, I was spotted spidering across the car park by the practice manager. Word got round. During the next hour a succession of nurses and partners looked in to show their 'concern'. Not one of them believed the Bristol suitcase story. And they all seemed to assume that I would never have dreamt of crying off work. Never mind. If I stood, supported by my supernumerary legs, I was almost pain-free and I psyched myself up for the onslaught. I had eighteen patients booked for my morning surgery session.

My first patient was a man with a shaving rash – 'sycosis barbae' – and he accepted my apology for my standing during the whole consultation with a mere nod. The second patient – a young mother worried that her two-year old had bow legs - looked, for some seconds, at my crutches and then flushed and rapidly moved onto a different problem. Perhaps she thought I might be having leg troubles myself and whatever she said could be inconsiderate. The third customer – a practice 'regular' – thought he was being clever and 'in the know' (or liked to think so). 'Been skiing again, doc?' I rather grumpily adjusted his statin dose.

I didn't want sympathy from my patients but had thought it manners, at least, to apologise for my evident disability. From now on, I thought,

I'll run a little experiment. I'll still be having to stand leaning on crutches, but I won't make any reference to the idiosyncrasy and I'll register what happens. Perhaps no-one will notice. And indeed, none of the next four patients made any reference to my situation: a drug addict needing a new prescription for methadone; the niece of an old lady worried about possible dementia in her aunt; a patient recently home after by-pass surgery sent for a prescription review; and a chronic depressive man who, I suspected, was merely wanting to impress on me that he was certainly no better in advance of the next review of his long-term sick certificate.

Then came a primiparous young woman who can't make it to our antenatal clinics (afternoons only) because of her job. She, at least, apologised when I struggled – away from crutches – to examine her 'bump'. Next was an unscheduled extra – a three-year old with otitis media. If the mother did actually comment when I struggled to bend down to use the auriscope I didn't hear above the screaming. So much for my first hour's consultations propped up on overgrown chopsticks.

I had to struggle, again, to examine the abdomen of the next patient. She had all the features of a very unhappy gall bladder not looking forward to Christmas. No mention of my crutches. After a phone call to accept the need to visit a child with abdominal pain and vomiting, the next three patients rattled through: an obvious inguinal hernia destined for the surgeons; another chronic depressive who recognised, herself, that she needed to be put back on treatment; and a young man with a tiny fatty lump on his scrotum – 'no, it's definitely not venereal disease.' My crutches still seemed to be invisible.

And now another old 'friend' who is reluctant to stop her HRT even though she has been on treatment longer than the oracle recommends. I try not to get shirty. The odd fact that I am standing over her while she sits doesn't seem to impact on her her self-centred orientation. And so ends the second hour of this unique, propped up, surgery session – fourteen patients so far. The staff kindly bring me some coffee and I scoff three paracetamol. I know – it should only be two - but I have the 'doctors make bad patients' reputation to live up to.

While the coffee is cooling, I see patients fifteen and sixteen – a persistent 'chesty' cough not getting better (worrying, this and I insist on a follow-up) and a then professional violinist who has found a hard lump on his fingering wrist. It's a ganglion and he's hugely relieved. Neither of them comment on my Douglas Bader imitation as I move around the room.

Midday is now fast approaching. I'm phoned to be told that two further 'extras' are being put on my list – bounced by nurse. And would I take a phone call – someone who has already phoned back twice. It's a woman asking for her father. He is Sri Lankan and flying over to stay with her for a few weeks. Will I be able to see him on the NHS – he's diabetic and she thinks his control is 'rubbish'. I tell her that he can only be seen privately but I would be happy to give her the names of a couple of specialists. I doubt I'll be getting a Christmas card.

The next patient, complaining of increasing acid reflux at night, requires another struggle, on my part, in order to examine the abdomen. I think he's drinking to excess but rather than confront him on flimsy evidence I book him for some blood tests and invite him back. Then I advise a woman, who works at a factory conveyor belt, on her shoulder pains. A change of job might be in the offing. My last scheduled patient also ignores my 'props'. She immediately embarks on an incredibly detailed description of her headaches. I suspect she's been rehearsing her lines for some days. Once I'm satisfied that any organic lesion is extremely unlikely, I try to persuade her to see our counsellor. She declines but then seems perfectly satisfied that I have listened to her composite story and simply departs.

The first extra from sister has a metal ring through her umbilicus that is an obvious focus of sepsis. There is a puddle of pus that is spilling over and running down the front of her abdomen to goodness knows where. She agrees to return at 3.30 so that sister and I can remove the curtain ring after she's had a couple of doses of antibiotic. Then I reluctantly give a young man with a dental abscess some antibiotics and a sickness certificate – he works with food. Both of these were in some discomfort and I'm not surprised that mine is not mentioned. Surgery is over at last. Now for prescriptions and house calls before it starts all over this afternoon. In fact, I find that my partners have distributed my home visits among themselves and there's a message left that I must go home for an hour's rest when paperwork completed. I am almost tearful with gratitude.

The receptionists are intrigued. 'How did your patients react?' 'Were they surprised to see you on crutches?' 'Were they sorry for you?'

'Well, after apologising to the first three of them and not getting much feedback, I thought I would do a little experiment.'

'How do you mean, doctor?'

'So, I made no further personal reference to my predicament and of the eighteen next patients who came to see me guess how many expressed surprise or sympathy?'

The staff looked at each other. Some frowned and others shrugged.

'One. Two at most. Why don't we put up a cut-out cardboard replica in my place for this evening?'

A long afternoon in Reception

UK General Practice is grounded in communities. Patients live locally, their problems often have a home-grown flavour, can relate to neighbourhood events and virtually all therapy is rendered close by. Occasionally patients will go to a district centre – to a main hospital – and even, though rarely, to a regional 'centre of excellence'. But trying to resolve an issue in the practice that is an immediate consequence of a world event is as rare as hen's teeth.

We all remember '9/11'. It was such a shattering event that we can probably also recall exactly what we were doing that lunchtime as the shocking images of the terror attacks on the World Trade Centre towers in New York appeared on our televisions. Believe it or not, the tentacular arms of the tragedy extended as far as our surgery.

It was one of the patients, checking in for an early afternoon appointment that first told us about the two crashed planes in Manhattan. By two o'clock very vivid images had been seen by those with access to a TV screen. Word spread rapidly around our reception area and in our main office. Staff interrupted their routines to follow events on a transistor radio hastily fetched from her car by Margaret, our practice manager. Then came the announcement of a further plane having crashed into the Pentagon and, about half an hour later, a plane plummeting into the Pennsylvania countryside. This was closely followed by a relay that United States airspace was being closed to all except US Air Force jets that were being scrambled. Commercial aircraft presently flying over the States or heading towards the US had been ordered to divert to the nearest feasible runway and land as soon as possible. The overall situation was very confusing. The US President, George W Bush, had been advised that 'the United States is under attack'. More planes falling from the sky, perhaps many more, seemed to be a strong possibility.

Janie, one of our most long-standing and valued receptionists was party to all the information but said nothing at first. Then, feeling very unwell, she asked to be excused from her front-desk duties. Some minutes later she was composed enough to remind the others that her daughter, an only child, was a British Airways cabin crew member – a 'trolley dolly'. To everyone's horror she then told them that Caroline was on a flight to New York that had left Heathrow early that morning. By now BA604 would be rapidly approaching the eastern seaboard of the US.

Janie and her husband, Chris, had been so proud when their daughter had successfully negotiated the tough BA recruitment hurdles five years before. Since then, Caroline had been all over the world, fulfilling a childhood dream. Today was not so celebratory.

Our practice manager immediately put Janie off work and said she would take her home. But Janie said she would prefer to stay in company. There was no-one at home and no possibility in view. Chris, her husband, a long-distance lorry driver, was somewhere in Belgium or Holland on his way to Hamburg. He would normally phone home each day but not usually until late evening. Janie was supported by us all but as the long afternoon wore on the news didn't improve. Planes out over the Atlantic were being diverted, it seemed, to Gander in Newfoundland, an airport with quite primitive landing aids and basic facilities. But it was impossible to glean any specific information on BA 604. Lines to BA Human Resources were all engaged. Two of Caroline's close friends and colleagues had no information. Then Caroline's boyfriend rang Janie. He was equally in the dark and in a near-hysterical state. Janie expended a deal of psychic energy counselling him and collapsed in tears afterwards.

Now all of the practice were sharing in the anxiety and the vibes diffused to the waiting room. Several patients came to the desk to ask what was wrong. Two even cancelled their appointments after checking in. By late afternoon, after an inordinate number of teas and coffees, Janie was exhausted. But the bush telegraph had not collapsed. A couple of off-duty staff heard of the trauma and came in to help out. The only positive news was that there had been no more reports of crashed planes and there had been no aerial clashes involving the US military jets, at least none that had been publicized. But both twin towers in New York had now collapsed and Manhattan was one huge cloud of toxic dust. Caroline's flight had, presumably, landed somewhere else. Hopefully she was safe, but we couldn't really reassure Janie with assumptions.

Then, at about 6.30, as we were closing the building and Margaret was preparing to take Janie home and stay with her, the phone rang. It was Caroline's boyfriend. Listed with BA as immediate next of kin, they had phoned him to report that BA604 was safely on the ground at Gander. However, the Canadian authorities were allowing no-one to leave the plane and all passengers and crew were being kept aboard overnight. Therefore, Caroline would not be able to get in touch personally; but she was quite safe. The sense of relief, for all of us, was enormous and the mood in a now darkened reception lifted above euphoric. It was soon punctured.

Robert, one of the partners, appeared in his overcoat and carrying his black bag, ready to go home. But he himself was very pale. He had, he said, just taken a call from his wife. Her cousin had flown to New York yesterday to attend a meeting, today, in the World Trade Centre. His office diary entry specified '98th floor North Tower 8.30 am.' It seemed very unlikely that he could have survived. He didn't. No trace was ever found of him.

~

Travelogue

During my three decades in general practice there was an obvious trend: more and more Mohameds were coming to the mountain. But every working day still involved the 'mountain' going out to Mohamed. The middle of the day was therefore on the move: infinitely varied, very unpredictable and peppered with hazards (intellectual more than physical). Coffee consumed, repeat prescriptions signed, bladder emptied, one donned a coat and set about the visiting list. Like many semi-rural practices based in a market town our population was centripetal, densely congregated in and close to town and then out through a scattering of farms and villages. Almost instinctively, we all seemed to first skid around town on our 'rounds' and then spin off to outer orbits.

On a typical day I started my 'calls' at the enclave of sheltered homes ('God's bus stop') next to the churchyard. Walking up the short path to number 6 I knew what to expect. I followed the four numbers on the front of the case record, punching them in sequence into the little key safe. I then pressed the star twice which allowed me to lever open the lid and retrieve the actual door key inside. I then put the key in the lock and, as I fully expected, the door opened at that very instant. Mrs. Cotter's little tease amused her, at the expense of my irritation, every time. I had tried just knocking on one occasion but waited for ages while Mrs. C pretended to have enormous difficulty getting to the door. The medicine was simpler than the mind game. Her disabled husband's latest exacerbation of his chronic psoriasis needed only an adjustment to his normal treatment.

On to one of the Edwardian villas marking the edge of the pre-war town. An old warhorse (his term not mine) was 'chesty'. It was significant because of his hemiparesis after a stroke. His neurological deficit made his speech yet more staccato and, since he was fond of pretending fluency in German after being a pilot in the Berlin airlift, perhaps appropriate.

'Danke Schön, guten reise, herr Artz.'

'Yea, guten tag.'

Then there were three visits for which I really can't recall the details except for the one where, on knocking at the door, I heard the owner shoo her very noisy and aggressive little terrier into the front parlour where I could watch, through the window, as he took out his frustration on all the cushions.

The next call was to a couple who were fortunate to live in a bungalow: ideal for Mrs. Simpson who had come home from hospital paralysed and in a wheelchair. They were well-known locally as regional ballroom dancing champions – well, they had been. A high-octane marital row, about a suspected infidelity, in the car coming home from a dancing competition, had resulted in a collision on the M4. Grace, in the passenger seat, had sustained life-changing injuries. Our nurses wanted me to inspect a growing bedsore and leave it exposed for them to re-dress later.

I next pull up outside a detached house on the very outskirts of town. It has an immaculate but rather municipal garden, a highly polished car in the drive and a thick coconut mat in the lobby asking me to 'kindly wipe your feet'. The door is answered by an old friend – in dark suit, collar and tie as if just going into the office or, perhaps, a funeral. He's a retired middle-ranking civil servant who looks after his rapidly dementing wife - rather well, I have to admit. As usual he has a list of questions – typed on card and categorised into 'A – important; B – not so important; C – only if doctor has time'. The pesky list and his tiresome habit of ticking the items off and making notes in the margin prevents me getting anywhere near my patient – again as usual. I push past 'Sir Humphrey' after the third question from paragraph B, latching on to something that I state, authoritatively, needs my immediate 'hands on' attention. In the end the real problem – Sir's overwhelming and deep-seated anxiety – is not touched. I walk out backwards knowing that I'll be back within days. I think I might then insist on starting the agenda at C6 and working backwards. Chaos might just bring up the truth.

I had never been to the next address – a semi-detached council house in a village. I knocked at the front. A man answered.

'Oh, good afternoon, I've come to see Mrs. Watkins.'

'Back door!'

The front door was then virtually slammed in my face. The kitchen door was opened by a very elderly lady who ushered me into an extremely cramped room at the back of the house. Mrs. Watkins was in a small bed with a temperature and a hacking cough. For a type-2 diabetic a prescription for an antibiotic was in order. No-one explained the bizarre social segregation in the property until I asked. Husband and wife had fallen out, irreversibly, over a year ago and neither of them was willing to leave. Old Mrs. Watkins negotiated the living expenses, cooked for them both and tried to keep the peace. She alone passed through 'Checkpoint Charlie' into the front sitting room. Would this Berlin wall ever come down, I wondered?

Further into the village I was due to call on Mr. and Mrs. Paxton. The cottage was notoriously full of cats and kittens. Emmy was in heart failure and I was convinced that she didn't take her treatment reliably. From the asphyxiating sour smell of cat pee, I wondered if she was actually pulverising her Lasix and putting in in the cat food. I tried yet another aggressive sermon on the benefits of regular therapy, the days of purring diplomacy long over.

The last scheduled visit – back in town – had become a daily one during the last week. Gregor Stephens, a Highland Scot, was dying and well aware of it. His lung cancer had spread to many parts of his body including his throat and his diction had become more impenetrable than ever. Our currently attached MacMillan nurse – from Lyon and with an Inspector Cluso accent – relies on Greg's daughter to translate but even she is having trouble at times. Today Greg seemed quite comfortable and relaxed, sticking up two thumbs in response to my obvious questions. His diamorphine pump is clearly working well. Was this, perhaps, the final calm that can often descend just before a death? As I left the room, he looked directly at me and rolled his eyes upwards. We both knew we both knew.

It was five past one. I would only be ten minutes late for the annual meeting with our accountant. An improvement; last year I didn't make it at all. As I drove back across town to the surgery, I mused that less than half of my actions in the last couple of hours had been based, remotely, on anything I had learned at medical school.

~

Do you know, I'm so busy?

'Dr. Beale?'

'Aha'

'Are you duty doctor this weekend?'

'Yes, I'm afraid so.'

'Morning. I'm one of the midwives from Fairways. I've been at a home confinement of one of yours overnight. We've had a lovely little girl – eight pounds at 6.15 and all's well. I'm just leaving – you'll be able to come out to do the full baby exam today? I'll leave the folder open at the page for you to complete, and I'll give Julia, your own midwife, a ring when she comes on at eight.'

'OK, thanks. No problem. What's the name and address, then?'

'Mrs. Corrigan at 42, Swindon Drive. It's her third by the way. She's a very sensible girl. In fact, she nearly caught me out. She rang at four to say that she was in labour and making progress. She said she could tell by her backache. I wasn't actually convinced that she was dilating when I got here – there seemed to be no regular contractions though she was obviously having strong pain. To my surprise she was fully at 5.30 and pushed like a champion. Sometimes patients know best don't they?'

'You bet. Anyway, have a good sleep and thanks for everything.'

I came out of a house call mid-morning and Julia was standing by my car.

'You know about Mrs. Corrigan?' I did. 'Well, it's not going to be easy for me to fit her in today – I already have a full schedule but I suppose I'll have to. I shouldn't really have been on duty this weekend but there are three staff off from the pool. How's your day panning out?'

I wasn't at all keen to stand in the street and discuss the problems of the midwifery rota – we had friction enough, from time to time, with our own. 'Well, I'm sure you'll cope, Julia. I must get on with saving lives. I'll certainly be going to number 42 to check the baby.'

'I might see you there, then. By the way, how is Dr. Latham's wife? I hear she's still in hospital.'

'Oh, she's recovering nicely by all accounts.'

'I hear it was touch and go.'

'Well, I don't know the details. I haven't seen anyone from the other practice for several days and perhaps it would be best not to speculate in the street.'

'OK, OK, but I did hear that things were dodgy at one point – she lost a lot of blood apparently. Poor girl. Do you suppose that she will ever have children now?'

'Well, who knows. Julia – I really must get going. See you later perhaps.'

An hour later, driving through town in the hope of getting home for some lunch I saw Julia talking to someone across a low brick wall in front of a house. She probably hadn't been there very long – her heavy black bag was in her hand. I was bleeped as I parked in our drive. I had to return to town 'post haste'. I passed Julia again – still talking, her bag now planted on the pavement. She was obviously so very busy. Seeing my car, she waved. I lifted one finger off the steering wheel. Two might have been more appropriate but, chinwagging aside, she was a very good midwife, an asset to the practice and, more importantly, to all our young mothers and their newborns.

At last, late afternoon, I was able to go to see our newest town inhabitant. The joy in the household was palpable and infectious. A girl after two boys. My examination went well until I flexed and turned out the little girl's hips. There was a slightly disconcerting movement on the left. Was the hip joint dislocating? Missing an unstable or dislocated hip in a newborn is a potential tragedy. I already had one patient who had limped through youth, unable to take part in anything athletic and who was now wearing a replacement hip which had not, sadly, corrected her gait. Mother, father and 'from next door' were all horrified as I punctured the euphoria. As gently as I could I outlined the problem; that we would need to arrange an urgent specialist appointment and that the baby's legs might need to go into a brace. Tears flowed, not surprisingly.

The paediatric registrar, next day, was more than happy to see our latest citizen in clinic and arrange an urgent scan of the hips. Unless we were all wrong, the baby would end up wearing a brace that would hold her legs in a frog-like posture and nature would put things right over three months or so. Later that week, being just up the road from no. 42, I thought I would call and check that the Corrigans had heard from the 'paeds'.

'Oh, it's you, doctor.'

The baby was in her arms and two small boys were clinging to her skirt.

'Sorry, I thought it was the midwife. We're expecting her any minute. She's been marvellous. The shock on Sunday seemed to upset my milk and she's been so understanding. She knew exactly what to do. Oh, sorry, doctor, so sorry. Look at me keeping you on the doorstep. Please come in, come in. Come on boys, out of the way and let the doctor through.'

'It's nothing. I was just up the road and wondered if you'd heard from the childrens' specialists yet?'

225

'Yes, we have. They're seeing us tomorrow. A very nice doctor rang up. I told him we were putting on two nappies – great-granny Brown told us it was a good idea – but he didn't seem impressed.'

'Well, it'll do no harm. It was once the recommended treatment but things are much better now. Anyway, you have an appointment and I'm relieved to hear it.'

'Yes, so are we. Would you like a cup of tea, doctor. Julia – sorry, midwife – has been having a cake and a drink with us about this time every day. She's a fund of local knowledge, isn't she? Mind you, she's very careful about people's names – as I suppose she has to be.'

'No, thanks just the same. I must keep moving. Surgery starts soon. I'll leave you to Julia. As long as you're lined up for tomorrow.'

'Well, thanks for all you've done, doctor – and for your being 'on the ball'. Oh, and for taking the time, on Sunday, to let us down gently when you're all so busy all the time, Julia especially. Mind you, as my husband says, she might not be so pushed if she spent less time telling everyone how busy she is.'

Yes, patients often know best.

~

Gee, thanks Fred

Northcote House. I hadn't been there for, maybe, ten years. I remembered Mr. Deverill having a stroke and not surviving. He had been well-known locally. He'd been the civil engineer in charge of the building of the Wiltshire stretch of the M4 motorway. Now his widow, Edith, had asked for a doctor to call, reporting breathing difficulty and light-headedness.

The drive and garden were nicely manicured, and the house looked well-maintained. At 82, Edith must have regular help if she still lived alone. It was Edith who opened the door and I noticed she was hanging on to it. We went into the large front lounge. For a sunny afternoon the room was cold. She apologised and bent down to switch on an electric fire. She got up slowly, using a side-table as a prop. Small-talking my way to a comfy chair I began to ask the obvious questions. Then the phone rang in the hall. With another apology, Edith tottered off to answer it. She came back with a cordless phone in her hand:

'It's my son, from New York. I'd best ask him to ring back?'

'No' I said, shaking my head 'assuming it's a brief call. Go ahead.'

She began to recite a series of 'yes' or 'no' answers and then, as just she was saying 'he's here now' she folded, slowly, to her knees and dropped the phone. I jumped up, but too late to prevent her flopping forwards face down on the carpet. Was this a faint, or worse? I took up the phone and explained to her son that his mother had passed out. Would he ring back in about ten minutes – after I'd had chance to examine her. But Edith had no vital signs; no respirations and no pulse. I rolled her over, checked her airway and thumped her breastbone with some force. No response. I began CPR but it was increasingly apparent that, entirely on my own, I was unlikely to be able to resuscitate her. After about five minutes of trying and with her pupils widely dilated, I stopped. Presumably her reported symptoms had represented a silent heart attack that had occurred some days earlier.

When the phone rang again, I had the unenviable task of telling Edith's son – currently three and half thousand miles away – that his mother had just died. He responded sensibly.

'I've been pleading with her for three days, to ask to see a doctor. She never liked making a fuss, you know. I'll make some urgent rearrangements of my business over here and get back in the next day or so. Thanks for trying your best, anyway, doctor.'

'Well, don't feel that you have to drop everything immediately. Your mother's death is unexpected and I'll not be able to issue a death certificate even though I was 'on scene' so to speak. This will have to be reported to the Coroner. It's almost certain that he will insist on a post-mortem and the body will not be made available for a funeral for, perhaps, a week. Give me a ring when you're back and I'll put you in touch with the authorities.'

I then rang the desk sergeant on duty at the police station to report what had happened, something that I've done, very sadly, many times in my career. Doctors and policemen share a private and protective backwash of black humour but I didn't get the usual friendly and supportive response. I was told, categorically and rather aggressively, to wait at the scene and not to touch anything. I'd never been told that before but, since I'd already touched it, I did use the phone to ring the surgery. I explained why I might be late for my afternoon stint and asked them to make the usual apologies and provisos. Something then told me to make a very careful, detailed entry in Edith's records.

Then the police were suddenly in the house; they didn't ring the bell. Two constables – one of each gender – looked me over very curiously and, in a rather cold manner, told me that the CID were on their way. To me, this was most unusual, and I said so. They didn't reply. The policewoman left and by craning to peer through the window I could see her speaking animatedly on their car phone. I made one or two inane comments to the remaining PC but he turned away and pretended not to hear me. I'd never known this type of behaviour before and was beginning to fret that I had no grasp of the situation.

After kicking my heels in the hostile silence for some ten minutes or so, two men in civilian clothes arrived. They introduced themselves as members of the regional crime unit. I've forgotten the ranks they quoted but one was in a very smart suit with an extremely shiny tie. Poor Edith was still on the floor staring at the ceiling, and I was staring at the reality of being treated as a suspect.

'So, am I under arrest or something?'

'No, doctor. But we hope you'll be willing to help us take a witness statement from you. You will need to think very carefully about your answers – that they are absolutely correct and accurate. You could be prosecuted if what you say is later shown to be untrue.'

I was briskly escorted out to an unmarked car. It was parked extremely close to mine and boxing it in. I wondered why. My wrinkly Renault was hardly an ideal getaway vehicle. Invited into the back seat of their car, one of the detectives put a hand on my head to protect it as I got in. He then got in beside me and the other officer took the front passenger seat and turned round towards us. I was interrogated, in great detail, about the events of the afternoon, every aspect being recorded, by hand, on a pad of lined paper. For some reason they were extremely attentive when I told them about the phone calls from New York. It sparked a long series of questions regarding any relationship I might have with Edith's son. Finally, they seemed content with the information they'd extracted from me. They asked me to read through their script and, unless I had any objections, to sign and date it.

I tried not to let the spelling mistakes distract me. The three sheets of paper did seem to be a true record of my narrative and so I signed. My signature was, probably, even less legible than usual but was accepted. I was then warned not to discuss any of the afternoon's events with anyone and that I should be prepared to answer further questions if necessary. I was able to reassure them that I would not be away from home and work in the near future. They then double-checked my contact details before letting me out of the car. The policewoman handed me my medical bag across the blue and white incident tape now erected. My car was released and I was able to drive to my remaining house call. I arrived at surgery over an hour late. But by then I'd managed to finish the jigsaw.

Doctor Harold Shipman ('Fred' to his close contacts), a Manchester GP, had been convicted of mass murder a couple of months earlier. He had probably put to death, using excessive morphine, well over a hundred of his patients, mostly old ladies and usually sometime in the middle of the day. It seemed that I was being viewed as his Wiltshire counterpart – alone, mid-afternoon, with an elderly lady who had died unexpectedly and who probably had a few bob in the bank. Boy, was I grateful that she hadn't been in severe pain and that I hadn't given her a morphine injection.

~

Attenshun!

Monday evening surgery used to be high season for 'morning after pill' requests. Sexual adventures over a weekend that were not planned create a collective anxiety by Monday morning and frantic phone calls to our appointments line. Ginny Parker was an exemplar. Having broken up with her long-standing boyfriend three months before she had, she said, given up 'the pill.' But that was before she had met 'Lewi' on Friday evening, and they had spent the weekend together. Post-coital contraception was needed – urgently as always. I prescribed. I think she absorbed the advice about following the instructions to the T – and to come back and arrange some proper contraception soon. She then broke precedent in not rushing away to get to the pharmacy before it closed. She hovered and asked if I could see her new boyfriend. He'd been very unwell today – violent 'trots' and had been unable to go back to base – he was in the RAF. I gave the obvious guidance and said that I would be able to see him if he really wasn't any better after 24 hours. She should ring appointments, take my name in vain, and I would fit him in somehow, somewhere.

The call came in and I found myself face to face with aircraftman Lewis Hills mid-afternoon the next day, Tuesday. He described, rather too vividly, I thought, a characteristic enteritis after a typically overindulgent weekend. There was nothing to find on examining him. I knew what was coming. He wanted me to certify him as unfit to return to base – he should have been through the gates by 6pm on Sunday.

'Perhaps you wouldn't mind, doctor, if you made it for a couple of days dated Sunday?'

Yes, I would 'mind'. I explained that an NHS certificate would not be valid in these circumstances but I would do my best to help him. I could issue a private certificate but dated, with probity, yesterday - at best. This was when Ginny had told me his symptoms had begun and he had inferred nothing different. He was obviously aggrieved and tried to soften me up. He thanked me profusely for helping Ginny with the pills. She had told him I would be very understanding and helpful. She had said I was a wonderful doctor. I said I thought I *was* being helpful. I was thinking, however, that it was quite unjustified for either of them to think I should be made complicit in their sexual marathon. Or was it just a sprint? A significant silence ensued. It was ended by Lewis picking up the certificate, plonking £2.50 on my desk, and leaving the room in a huff.

I heard no more from either party of this particular union but I did get a phone call, about six weeks later, from a Wing Commander Binns. He introduced himself as a prosecuting counsel of the RAF military police. I paid full attention to this one. He wanted me to offer him a date and time when I could give him half an hour of uninterrupted attention – completely at my convenience. He hoped he would be able to take a statement from me about one of the young men serving at the nearby RAF base. He understood that the aircraftman had consulted me professionally but was not at liberty to give me more details 'at this juncture.' He would be very grateful if I would be so kind – it would avoid a subpoena.

Wing Commander Binns came to the surgery a couple of days later. The large RAF blue limousine caught the attention of the receptionists who watched a chauffeur open the rear door and a tall, very well-dressed officer emerge. He was accompanied by a Sergeant Robinson, also of the RAF police, who would witness my giving the statement and countersign. Both men seemed very stiff and formal and I think I upset them by my rather light-hearted greeting. Binns put me in my place.

'This is, I'm afraid, a very serious matter, doctor.'

The 'case' was, as I had guessed, Ginny Parker's 'fling' – Lewis Hills. The Wing Commander said he well understood the matter of medical confidence and that I might be very apprehensive in its context. However, they had, in their possession, a document about which they hoped I might be able to confirm some simple facts. As officers investigating a crime, they felt obliged to probe as far as I felt comfortable. Although I felt uneasy, I said I would cooperate as far as I was able. Binns prepared himself with a clipboard on which there was some foolscap and he then produced, from his very smart attaché case, a small piece of paper.

'Was this the certificate of illness that I had issued to aircraftman Hills' he asked, quoting the date.

It was, indeed, the private certificate.

'And can you confirm, doctor, that it is exactly as written by yourself?'

I looked at the document, now dog-eared, stained and creased. The outstanding inconsistency was that it now stated 'unable to attend work for 12 days.'

'No, I laughed, this is not as written by me – I issued a certificate for 2 days – and with some reluctance. I wasn't best popular.' I then hesitated – perhaps I had gone too far, ethically.

Binns stayed strictly on track. 'But it is (a) in your handwriting in black ink and (b) your signature, doctor?'

'Yes, certainly.'

'Do you notice anything about the number of days besides the numerical discrepancy?'

I looked again. A number '1' had been inscribed in front of my '2' and, in good light, it appeared to be in pencil.

'Yes, that's what we thought, doctor.'

'Well, what a cheek – I suppose the young man will have his pocket money stopped for quite a while for doing this?'

'I'm afraid going absent without leave is a very serious offence in the Services, doctor. If the Court Martial find him guilty, he will be imprisoned for two years - minimum.'

As they rose to leave, I found myself standing rigidly to attention. I wonder why?

~

In the cross hairs

When I first dreamt up the idea of researching the effects of compulsory redundancy on general practice workload it was an esoteric topic. Some years later, when my statistician colleague, Sarah Nugent, and I had a paper published in a reputable medical journal, UK unemployment was the hottest potato in town. Our discovery, indisputable evidence that the mere threat of redundancy was caustic for the health of families, was a new tun of gunpowder under Parliament. For the previous half-decade an earnest and powerful government led by a lady 'resistant to rotation' had pile-driven monetarist doctrine to its inevitable consequences. Huge tranches of heavy industry had become a wasteland. Millions of workers had lost their valuable jobs, whole communities had been shelled out, and national unemployment had risen to well over three million. In fact, it would have been nearer five million if the cabinet had not approved a string of changes in the definition of UK unemployment, all of them suppressing the declared total. The arcane and academic had transmogrified into topical and very controversial.

Breakfast television was first but not before the two regional TV news channels had descended on me. BBC Points West won the race. They asked if I could be interviewed in the very room where I had done the research donkey work. This was the upstairs study at our home. They swarmed in. Furniture was moved, windows and doors firmly shut against traffic and household noise and my squeaky desk chair swapped for one from our dining room – I was having trouble keeping still in the stress. I don't remember how I answered the probing questions but clearly my responses were not good footage. My interview was canned in favour of a 'voice over' on shots of the now half-demolished factory whose workers I had studied before and after closure. The ITV West crew were no more empathetic but at least they did transmit some of my interview – after brutal editing. Perhaps after my dismal BBC 'rehearsal' I was learning to be media savvy.

Breakfast television meant a late evening train ride to London, to an anonymous hotel in Camden ('take a taxi, doctor, we will repay you all expenses'), an abbreviated near-sleepless night, and waiting for a car at 6 a.m. Knowing where he was taking me, the driver launched into reassurance mode – he often picked up people for the studio and said there was nothing to worry about. All of his passengers had always done 'fine'. No, he never collected people from the studios. So how could he know? Some reassurance!

Inside the studio – a vast building – everyone was as awake as the rest of us tend to be at midday. After security had checked my identity a man with a clipboard took me to a small, window-less room with comfy chairs and a coffee table – the sort of room that I knew from hospital days. The sort of room where one met with relatives to issue very bad news. I waited, very conscious of my adrenaline tremor. Then, like the condemned on their last journey - to the gallows - I was suddenly bustled into another room where I was hastily primped and powdered and then quick-marched onto the 'set.' What was it Pierrepoint proudly claimed – that death row to oblivion took less than 45 seconds?

There was the famous sofa. There was Ann Diamond and Nick Owen. I was wired up and placed on a very precise spot, greeted warmly but told not to squirm or look at the cameras. I was introduced to another guest – a young female Labour MP (who would grow up into The Rt. Hon. Harriet Harman). The rest is a blur, but I think I tried to explain how our research had been an exercise in gleaning anonymised consultation rates exclusively from our practice records. And that, as a consequence, the patients of our practice would be as surprised by the broadcast as anyone. To my amazement Harriet Harman then asked me how my patients had responded when I 'sat down with' them to 'fill in' my questionnaires. I was rescued by a swift intervention from Ann Diamond. She, for one, had actually been listening to my bumbling. Then it was over. I was unleashed and shepherded away from the lights to be replaced on the sofa by the next guest – a life-sized Rupert Bear. I hope he enjoyed it more than I did. Another bod with a clipboard arranged a taxi for me – to Paddington Station - and I was quick-marched out into the street.

Morning surgery started at nine as usual. I arrived, direct from the station, at five to. Then it started all over. A string of impertinent national newspaper journalists was on the phone. They were all armed with the press release issued by my Royal College but wanted more intimate details – sometimes even of our research. 'How old was I?' (All the reporters). 'Was I married – and for how long?' (Daily Mail) 'Did I have children?' (Daily Mirror) 'Was I a paid-up member of the Labour Party? (Daily Express). 'Had I ever been unemployed and who had paid for our research? (Daily Telegraph). 'How much time had I taken out of my practice and when was I giving up doctoring to join academe?' (Guardian). On and on it went – all day. 'Hey, doc, can you just give me the names and addresses of just ten of the patients in your study, and would you happen to have their phone numbers?' (Several papers). 'Could I be available for a phoned interview in about ten minutes? (Western Daily Press). 'What, exactly, was my relationship with Ms. Nugent?' (The Sun). 'Was there an 'everyman' version of our paper that didn't contain quite so many numbers and graphs?' (The Times). I had never known a day be so interrupted – before or since.

Then the BBC Six O'clock News team arrived at the surgery car park after fifteen minutes' notice. Surprise, surprise: they had a six-p.m. deadline. I was to make myself available at ten to six, no matter any waiting patients. All phones in the building were to be disconnected, never mind emergencies. I was prepped by a twosome team with a powder puff, comb and clothes brush. I was to drape a stethoscope from my neck. I suggested wielding a biro would be more apposite but, like the famous queen, they were not amused. Hardened now, if not cavalier, I did another interview that I don't remember. It was peremptory anyway. I eventually arrived home – exhausted. It was the weekend. Thankfully I was not on duty. We packed a couple of bags and took off for the weekend.

Monday morning brought more phone calls but less impetuosity. 'When could you be available to make a film with a crew from 'World in Action' – it would only take two or three days.' And 'could you drop everything and be in London on Wednesday as a guest on the Jimmy Young Show' – tomorrow would be better but perhaps you'll need a little more notice!'

I managed to find a locum for Wednesday and took an early train, packed with commuters, to Paddington. Having arrived at the BBC, Portland Place, in good time they kept me waiting for an hour and a half. Jimmy Young was friendly enough when I asked him 'ow bist?' (both of us from the Forest of Dean). And I was fascinated to watch him throw across the studio the vinyl that had been played – like a boy skimming stones over a pond.

Two weeks later I engineered some annual leave and spent three days with a 'World in Action' team. They wanted me to be 'totally natural' and do some of my familiar 'everyday' things. It seemed they did not mean sitting on the toilet. I mowed the lawn, walked the dog, went to the pub, drove the car through the village (very slowly as directed), picked the kids up from school and pretended to answer the phone. I think they were surprised, if not totally disillusioned, that I didn't play golf, shoot, ride to hounds, or fish. Oh, and they even filmed me sitting at my desk in the surgery – hours of celluloid that turned into a few minutes of 'erudition'.

By now it should be obvious that I'd become completely scornful of the media and I was convinced that our home phone was tapped for some months. But there was to be massive compensation. The 'World in Action' director had been mingling with the locals in town – in the pubs and the shops. Some good old-fashioned snooping had landed him the names and addresses of a list of people who had been made redundant from my study factory. Unbeknown to me, he had approached them and most of them had agreed to be interviewed on camera. I was able to join the crew for the interviews. It was a joy for me to actually meet many of the families who had, until now, just been ciphers on our spreadsheets (most of them not my listed patients and therefore strangers to me.) Hearing their personal stories put a very human and touching gloss on our exercise in statistics; numbers to encounters, prose to poetry. I was Dickens actually meeting Magwitch.

CLOSURE

I retired in May 2005 – at lunchtime. I went home and washed and oiled my bike. In the evening my erstwhile partners very kindly organised a party to celebrate my departure. They invited all our staff and spouses, past and present, attached staff, past and present and previously retired partners and spouses. It was a very warm occasion, valued gifts were received with thanks, and speeches were made. I interrupted mine to make a foray into the crowd – to give back the biro (OK, not the same one) to the widow of my late senior partner. By the end of the evening I was wearing a straw hat and walking with a stick. Was I really as old as the part I was playing? Anyway, it was euphoric occasion – for both myself and my wife, and we felt very honoured.

Next day I received a proforma letter from the Wiltshire Practices Committee. Although I'm not bitter about it, I did rather think that there might have been a scintilla of gratitude. The letter simply said that my name had been removed, forthwith, from the list of approved medical practitioners for Wiltshire and that I was to send in all prescription pads, my death certificate book, and my stillbirth book. That was it. Adieu.

ACKNOWLEDGEMENTS

First and foremost, I am grateful to all my patients, their relatives and friends. Their participation may have been inadvertent on their part and intrusive on mine but there would be no memoir without them. And without all my practice partners and staff I could not have survived to tell the tale(s).

Then I am very grateful for the help within my family – from Elaine and our two boys, Alick and Huw. Thanks are also due to Diana Dalton, my sister-in-law: for years she pestered me to write up my 'funny stories.' Thanks, also, to Lesley Scholes, Chris Greenwood, Rachel Barnett, John Chandler, Roger Jones, Professor Andrew Finlay and to Phil Hammond, another veteran of 'moonraker' medicine.

ABOUT THE AUTHOR

Dr. Norman Beale MA, MD was a full-time GP in Wiltshire for 30 years, latterly senior partner, in a semi-rural practice based in a market town. He was a trainer and involved in primary care research. He had published over 20 papers in refereed journals, the bulk of them on unemployment and health and on Council Tax Valuation Bands as a marker of socioeconomic deprivation. For his Cambridge MD dissertation on redundancy and health he was awarded the Raymond Horton-Smith prize for 1989 – the best MD thesis submitted to the university that year. He also shared the Sir James MacKenzie prize of the Royal College of General Practitioners and was elected a fellow. He became a journal editor and a referee, activities that continued after retirement from clinical practice. He has also published five books on various topics – one of them with his wife, a historian, (and with the encouragement of the late David Bellamy) – a 600-page biography of Dr Jan Ingen Housz, FRS – the eighteenth-century physician who discovered the essentials of photosynthesis. Dr Beale still lives in Wiltshire.